A Woman's Odyssey
Journals, 1976—1992

A Woman's Odyssey
Journals, 1976—1992

Linda Aaker

To Tiana,
    whose mother had a tale, and
shared it. Perhaps you should write
your tale, too. Enjoy.

Linda Aaker

D. C.
1996

University of North Texas Press

First Edition 1994

10 9 8 7 6 5 4 3 2 1

The paper in this book meets the minimum requirements of the American National Standard for Permanence of paper for Printed Library Materials, Z39.48-1984.

Library of Congress Cataloging-in-Publication Data

Aaker, Linda, 1948–
        A woman's odyssey : journals, 1976–1992 / Linda Aaker.
            p.   cm.
        ISBN 0-929398-74-2
        1. Aaker, Linda, 1948–   —Diaries. 2. Women—United States—
Diaries. 3. Women lawyers—United States—Diaries. I. Title.
HQ1413.A24A3 1994
305.4'0973—dc20   94–16038
                                                                CIP

Cover photograph by Ave Bonar
Cover design by Amy Layton
Title page art by Dana Adams

For my soulmate, Bob

Contents

✿ Prologue

I didn't set out to write this particular book. In December of 1992, I gave an off-the-program reading from the Road Warrior section to women attending Leadership America in Seattle. Fran Vick from the University of North Texas Press listened. When she called me two weeks later to ask if I had any more journal-type writings, I was stunned. "Yes," I told her, "but they weren't written for third parties to read." They're not like the "Road Warriors" which I wrote to share with my law firm. My journals are more hormonal in nature, perhaps suitable for Harlequin, not a University Press. Besides, who would be interested in the life of a forty-four-year-old regular working mother? It sounded awfully narcissistic, and made me uncomfortable.

Fran persisted. She assigned me an encouraging and perceptive editor, Charlotte Wright. The result is this book. I'm grateful (I think) for her willingness to risk. One of the risks is telling this story in journal format, especially because I did not keep the journals consistently, and gaps appear. Also because truth, reality and memory sometimes become confused in retrospect. Perhaps the most difficult task has been to resist the urge to make me and my contemporaries, particularly in our early years, seem wiser, more mature, less egocentric. But the vast majority of this book was written contemporarily with the events chronicled, and has been left largely intact.

Reviewing the journals, I was often struck by how differently I remembered an event now from the way I wrote about it then. Also, when I came home from work, I didn't record my three best lawyer arguments for a motion for summary judgment, but rather, wrote of the personal decisions and searching that engaged so many of us in the 70s and 80s as we tried to find meaning in our lives, work and politics.

Most of this book actually occurred, but some names, dates and stories have been altered. The opinions, the reminiscences, are, of course, only one woman's version of her life.

Introduction

My stepson asked the dreaded question: "Why would anyone want to publish the story of your life?" Daunted, I replied, "Well, I guess because I wrote it down. It's the story of a woman's life in a particular time of history, after birth control, before AIDS, when most of us were trying to figure out how to achieve and live with our personal freedom."

He reflected a moment. Understanding brightened his face. "Oh, like those diaries from the Civil War days!"

He's about the age I was when I began the journals. I wonder what his journey will be. I hope he writes it down.

Journal I

🌿 *Linda*

❧ *Linda*

October 14, 1975

Dinner with Kay. "You must learn to create your own happiness." To date, I've only learned the rudiments of creating, in the sense of choosing my life, thus controlling more significant portions. I know that I alone am responsible for enduring, of choosing what I do, but now I must learn to do more than just endure.

Thought: Laughter is a good way of sublimating, not only sexual needs, but loneliness. Losing a generosity of spirit—the capacity to feel joy at another's happiness—is almost as bad as losing one's sense of humor. I wonder if people like Kay know, or sense, the impact they have on others' lives by their mere existence or a chance encounter with them. Perhaps just growing older (I can't believe I'll be twenty-seven in two weeks) makes me appreciate nights like tonight for the high that they are, and not regret the moment by wishing for more. Is that "settling" or just learning acceptance?

December 16, 1975 (Santiago, Atitlan, Guatemala)

This vacation trip is exactly what I've needed. Not that it has been without fears and trepidation. Traveling alone is an experience I've needed—to give me time to reflect without the distractions of other people. I was scared and lonely coming into Guatemala City—so big, hassles with customs, etc. But Serendipity occurred and I met a professor-turned-import salesman who rescued me from the barrage of Spanish and took me to dinner. Sunday morning, as I was leaving the hotel to find the bus to Panajachel, three men offered me a ride. I took it, a bit surprised at my daring, and felt old. (My hitchhiking days are over.) The trio: a black, a brown and an Anglo, who drove like maniacs through mountainous roads while speaking "jive" English. Quite a crew. Civility and polite demeanor count a lot in the ordinary day-to-day living.

Panajachel, called "Gringo Tinego" because of the high concentration of gringos passing through for a few days, was fun. Good food, nice people. Took a long hike to a small restaurant called Mama's.

February 15, 1976 (Austin)

More often these days, I think having children is in the long run "where it's at." Scary thought, since there's no prospective father in sight.

On the plane returning home from El Paso and an airport interview for the steel case, I read that Heisenberg had died. If mere observation and measurement can change what is being observed in science, can mere *thinking* about an event change it "backwards" in the past? For example, my week with Alfredo: Does thinking about our time together alter what happened? I know I can think it into more romanticism than was there.

March 20, 1976

Sunday spent with Don. A lovely day. The ending thought was one of pain—although slight. For life to be rich, the risks necessarily entail moments of hurt. People are so fragile—just like me! I've learned not to take some of the small stuff so seriously, but I get mixed up about which things are small.

Good sign. The hurt leaves quickly. Maybe Don is right—if we talk about it, it stays under control. Am getting stronger, though tenuously.

The new stereo gives me joy.

April 3, 1976

Flying from Houston to Austin, toward home. There are other geographical areas more beautiful, but Austin is home. Not only in a people sense, but in a place sense. Also, was content (happy is too strong a word) with my life for now. I know the joy of having someone meet me at the airport and the combination aloneness and strength of not being met, of handling by myself both me and the baggage.

But lately, I fear that the strength is hardening a piece in me. And I understood that for the first time in a long time I didn't love anyone. Care for, yes, but without that "connected" feeling. Or is love about something I don't even understand? Could I have been mistaken about the rushes of feelings I've had these many years?

Also flashed on Dennis. I miss the learning and realized my fascination with him was due to the worlds he opened up for me. I miss people to talk to—not just about feelings but ideas. What is curved space? But even though I miss that, this alone time is productive. Amorphous things are settling out—learning that preparation is constant, that perhaps I'll never (shudder) be able to share much of this with another, but I long to. Strange, but I think my sexual/sensual reachings out for men—they're my way of trying to connect, be close to another person, to try to bridge the chasm, but I wonder if it can ever be done. Rod and I almost did it once. The absence of passionate emotion frees me to savor the subtler ones.

Have had discussions with Julius about social responsibility versus personal responsibility. Lately I've become more aware of social responsibility, yet further from taking personal responsibility for another. For me the latter is the more difficult.

Wish I didn't need so much sleep. Please, body, behave!

April 14, 1976

Assorted thoughts:

1. My friends don't make nearly the demands on my time as I convince myself they do. I think I make a lot of it up, so I feel needed.

2. I'm bored with my job. There. It's on paper. Soon I shall deal with that.

3. It is difficult for me to be friends with men as opposed to being lovers.

4. I refuse to let myself be just ordinarily "down." I have to make it into a big catastrophe—or take the down and find deep psychological causes, when it could be just a mild blah.

5. Today for the first time I called up a strange man (a doctor who treated me at the Health Center) and asked him to have lunch. Figured I had nothing to lose. Am more excited about having done it than at the actual prospect of meeting him. Query: I'm more excited about the challenge of almost anything than I am about it when (if) it's attained. Does that mean I should set higher goals?

May 30, 1976

Reading *Small is Beautiful*—when Shumacher set out his three goals for economics: health, beauty and permanence—I had a mental wince at the last. Change has always seemed to me to be a universal condition. But what I was doing was witnessing myself exhibit mental/psychological bias/prejudice. It is most alarming to think my mind has become so closed to new concepts which challenge my basic assumptions.

June 6, 1976

National Association of Attorneys General conference. San Antonio this weekend. Met Bud. My emotions are opening up again, slowly. I feel tonight the slight ache of loneliness for someone, a precursor to knowing love again, I think. I used to call these "self-indulgence evenings." Now my attitude is changing. They may be just *living* evenings. The conference was good for me. I felt confident of myself more than in a long while. Is it possible Bud was right and I am a pretty together lady?

My work is becoming more important to me. Will I go to Washington? There are several young Attorneys General here. One from Arkansas named Clinton will be sworn in in January; a friend of Liz's. Could our generation be starting to lead? Interesting thought.

June 15, 1976

While listening to Jim Croce's "Photographs and Memories," visions of Rod and "bedroom talks" came, painful in a wistful sense. I don't feel like a "divorced woman"—whatever that is supposed to mean. Seven years of marriage memories don't disappear a year later. But maybe it takes such memories to fully understand and *feel* songs and other art forms.

July 4, 1976

I've put off writing in this diary all day. Why? Don't know.

Yesterday I *ran* (not walked) a mile. The first time I've ever done that, in about ten-and-one-half minutes. I'd like to lose some weight, maybe quit smoking, but so far haven't. Watched the Washington fireworks on TV and thought of Bud there. Or perhaps it's just being lonely for someone to share my life with. Yet as I write this, I am content—ready to sleep alone. The contradictions of my life amuse me.

I cut my hair. Still looks the same, but not quite the "young hippie chick." Today, while reading some Lessing, I realized I was getting old and have (probably) passed my prime. At least in body.

Jackie called. We mused a while on living alone. There is a chance I'll be a spinster. Although I've not perhaps been "happy" this last year-and-a-half of living alone, I've been, all in all, strangely content. However, I don't wish to become like Susan—enamored of my aloneness. (Not to be confused with independence—which I hope will continue to grow despite my physical living conditions.)

My mind is restless these days. I read with half a heart. It's as if my life had gone into hibernation for a while and is now beginning to crave breaking out. For two-and-a-half weeks I had a "fling" with Luke. Yet I have a feeling it's not the end of things. He's gone to Europe with his girlfriend for a month. I wish he were in town. Today I didn't want him with me in the house all the time, but I wanted him to be reachable. I'm learning to control the excesses of intimacy. Not to give all at once, but hopefully let it grow. I needed these last two days to calm down, take things slowly and just live a bit.

Good thought on America: We've built a nation on principles/ ideas rather than nationalism. Corny, but it strikes me as true.

Thought: In the midst of the bicentennial, my concerns still focus too much on the personal.

Query: Do I really want to be an antitrust lawyer? Is my career on a dead-end path? Lately, I've found a place among the Austin legal community. Hope I do a good job on the Grievance Committee.

July 10, 1976

While listening to a Steve Fromholz concert last night, both Al and Don were there, and I felt alone. At the time, I missed Luke, but am unsure if it is Luke himself or someone to be "in love" with that produced the ache.

Reading *The Second Sex*. Why are women always looking for a man to complete them? Sheila and I spend interminable hours discussing our men, or lack thereof. Do we really *need* them so much? It must be possible to be a complete person alone and then share with another. But to suggest that friend or family is enough, or should be, is perhaps to deny some fundamental part which does want completion in another person. Sometimes I feel on the verge of discovering some insights into the man/woman friend/lover problem, but then a new setback occurs. Thought: Usually I feel close to understanding when I'm not "involved" with a man at the moment. Don't know what that means.

When I listen to music, I listen for the familiar—tunes I know, etc., rather than listening openly, responsively for new sounds. The same is true in reading. One really does like confirmation of already held tastes, thoughts, ideas; I must learn and train myself to be open to creativity, to newness.

July 16, 1976

Bought my Canon TX camera today. Candice Bergen, here I come!

Lately, I've been jealous of other people's happiness and good work at their jobs. Sheila did an excellent job trying a case today and as she bubbled, I was happy for her, but jealous that she was good. I don't like this feeling. Am I losing generosity of spirit—or is that merely a comment on my own abilities at my job? Thought: I rarely am that kind of jealous about others' personal happiness, maybe because right now, for all my lonely complaining, I am content with my lot and wouldn't basically change it. I've tried hard to be more efficient and productive at work and to leave it alone when I come home.

September 6, 1976

Things that have occurred since my last entry:

1. I won the cooling tower case—notices in the paper. I was surprised and at first it didn't register. However, I do like winning!

2. While on my last D. C. trip, I realized I had become a pretty good lawyer and am learning to be relaxed in meetings. Not afraid to say things or get a cup of coffee.

3. I started to swim again. Can now do a mile! It's good to be in touch with my body.

4. Met Wes. He's a comfortable person.

5. Liz got married and moved to Virginia. I'm not sure I want to get married again, at least till I want to have kids. That used to be something I *said*, now perhaps I mean it.

6. I think I'm straightened out a bit about Luke. There's no real future in terms of an exclusive relationship, but I like knowing him. Unfortunately, he fascinates me and makes me confused. There must be somewhere a combination of Luke the newspaper man, and Wes, the doctor.

I think I'm getting better and better. My next goal will be to stop bitching about stuff at work and stop making snide remarks about people's bad points and instead concentrate on the positive. Sign I put up on the inside view of my IN Box: Bitch only if you mean it! Maybe its okay to be moody!

September 19, 1976

Luke doesn't know what he wants from me, or so he says. Now

after thinking about it, I think he basically just wants me *around*, as a good date, easy-to-get-along-with type. He doesn't understand that I want him to want *me* around.

October 4, 1976

From an antitrust bulletin: "The tasks of social change are for the tough-minded and the competent. Those who come to the task with the currently fashionable mixture of passion and incompetence only add to the confusion."

October 10, 1976

Decision making is entirely too difficult for me. "It's better to make a wrong decision than to wear oneself out with no decision."

I am deciding to see a shrink. I need help with tension and anxiety, allowing myself to make mistakes and not be perfect.

Am finally pretty much over Luke. Met Sean and was infatuated last night. I don't trust my reactions with men. (Or people for that matter!) Wouldn't have sex with him, although I slept with him. Sean physically is tremendously attractive to me. I can understand how men must feel about pretty women—it helps!

Had my last cigarette September 12. (Nana's birthday.) Now have problems with weight.

October 17, 1976 (Sunday)

I may perhaps begin to write daily in this diary and try to have a record of one month in my life. Today I woke up and felt fine. It was good to wake up and not be depressed, but I keep taking my emotional temperature to see if the good feelings would last. Susan's friend appeared out of the blue. The assistant federal public defender in Albuquerque—I liked him. He wrote a novel once.

Went to the art museum and saw a hologram. Mind expanding to think of creating an "extra room" which isn't there.

Don came by. He glanced through my responses to Paul (the psychologist's) questionnaire and saw my response to the sex life. Don't think he liked it.

I think I'm rebelling against discipline.

October 18, 1976

Lynn won the Roloff case! Watched part of the trial. Talked with Wes last night. He cried when he began to realize I meant we were going to just be friends. Why am I attracted only to men who give me a hard time and are abusive in some way, and am not attracted to the "nice guys"?

Sheila was down. I hope her downs aren't rubbing off too much on me.

October 19, 1976

I'm trying a new system at work. Until 9:00 I take care of personal life details, write in diary, etc., and then work very hard afterwards. Do a few minutes of meditation, currently about eating.

I called Bud and recounted my conversation with Sandee. He asked if Sam knew about "us" and got angry. I felt defensive about my reputation and it pissed me off. Had visions of Sam and Buddy chuckling over my "illicit" relationship with Buddy. Why is it that men can screw around and women just can't? The double standard really hacks me.

Last night I went to a neighborhood association meeting. Thought I ought to go and meet people, etc. It was boring and afterwards I drove all over town rather aimlessly looking for someone to drop in on. Tried to keep myself from calling Sean. I'm tired of holding back, of being rational about feelings, although I guess things like dropping in on Luke in the middle of the night show a certain lack of consideration. Wish I hadn't done that.

October 20, 1976

It's Thursday and I'm in Houston at the Hirschorn trial. Yesterday was a good day. I worked hard, swam a mile, Don unexpectedly took me to dinner, then I went out to a party for clerks who passed the bar exam. Talked with Eileen. I like her and I think she really likes me! I never expect that people might like to be my friend also. I miss having someone in my life. For the first time in a long time I'm ready (almost) to wake up with someone next to me. Sean is the current person I focus these feelings on. My reaction to him surprises me. I'm like a high school boy with a crush, afraid to ask Sean out for fear he'll reject me—or laugh at me. Hard to determine how much one should listen to other people.

October 23, 1976 (Saturday morning at the office.)
Thursday and Friday I spent in Houston, watching the trial of the big steel company executive. Had a long interesting conversation with Danny about becoming a really good lawyer and bringing myself to the Attorney General's attention. Need to think about those things.

October 24, 1976
Friars weekend has proven seminal for me. There was a presentation of letters of a thirty-three-year-old Friar who died climbing a mountain soon after he wrote them. They reflected the sense of the world around us, of beauty in nature and poverty of people and of spirit that can occur. He was committed to working at his chosen field, to try to correct the evils, yet remain questioning of them.
Perhaps the crisis in my confidence concerning the lawyering path is becoming resolved. Lawyering is a tool to accomplish some objectives—objectives which I want to be consistent with my values. But there is more to it than just *stating* the fact. The act or actions of lawyering require excellence in their execution in order for me to *enjoy* the job and feel pride in using the tool. It is this rather tremulous line—between concern for the purpose of the lawsuits and their effects on real people and the ego involvement in lawyering—which I find difficult to walk.

October 25, 1976
Long conversation with Liz about herself and office. Feds lost their case against Hirschorn.

November 3, 1976
I keep losing the thoughts that come into my head. Need to learn to jot them down, yet don't want to be a slave to a diary. Don was

nice last night, told me to quit trying so hard. Today, I quit trying and did feel better. Paul says I don't trust me. He's right. Sometimes I blame things on sex which aren't sex at all, e.g., I feel alienated from men, yet sex doesn't really help it one way or another. What confuses me these days is that I don't know who to believe—or at least don't trust my feelings. I think everyone is "good" and then when they aren't, get upset.

November 6, 1976

At a meeting at the Law School yesterday, I gave a short speech on the New Century (scholarship) Fund for minority students. I was asked by one student if the student initiators of the Fund didn't get paid! I was amazed.

Qualities for a leader—from TIME symposium:

1. Purpose.
2. Integrity.
3. Tolerance—"which is just a willingness to keep enough of an open mind to admit that you may be wrong."
4. Personal security and stability.

At work I too often berate or look down on the clerks. They need to be inspired. So do I sometimes!

Slowly I'm awakening to the fact that we are the grownups. Is leadership really to be learned and exercised on the local level first? I dream of power at times, but am bored at neighborhood meetings. Is this preoccupation with power and politics merely another passing stage in my life? And do I want to be a leader *for* something or just to be *known* as an "important" person? The hard truth is the latter, to a degree which makes me uncomfortable.

(Played my first soccer game today—fun!)

I must be careful with Attorney General Hill (John Luke Hill) because I want to be committed and perhaps to have someone else give my life meaning. That's a vulnerable position to be in, and is potentially dangerous.

Talked with my parents. A lost cause. They really don't understand about me. Daddy dominates, Mother lets him. Are there no people who understand? Maybe I need a women's group again.

My anger level is increasing. Funny, I'm being radicalized at such a late age.

I keep looking for answers when there are no stable, immutable ones, only an acceptance of change.

November 16, 1976

Matt told me everyone thought I slept with two people to get my job. I was hurt, then *furious*—I HATE MEN.

November 18, 1976

Rereading this journal, I'm struck by how cold and unfeeling I sound. It's scary. There seems to be no compassion for others. I'm so caught up in myself. What's happened to me?

December 12, 1976

Things I want to tell/talk with Paul about:
1. Anxiety attacks. I have times when I'm immobilized, feel the blood running through my body very fast and I can't control it. I had some at work this week, then one when I spent the night with Luke. It's different than just being upset or alarmed for a moment. I think I used to have them the night before exams or a first oral argument, only then I learned how to use (or tell myself I was using) them constructively.
2. I am sorry for the way I treated Paul last week: ". . . pay you to be my friend." He was right when he said I push people away if I sense them coming close.
3. About work. Diane said that at her job as a social worker, women were always taking the caretaker role and then people treated them that way rather than as bosses or even equals. She said women should use their intuition constructively.
4. Weight problem—tied in with *moderation*, something I need more of!

December 14, 1976

Last night I realized that the reason I get so anxious is due in large measure to my being so terribly concerned about what other people think rather than what I think. Also I don't really like the person I've become lately. Too selfish and introverted.

December 21, 1976

Spent the day with General Hill in Corpus raising money for the New Century Fund and then met with Ed, publisher of the local paper, and did some politicking. I used to be totally an issue person and not loyal to or especially attached to a political figure. Issues are still what it's all about in the end for me, but I'm beginning to understand that it takes people and specifically politicians to implement the ideas. Therefore, it makes pragmatic sense to work with politicians or power people to see that goals are achieved.

Which once again brings me to a second thought; what's important is the way and the end for which power is used. That means relatively clear, defined goals or objectives. Otherwise, it becomes a game, an ego trip, and if that is all it's about, then to be rich and powerful doesn't seem to be all that appealing (except for the rich part). I'd be happier making less money and being my own person, taking pictures, reading books, etc. Ah, balance, moderation!

If I were ever in power, I'd have issue people around me. Then if they gave their opinions on things, I could attempt to screen it a little for the bias that is up front on their issue and which probably colors the advice. I think even with screening, I'd get more honest advice. It's difficult to read through all the self-interest, but with cause people, the *self*-interest is minimized. This past year I've begun to understand about self interest on a professional level, and it's been a chaotic experience. One of the reasons I haven't been in control of my life is because I haven't known enough of myself and my own goals to see what my best interest is. I'm still working at it.

Lately I think self righteousness is one of the overwhelming attributes of my character. Ugh!

December 26, 1976

A relatively calm Xmas at home. My sister Cathy really is a giving person. I have guilt feelings about not putting others before myself, yet there really isn't anyone to put before me! So why feel guilty? Tonight I stayed home, read the paper, talked on the phone, played the guitar and spent quiet time alone. At these times I truly *like* my life and don't miss having someone. It just might be that I won't have a special person, but I think I could live with that. I need to find out what I really want, what's important and do it! Certainly lawyering isn't so important that it should run my life like it has lately.

January 3, 1977 (Soda Springs, California, skiing vacation)
New Year's Resolutions:
1. Lose fifteen pounds—weigh 110 by March 1.
2. Take photography lessons.
3. Take guitar lessons.
4. Save money.

Tomorrow I attempt to learn to ski—wish I were thinner and in better shape to do it. Something is not right with me that I am this heavy.

I don't envy Jane at all. I don't want demands made on me like her family does, with no time or place to be alone. Part of my reaction to her family (like Rod's) stems from the fact that I have no background like that. My family didn't do those kind of things together.

I'm beginning to appreciate my Austin life and job. I don't mind not having someone as long as I'm fat!

January 24, 1977

It's a Monday and I'm the right kind of sick—too sick to work well so I can justify staying home, and yet well enough to enjoy reading and lazing in bed. This morning I read some more of the *How to Be Free in An Unfree World* book and was able to do some thinking about my life while not in a state of anxiety or depression. I'm still not ready to look full face at myself or my life, but I'm snatching glances and learning to assimilate them. I'm afraid of the darker sides of meaningless activity and selfish nature on my part. But as the book suggested, the first step toward changing or improving your life or self is to find out about it, and accept yourself.

Hard to face, but true: I'm selfish and right now at least, not very interested in other people's lives. I'd like to change that piece a bit, but that's not just all of me. A part is very concerned about others.

I'm going to determine how I spend my time and whether I like it that way. One trait I have is to be afraid to find the BAD so I just avoid it. That habit will take a while to break but I'm getting there.

Today and several mornings last week I woke up happy! I even like me okay much of the time and am discovering that others do too. I guess it really is true that we put out vibrations of the kind of person we are and attract people who like that. Paul said it was an ego trip to put on a fake face, so that if rejected, I could say he really didn't know me.

I learned about being direct: I asked Cliff at a party, "Are you mad at me?" and he responded, "No, should I be?" When really the question was, "Why aren't you paying any attention to me? I feel slighted."

Things to face up to:
1. I'm selfish, but no one in this world is going to look after my interest as well as I will.
2. I only have one real friend—Sheila. I'd like more women friends. Diane P.?

Things I like to spend time doing:
1. Lying in the sun reading junk books.
2. Riding my bike.
3. Being alone in my house (when it's cleaned up) and reading or listening to music.
4. Listening to good live concerts.
5. Having long intimate talks with friends.
6. Swimming, if I can get in shape.

I have ambition without a definite goal. I think I want either a profession which has no outward definitions of success or else one which entirely does.

February 1, 1977

Being in therapy is like getting married—if one knew ahead of time what triumphs and heartaches were involved, one might think twice and not do it. Today I understood for the first time that I was "in therapy" and not just seeing Paul to get through a difficult time. Wish it weren't so expensive. If it helps, it certainly is worth it. I cried today and we talked about my father. I really don't have much reason to like men or trust them. I think I understand why I have such a tremendous need for physical affection which isn't related to sex—Daddy wasn't physical with us, so I constantly want and seek out men who will "cuddle" me, then get upset if they want to make love (or if they don't!).

Funny to be so blah—not really depressed or down, but not up—sort of disconnected from other people and life.

February 6, 1977

Last night while eating a GIANT sundae at Swenson's with Al, I got irritated with him when he started talking about going to church as a promise to God. It didn't fit my romantic mood or my vision of Prince Charming which I want to force Al into. Tonight I realized that I use men as emotional objects in much the same way that I've accused men of using women as sex objects. Men are not real and 3-dimensional to me like women are. I have strong urges/needs for emotion in my life which I think can only be met by a "love affair" relationship. Rather than letting a man be just who he is, I try to see him through emotion-charged eyes. That's one reason I'm attracted to men with strong outward personalities—they make me take them on their own terms and I can't manipulate.

I'm learning to use my sexuality or femininity. That's not all bad, but I'm a little uncomfortable with it yet—the using it.

Started a fast today. I have got to come to grips with my compulsive eating.

February 21, 1977 (The week of Dealing with Weight, maybe)
1. Fundamental truth: To constantly be jealous/envious of others' attributes, whether a skinny, talented Emmy Lou Harris or a "bright law clerk," is a fundamentally egocentric way of looking at the world.

2. Walking along Pease Park yesterday, I *understood* that money can't buy happiness. I was content to just be me.

March 2, 1977
1. Food won't give me what it is I am craving.
2. Neither will being thin make me happy (although it's a contributing factor! As a matter of fact I don't think I can envision being *fat* and happy.)

There is not much happening in my life these days. I seem on hold and small things assume a significance out of proportion to their actual place. Conversations loom large which should be shrugged off.

I can't stop my relationship with Cliff, but we really aren't alike. I need to just leave it alone, worry less, do what makes me feel good, let him be responsible for himself and think free thoughts.

Driving to work today I was thinking about change. Part of my frustration is thinking that I can try to be perfect and then when I don't achieve it, getting depressed. Also I impart the search for perfection on others and am upset when they don't either try or achieve it.

I'm also learning about (perhaps accepting?) personal limitations. I was catty, jealous about C and Cliff. But running to C and apologizing for the way I'd "thought" and talked to Kathie wouldn't really change that or atone, wouldn't make me perfect. That's why I go around justifying everything I do, if not to others, extensively to myself.

I am so afraid of over-romanticizing Cliff. We really aren't at all alike. Not sure Paul is right on this one—maybe I shouldn't run away.

March 10, 1977
Re-reading the last entry, I liked me! Today I started a crazy grapefruit/egg diet—guaranteed to lose ten pounds in two weeks. We'll see. Anyway, I've begun to swim again, work a bit better and generally take things a bit easier—but barely. After numerous long

discussions with Cliff, a nice weekend culminating in my leaving for Dallas on business, I finally couldn't take the trapped feeling anymore and told him I wanted a two-week vacation. It's been hard at work these last two days, but he's been great. I think I'm in love with him, but I don't need a father figure and right now, that's too large a part of our relationship. I'm torn because as Kathie says, no one is perfect. But I really need an emotional equal—not that I'm all that great, but I'm further than he is.

Even though I don't have any plans for the weekend, I feel curiously good, weightless. But strangely I don't have any other men in mind to see.

March 15, 1977

Have stayed on diet! But only lost four pounds. Ugh—ten more to go. I hate being fat. At exercise class we were to imagine sometime in our lives when we were pleased with ourselves and I couldn't think of any times. It upset me. The closest I came was when I first swam a mile.

April 17, 1977

Off to have dinner with David, Debbie and Cliff. I feel pleasantly tired, slightly anxious about seeing Cliff.

Paul said I am on the threshold of breaking out: I think he's right. Also, I think I need to apply the diligence and hard work toward therapy and weight that I do on other areas. I've been looking in the wrong places, says Paul. Learning to feel is tough!

May 1, 1977 (On flight from Honolulu to Austin)

I've done a crazy, impulsive thing—going to Hawaii for the weekend, but it feels perfectly normal, just fine. Luke and I were having dinner with Mariotti Thursday night when Mariotti said he was leaving the following morning to go to the Annual Meeting of the Society of Newspaper Editors. He suggested Luke go and Luke asked me.

The more I see of Luke, the better I like him. The patterns of growth in our relationship are interesting. The infatuation is still there, but much different than last summer. He's grown also. I must be a bit careful not to fall too hard this time. I knew when I first met him he would be an important person in my life, but I'm still not sure in what capacity.

Luke brings out the better pieces of me. Around him I feel pretty, competent, and generally like a good person. Somehow even though he's filled with nervous energy and works too hard, there is always enough time. When we're going out, I seem to be able to get ready, look fine, and still be able to wash last night's dishes before his arrival. If he asked, I would seriously consider marrying him. Rereading this diary, I realized how far I'd come since Christmas.

It was worth spending the money on the white dress.

May 3, 1977

I get better by spurts and then revert. I need to learn to stay away from people who make me feel bad. Like Matt and office politics. Just do my work and don't care about the ins and outs. *Slowly* I learn that.

May 4, 1977

Sitting in Paul's office, waiting. For a change I'm early!

Every once in a while the understanding dawns that one must enjoy the process as much as the end result to make everyday life more than merely bearable. It's like running.

May 8, 1977

After eating breakfast with Diane, Mark and Luke, I went *alone* to the exhibit of Women Artists. Doing things like that requires an effort. But after seeing the paintings I was so proud to be a woman. Blacks must feel that way in black literature/artists' courses. It's as if a part of my heritage I didn't even realize existed suddenly came alive for me.

I've almost seen too much of Luke, or at least too much on his terms. Driving to the pool to meet him, I was slightly irritated at myself for letting him run my life. Tim had come by. I knew I'd be sorry I missed him, but also didn't like it that I felt cornered and trapped by my own feelings.

May 9, 1977

A bad day, bored at work, hating Cliff and Matt. Running went poorly; I stopped after one mile. Sometimes I just get tired of trying.

I'm not myself with Luke. I'm afraid to dump on him the insecurities and the "clutchy" piece of myself. Afraid I'll lose him, but that's silly. I never had him. And if I ever did have him, that's not the kind of relationship I want.

May 11, 1977

After writing the above entry, I went to Luke's house and cried. He was nice, but just doesn't want to give me what I need. Somehow I tend to pick men who aren't affectionate and simply keep themselves removed from me.

Dreamed last night I was pregnant. Luke and Al were there. The baby was a beautiful girl—and then her head fell off to one side because I picked it up wrong. Not intentional on my part. I felt awful waking up.

Yesterday I went to the fortune teller:

1. Nana would die and leave me a piece of jewelry.
2. I was torn between two boys. One about my coloring and the other darker. Both had good qualities and I kept weighing them and being confused. Either one would make a good marriage.
3. One of them would get computer training.
4. Daddy, if he lived to be fifty-six, would be in the hospital with liver and gastric trouble. He'd recover and try to make it up to Mother.
5. My work environment was filled with dog-eat-dog competition. I felt as if I were getting a raw deal and I was.
6. I'd leave government work. Go into practice with two lawyers, a man and a woman.
7. The light-haired lawyer was honest with me.

8. My sister Janet was happy; Cathy may be divorced in two years.
9. A child, a little boy, was running around.
10. Luke would invite me to go on vacation to a coast in July.
11. I'd buy a new car.
12. I shouldn't leave this job till I had something definite.
13. I'd make the decision to leave this job in two months.

May 14, 1977

Will gets married tonight. Andrea, not I, will be Luke's date.

Emily told me she had had Hodgkin's disease for three years. She's one of two people who've lived after having it. I asked how she felt—"scared." All the problems recede a bit in that context. Yes, I do love being alive!

Paul said he would hurt with me if after all these months of discovering my identity I'd let it be submerged into another's.

Why I like/love (?) Luke:

1. He's strong as a person.
2. He makes me be the best person I am when I'm with him.
3. He has a strong sense of family.
4. He tries to understand and learn from his actions.
5. He's not afraid to cry.
6. He's incredibly honest and direct: "There isn't any spark between us." "Someday you'll find someone who'll light up the whole way, not halfway like I do." Example: He forgot an 8:00 a.m. appointment. Rather than have his secretary lie for him, he got on the phone with the appointment person, explained he forgot, felt embarrassed and offered to meet again at *her* office so as to save her the trip.

I think I want to marry him, but I'm not sure yet. He's certain we'll always be friends, but not "lovers/long range exclusive partners" because our backgrounds are too different. He may be right. I feel rejected that Luke feels no sexual desire for me. Funny thing is that I don't feel that kind of sexual feeling for him, either; rather, a lot of affection.

Things I don't like about Luke:

1. He's selfish.

2. He works too much.

3. Although he's in good touch with his own feelings, he's not very sensitive to mine.

May 20, 1977

In Houston for the first pretrial conference in the steel case. Since all the major producers were involved (U. S. Steel, Bethlehem, Armco, etc.), there were at least two representatives for each of the nine company defendants. Lawyers, lawyers everywhere!

May 22, 1977

This morning, I put Luke on a plane to Seattle. It felt good to be alone and in my house with no plans.

Tonight driving from Luke's after dropping off his paper, I felt the in-love ache. It came as a surprise to me. I have to hold back. He's told me so often that he didn't think we'd work. Should I believe him? I don't trust men very well. I'm afraid to rely on their words since so many have lied to me. Yet Luke wouldn't lie and he says so clearly that he only wants friendship from me. Why must I always hear what I want to hear rather than the truth? I've not been totally honest in words with Luke. He knows I'm in love with him, but since I try to downplay it, he does too.

From Rod and Cliff, I learned you can't change someone. So I must take Luke as is. It's difficult for me to separate what Luke is *really* like from what I *want* him to be like. For example, I didn't think he was particularly affectionate, but that's not true. It's just that sometimes, especially in public, he doesn't want to be affectionate with *me*.

No wonder Luke thinks I'm a wonderful, marvelous woman. If I devoted a month to any one person the way I've done with Luke, of course they'd think I was wonderful! It's hard to stop being obsessed by Luke. But my life continues and I must "center" again.

Timing is of the essence. I'm ready to settle down, be committed. The next man of the proper kind I'll probably fall for. That's a scary thought, but I'm better prepared this time.

June 1, 1977

At therapy the other day, Paul told me he liked me and that but for the client relationship we had, he would enjoy having me in his "life space." I gave him a hug. He also told me to think about other people as being lucky to know me, that the men in my life were getting a good deal. That conversation has given me strength this week. We discussed how I'd feel when I finally realized that men were just people like me.

Bud has offered me a job in Massachusetts. I'm flying up there. We'll see—its flattering. Slowly I'm learning about being aggressive with my career. Luke is good for me about those things.

Luke? I think we may have missed the magic. I'd like that in my life again.

June 2, 1977

While driving to work, I was stuck behind a city garbage truck. Two muscled, middle-aged black men lifted large cans and with graceful swinging movements threw yesterday's egg cartons and lawn remains into the truck. Conflicting feelings of "sorry for them" and appreciation not only of the function, but of the ease with which they performed their job. But why are garbage men always black, and am I a white liberal snob to even feel sorry for them? People don't need that kind of patronizing.

June 5, 1977

General Hill made a speech Friday to the Houston Democratic Quorum and mentioned my name—to 850 folks! Also said today at the ranch he wanted to make me a chief or assistant chief.

Dinner in San Antonio at the Institute for Texan Cultures with Luke and the Maguires. I've come a long way. Wore my white Hawaiian lacy dress and mixed with the guests. They were delightful.

Luke is getting better and over Andrea. But as he does and learns to fly again, he doesn't need me anymore, and like a frightened parent, afraid he'll never return, I want to keep him weak and mine. But I can't and I won't. He's gaining himself back, spending time with male and female friends and putting his life back together. Soon he'll feel the joy again.

If this relationship ever works as a lover relationship, he is going to have to come to me whole for his own sense of self-worth and frankly, for my continued respect. I'm afraid to admit that Luke just might not be the right person or kind of person, because then I'll have to start all over. But maybe that's okay. We'll try again for an equal relationship.

I've been in a good mood for several days now. It's nice to be up.

June 14, 1977 (With General Hill at a convention in Indianapolis)

JLH: A sense of the weight of unknown issues, facts, life-affecting decisions; yet one man, rather short, tired, a bit sick, must have the ready smile and twice-winded vitality to remain decisively compassionate.

June 15, 1977 (On plane from Indianapolis-Boston)
Quick random thoughts:
1. To grow old will put me beyond the reach of sex. So much of my life, of relationships, is based too much on sex or the possibility thereof.
2. It really doesn't matter what I do. Life is establishing the world around you in a way to make you feel useful, secure and challenged. Whether that takes place in Austin, Boston or Guatemala really doesn't matter. So I can take my around-the-world trip.
3. I spend too much time leading up to actions: e.g. walking up the aisle to give my resumé to the Boston AG. All confidence leaves and I become a supplicant. Where did I learn to be so afraid of failure?
4. NAAG-General Hill: Politics. It's heady, but once accomplished, or seen as accomplishable, I'm not interested.
5. Texas is my heritage, my home; the South, my lingering pride and shame.

June 20, 1977

Note to myself: Anita Bryant, civil liberties and free speech: an uneasiness about absolute freedom to say what one believes when it leads people to do things so contrary to my value system. What of Hitler?

Second most significant book: *The Golden Notebook*. Just finished the *Four Gated City*. (First was *The Brothers Karamozov*)

Lately I've been growing and thinking by leaps and bounds. There is a distancing process I engage in at various times in my life.

A prayer I wrote for JLH on plane to Indianapolis—he had to give it at breakfast:

In a time of divisiveness, we pray for unity.

In a time of intolerance, we pray for understanding.

In a time lacking leadership, we pray for guidance.

In a time of the whirlwind of issues, debates, arguments,
    we pray for insight.

Center us, oh Lord.

June 30, 1977

It is possible to arrange my life to meet all my needs, but to do so runs me ragged; therefore, I must decide priority needs. Simplification of my life is in order.

Yesterday, the responsibility of being named assistant chief dawned on me. No longer can I pass the ultimate feeling of responsibility on to Cliff. Need to learn more substantive law.

Susan explained that in politics the trick is to ascertain what motivates other people to do whatever it is you want done, and then play to *their* reasons, not yours. "Other people might not be following your agenda." Otherwise one wastes effort.

July 7, 1977

Notes from 4th of July weekend in Dallas with Rod, family, Jane and Bill:

Following my younger sister Janet through the house converted to her office at the Recreation Center, listening to her bubbling explanation of Lewisville's bond plans, the Park Board Senior Citizen programs, I suddenly realized that my baby sister and those like her in communities throughout the U. S. provide the real background/backbone of American democracy.

July 11, 1977

An amazing phone call from Daddy. While reading Jaworski's book last night, he realized that I was one of the young lawyers like those mentioned in the book—that I was not a "kid." He said he wanted me to know that one can teach an old dog new tricks and that it was a humbling experience. I was so touched; tears sprang up and I told him I loved him. He said he needed that; we both became embarrassed.

July 12, 1977

I ran two miles today for the first time in several weeks. Once again running is serving as the physical outlet for my anger and frustration. I had sought Cliff's advice on drafting motion responses for summary judgment in the steel case, and he began screaming at me, rather than helping. Instead of ignoring it—or taking it, and trying to calm him down—I raised my voice and told him he didn't have to scream at me, that what he was screaming at me about was precisely the reason I had asked his advice—to give me help in getting out of the particular logical/legal box our posture on the motions required. He didn't acknowledge my comment, but stopped yelling and came up with a solid solution, BUT he talked to Matt and ignored me. Christ, I'm tired of these games. Or is it possible I thrive on them? One problem in never working in a "normal" situation is that one gets used to the abnormal and loses track of how to operate in the "real" world. Wonder if that is true of dating uncommunicative men as well.

At the Y after running, my feet were hot and tired, but they could *feel*. The toes separately felt the smooth yet crunchy artificial turf mats outside the showers. And I said a small prayer on how lucky I was (1) to have toes and feet and (2) to be able to "feel." Sometimes my head becomes too cluttered. One of the major positive effects of running is that it teaches the wonder of my senses. I'm learning to "see" the shades of green in the trees and feel the blood in my veins and air course through lungs. Slowly a respect for this humble body is dawning on me. Looking down at my knees as they support my diary, I'm struck by how frail and intransigent a vessel my body is. This is going to carry "me" for the rest of my life? I should remember that the next time a longing for an entire box of Wheat Thins hits!

I've started to pray again. Why? Perhaps unconsciously the thoughts of Bruce Wrightsman, an old religion prof from college, return. The triggering event was seeing John O. at the Hill BBQ who had recently undergone surgery for cancer. I told him I'd pray for him (though what possessed me to say that I don't know) and having so promised, I began to do so. I stood before my locker at the Y, having run out my anger, and let the rote words of the Lord's Prayer float across my mind.

Old childhood prayers returned: God bless John O., Mother, Daddy, Sheila, Luke, Cliff (yes, even Matt). And the list of friends who enrich my life paraded by. What does it mean? Has faith returned? I doubt it. But for now it is comfortable, and real.

Can't sleep tonight, so reread diary entries and then began *The Golden Notebook*. Lessing was absolutely correct when she said that one shouldn't read a book until one is ready—don't force feed the "ought to" books. I'm glad I waited to read Lessing.

Tonight when Al was here, I had a sense of freedom in knowing that it was okay to take relationships with men for what they are and not to try to make them "loves" of my life and then be upset when they aren't. Also I'm learning that men can be my friends, and I don't need to "buy" friendship with sex. I don't think I've ever really believed that before. I use sex to get close, but I don't think I have to do so to be friends. A lot of my confusion about men comes from this.

August 13, 1977

A quiet morning of Sunday tasks, letters, thought. Feeling relaxed all through. Can I tell Doris Lessing that I almost lost my life to lists?

August 29, 1977

1. I think I'm falling a little bit in love with Tim. At least sometimes I think of him and smile.

2. Realization that I normally associate love with pain. Or at least attach the words "in-love" with the dreadful feeling of anticipation of rejection.

3. The pattern repeats. I am involved with one person whom I let keep me from opening up my life the way I want it. But damn it. Who cares? It's my life and I'll order it as I please! So what if "people" think I'm climbing the social ladder to date Tim. If it makes me happy, it's my business. Tonight another small breakthrough. I understood that Cliff loses his place as "authority" figure as I get to be a better lawyer, so his hold over me goes away. I can do most of the things as well as he can, or will soon be able to do so.

September 2, 1977

Cliff and I broke up tonight. I feel sad, relieved, frightened at the thought of being alone. There's no place to turn anymore but to me, inside myself. This is a strange feeling, not as immediate as most of the hurts I've gone through. Any pain I feel for Cliff's absence is either slight or more deeply held down. It is okay if I get over Cliff sooner rather than later.

I'm taking my life back, or perhaps it's more accurate to say I am just starting it. Singlehood is frightening. As I write that, I think of having a child, but that really won't do it.

Sheila was told tonight that she had the talent to be the city attorney some day. I was proud for her, and jealous. They said it was in part because she's so honest. That's really true. She's a remarkable person.

September 30, 1977

An important month in my life has just passed. Immediately after I broke up with Cliff, Tim and I went on an incredible trip through Central Texas. I bought new hiking boots; we stopped at the Hill ranch and heard JLH rehearse a draft of the announcement speech. Then to Luckenbach (where Tim was attacked by a chicken). Kerrville, Balanced Rock, Enchanted Rock, Pedernales Falls, Longhorn Cavern. I fell in serious like with Tim while climbing down the back of Enchanted Rock. It was dangerous and wonderful all at the same time. That weekend was some of the most fun I've ever had.

The political arena occupies a major position in my life now. Through Susan, Tim, Stan, etc., I'm involved. But as usual I'm concerned about adopting someone else's dream. With Luke it was his world of the paper; with Tim, it's politics. But probably what I'm best at is lawyering. Only at times I get tired of the inaction. Last week it was fun because I had so much to do. I am just too scared by the trial lawyering part. But I bet I could be good. Maybe the secret is to stop fighting the things I do well and work on improving them. Lawyering also gives me an independence from the political arena I think is essential. Luke has his through his financial resources; Tim through his business possibilities. That's in part the lure of private practice—to learn enough to really become good, thereby gaining independence.

Part of my fear with the increasing involvement with Tim is his inner sense of commitment and direction. His life has a general plan and it is (as usual) all too easy for me to adopt his interests, his goals.

My vision of a better world has been tempered. A lot of it has become personalized. I want the process and instinctively know that for me that's the most important part. End results pale in comparison. Analogous to marriage with Rod: the years together are the significant moments, not the end result of divorce.

If you tell a few select people your visions, they crystallize and seem not so far fetched. Yes, I'd like to be AG. What do I need in order to do so? More solid lawyering experience and a political base. But I don't *really* want to be the candidate; I want to be the candidates' best friend/wife. Is that a cop-out?

Why have a specific career goal?

1. It's more fun to control that aspect of my life than to be controlled.
2. It's fun/challenging to make the decisions and know they have impact for the good I want to see done.
3. It's stupid and wasteful to ignore that sense of potential.

Money—I have enough now for regular needs to be perfectly comfortable. More money is for future security. I'd like to buy this house and add some rooms.

I'm getting thin again and my handwriting is improving. A sure sign of getting healthy. Slowly, I've noticed that I'm starting to associate eating with my body.

Still very prominent on my lifetime list is having a baby. (I think.)

October 3, 1977

Ran three miles with Luke at lunch. One mile too far. He'll always be special to me, and the blue eyes beckon; probably always will. I think I understand better where he is these days and I'm somewhere else further along the path.

Filed my first lawsuit that I worked up all alone! Splitting from Cliff was good.

I've been smiling a lot—Tim.

October 3, 1977

A wonderful letter from Lee S. in Dallas at the end of a grueling day at work and then a grievance meeting. And I was worried that he was disappointed or upset with me. Points out how much my frustrations are created out of whole imaginary cloth.

Quote from Loren Eisley's autobiography, strangely mentioned in Lee's letter since I too had been reading it: "One must somehow find a way of loving the world without trusting it; somehow one must love the world without being worldly." G. K. Chesterton

There is a network of men in my life with whom I've shared joy and who, like Lee S., have been truly touched by my presence in their lives. This quality to reach out and secure for a moment a connection with what lies at the heart of someone is my gift. It doesn't take any effort on my part—at least in a work sense. It's like Susan's facility to help different people—who have common goals but varying methods—come together.

In a flash I perceived this quality and simultaneously realized that's one of Tim's qualities too. We both attract friends.

October 12, 1977

Last night was my parents' thirtieth anniversary. Daddy left Mother alone and went drinking. When I called later, he got on the extension and after being wished happy anniversary, told me the "anniversary doesn't start till Saturday. You've ruined everything."

October 19, 1977

Events:

1. "Graduated" from Paul.
2. Major run-in with JLH. Lesson: he can question our judgments (mine, Stan's, Tim's) but not our motivation.

Tonight I said yes to Tim. He doesn't know it yet, but I made a commitment. He's a part of my life in a long term sense. The fears I have center on my place in his world.

Tim has absolutely no lack of self-confidence. That was a startling revelation to me tonight as I lay alone contemplating this relationship. One piece of myself I'm so reluctant to share with him, is my insecurity; he values self-confidence incredibly. Stan's arrival has also brought the old fears and jealousies back to the forefront. They never disappear—just become background. (An aside: I trust Susan. She is one of the rare, essentially good people. A natural, not learned one, like me.)

It is terrifically important for me to remain *my own person*. I become too chameleon-like when I am around my men. Assume their posture in life. My dreams on the outside (external success) are modest; on the inside (personal success) grandiose.

October 23, 1977 (Approaching my twenty-ninth birthday)

Last week was one of the hardest (in a work sense) that I've ever encountered. Decision after decision, crisis upon crisis and eventually an anxiety attack about my capabilities. But I got through without falling apart; enormous physical exhaustion, however. Thought: It takes physical energy to stay on top of things psychologically. I've known but not really understood that before.

Tim and I have had a difficult time this week. Just not enough time to be together and alone. I'm a bit scared, but this morning I thought that this period was just part of living and loving between us. We can't always be madly in love, and sometimes we'll both be insecure. What's tough is both of us having such tough weeks at the same time.

He's asleep beyond the leaves beside me, tucked away in my quiet white house. My skin has memories of its own which come unbidden by brain and I feel the tautness of his soft skin next to mine. Sleep patterns have changed; where once I held the little boy in him, he now cradles the woman in me.

Autumn arrived. Twice in as many days I've been barraged by onslaughts of yellowbrown leaves. In the Capitol area they fall, small and soft—brown snowflakes. Here on my picnic table they are large and pound my head hard when windblown. I love this short season we call "fall." Cool breezes, yet warm sun on my back.

Qualities I strive for:

1. Judgment.
2. Empathy—to exchange souls for a moment is the key to understanding, and only through understanding can we truly make changes toward a better world.
3. Stability.
4. Competence.

These moments, alone outside, are the source of strength for me. I must feel the wind to become part of it. Someday I'll learn to evoke this state of mind at will. Already, I sometimes can. Since I can't slow down some of my activities, I am going to approach the days in ways that afford moments of peace. Otherwise, I'll burn out. And I *won't* do that.

Talking with Eileen about her anger with JLH. She believes he's out of the office campaigning too much. I disagreed; he needs to win the election to make Texas a better state. As I said that, I realized I have truly become caught up in the political. Shocked at how my perceptions had become pragmatic. But we need both sides.

October 31, 1977
Why go back to Paul?
1. Fight with JLH.
2. Work tensions.
3. Daddy, DWI, etc.

Went back to Paul:
1. He said to trust my own judgment and don't go back on decisions.
2. Assume if problems arise, they can be fixed and I'll fix them.

November 8, 1977
Mother called last night. Daddy, given the choice between her and the bottle, picked up his glass and walked out of the room. She's talking of divorce. I must stay away from that. It's their lives. God, I was angry. Instead of parents, I feel as if I have two children to watch and care for. It isn't fair.

Tim had had a terrible day. I raged inside, felt lonely, and didn't tell him until this morning. I think I'm so afraid of confrontation, of rejection, that I not only don't know how to fight, I don't know how to ask openly for help. I need to be direct, but I'm so damn scared.

Tim? I'll screw it up if I'm not careful. Both try, but there's so little time. Part of the problem is that I understand the decisions he's making. I'd protect and nourish my job, too. I want to run his life, tell him to teach JLH consideration, because otherwise, I'll leave. (Absurd thought.)

November 12, 1977
Amazingly, that last entry was written in Paul's office waiting for my appointment, and both staying out of my parents' lives and

demanding my needs from Tim were themes in therapy. Guess I need to go back to block one and re-learn to trust my own judgment.

Tonight Mark and I went to the Symphony while Diane kept the baby. Japanese night; interesting to listen to the dissonance. I'd earlier run three and three-fourths, so was pretty beat.

Al stopped by Mark and Diane's afterwards too. He unsettles me; instead of feeling good about him, I let myself be on the defensive in an argument. When I told him of my massive fight with JLH, Al said I lived in an unreal world and that the real world was one of power (and putting cronies rather than ideals first). I'm tired of justifying idealism. Thought: Mark doesn't justify his "niceness." But since he bought the big house, no one gives him as hard a time.

Tim: I sense my friends disapproving. I'll have to ask if that's true. I try harder with his friends than he does with mine in general. I'm scared these days. This is serious. My loyalties are switching; I'm beginning to put Tim and me against the world. Maybe part of why I'm scared is that I fear Tim doesn't really know me, so he can't really love me.

We'll find out in Mexico.

I've come so terribly far from lawyering; and I'm not really interested in it anymore. Listening to Al talk, it hit me that I resented the lawyering and want to do something else. What? All of this politics is burning me out. I'm not that enamored of power anymore. Would rather be my own boss and lead a simpler life. To do that, I may have to try to become rich. How? Do one very large antitrust suit. My God, how callous I've become.

Luke? When he's sweet, he makes the butterflies come, but in the long run, he doesn't love me. I understand why we can't be together, and think of Tim.

November 14, 1977 (Middle of the night)

Anxiety has returned; the stomach churns and I can't sleep. Immediate cause, the arts speech. Yes, I'll fix it, and in my head I understand the principle that if problems arise they can be fixed and I'll fix them.

Mother sounds scared on the phone. She resents Paul, I fear. Perhaps I'm too tough on her, but talking to Cathy, Janet and me instead of openly talking to Daddy is part of their problem. Sometimes it seems so clear to me that they need help and their patterns are obvious.

Tim backs off; L: "I told Luke we were serious; he asked if I were going to marry you; I said not yet, but I'd thought of it." T: "Well, one thing is for sure, we're not going anywhere in this relationship until I get myself together and I'm not there yet." L: "I don't want you unless you're there."

I'm impatient. I want to be loved madly, passionately, romantically. Tim says he doesn't feel that way, rather his love for me is like a river, very steady. I thought that eventually he'd "fall in love" with me, but I admit there are more rivers than torrents on my side too.

The politics hurt. I'm not sure I can live like this; we'll never be free. I'm reassessing lawyering. But this is not productive thought time. I'll give it until May.

November 15, 1977 (After a visit to Paul)

I'm falling back into old patterns because "it's the first time since making a lot of changes that I've had so much pressure to deal with." It's the campaign. Sheila and Paul were both right. That's what started the anxiety attack again on Friday! So maybe if I get out, I'll feel better. One full-time politician in this family is enough!

Am I an elitist? Yes. Is that *bad?* I don't know. I try to live my life *not* to be.

I think I've calmed down again. Had a peaceful day with Tim, reading, a long walk. Our best times are outside walking after we've jogged and in the morning. We're both in some turmoil about jobs, life, each other, etc. But I feel a fundamental thread of security and solidity for us. I think we'll always be close friends, regardless of what happens.

Tim says he loves me for my "goodness." I know he knows the pettiness, but does he know the blackness?

Thanksgiving, 1977 (Zihjuatanejo, Mexico)

With Tim; we learned. "You're more in love with me, but I'm more serious." Perhaps I cried on the balcony, but didn't run alone to the waves constantly crashing on the sand. Turning to Tim, I threw my arms around him. "Each time I try, I think we aren't alone, but then it always comes back to being cold and very lonely." His face close to mine, the blue eyes intent, "That's not true! We have something good here. Hold on to that." And I collapsed from the churning emotions, was led quietly into our room.

And he learned. In a quaint Mexico City hotel (the Geneva) shadows danced lightly across the ancient antique furniture, the lovemaking candle still casting glows. Tim, fumbling with a cufflink (I recall?) glanced up, and oh-so-casually asked, "Would you love me even if I didn't do politics?" Lying on the bed, I felt my body fall deeper into the covers. I was dumbstruck. He did not understand I love him despite rather than because of politics!

Am finally reading *The Golden Notebook* again. My God, that woman understands!

November 30, 1977

The first cold, blustery winter day arrived, and I secretly congratulated myself for having a dreadful cold and staying home from work, curled, cocoon-like in my bed. Glancing from these pages, I see his flowers and smile. This morning Tim packed frantically, and we said words.

November 31, 1977

After two days at home, I am only now really beginning to go inside myself, to think about why I spend my life's time in this manner. I do want to get out of lawyering, but how? Am I being totally unrealistic to imagine a life of writing/pictures/songs? I must attempt to write some more if that's what I want to do. I'm afraid I'll fail, but then if I don't try now, I will always wonder.

I feel as if I'm entering a new stage in my life. I love this little room, inside my quiet house. It's finally me. If I only had this little place the rest of my life, it would be okay. This house contains peace.

What I really like to do is be lazy. And read, and think of "personal" things. This good feeling is contentment.

December 1, 1977

Sometimes I turn myself on more by what I look like than by what my sexual partner looks like. For example, if I am thin, I'm turned on, even if my partner's slightly heavy; but not true in reverse.

December 2, 1977

Dear Ms. Lessing: I would like to write you a letter about *The Golden Notebook*, but suddenly I hear my breathing and am distracted.

What a remarkable period of time I've just experienced. Being ill and alone this week, I've lived inside and rather calmly. I think I'm becoming less afraid of what I'll find inside. My emotions and ideas range; the very diffuseness saps energies when I fight to be centered. Like a bubble pushed into too small a space, some piece protrudes out while I gallantly try to stuff it in; excuse me world, while I subdue this embarrassing thing that snuck out.

Thought: I like this me; I'm at home with this me; it feels right. I respect the part of myself that thinks/feels creatively. It's not like putting on lawyer clothes and making a "fakey appearance."

December 3, 1977

At the beauty salon, I turn meekly into a woman led: my entire body given to the ministrations of strong-fingered, strong-voiced ladies scrubbing hard on my scalp.

December 4, 1977

Too much emotion today. My eyes red and tired from tears. Tim: "I used to be able to give one hundred percent of myself to my dream, but now you take some of that energy, so I've less to give." Linda: "I think your dream is pretty narrow if there isn't room in it for you to love me, or someone." I told Tim there was something wrong that he felt drained by our relationship rather than replenished.

On a hill in the golf course, the sunset was brilliant pink/orange.

I felt the distance and thought I wasn't going to be the one with Tim. We have a fundamental difference. I know that what's most important next to myself is having, loving one other special person. What's most important for Tim is his vision to leave the world a better place. It's almost messianic in fervor. But that strikes me as such a sterile way to live.

When Tim left, I called Luke and we walked in the park while I cried. Luke has been where Tim is; the campaign is Tim's wife and I'm his mistress. Luke: "If you wait long enough, someone will change to your point of view—that loving one person is most important." But probably not Tim (and besides I love him for his dreams).

Writing this, I think campaigns come and go. I'm at least as important as JLH. If and when Tim finds the position of his dream, I don't think he'll be lonely. He draws strength from friends, and will always have women.

I write in the past tense mentally; I think it's over, although the complicated dance of the ending must play out. I went too fast, now must slow down. The tears tonight will ease the pain of parting. I've been hurt by Tim's absence, but there's a strong me deep inside. I think when the campaign is over, I'll go to Mexico for the summer and learn Spanish. Why do I feel as if it's the end? Am I merely working myself into a state? Of what? I miss him.

Vicki called. She and Jay made the trip to the Far East that I want to make. Serendipity!

December 8, 1977

These men in my life confuse me. Tonight drank beer with Stan and Rod, then later Luke wanted to talk, so went to Jeffrey's for dinner.

Luke, and I think Tim, want women who are independent and active in their own lives, but who are also willing to help them with their ambitions. But they really aren't willing to give quite enough back to make the trade-off. With Luke there would be the lure of financial security.

I think I'll plan my China/India trip.

December 9, 1977

I'm pregnant. Calmly I put two potatoes in to bake, pour out a measure of Diet D.P. and allow myself the luxury of Wheat Thins. Kathie called me in San Antonio just before I went into Kelleher's office to negotiate a lawsuit, and told me the test results were positive. I marched down the hall of the law offices, thinking how strange a world I live in. How much more can my system take?

I very carefully arranged the details (which have now gone awry) in case Tim couldn't be here. I realized I was afraid to lean on the man in my life. I feel very distanced from everything and very alone. And tired.

I want someone else to make arrangements for me.

I'm not sure I can easily forgive Tim for not being here. There could be so many times in our lives when things like this happen and he has to choose to come home. The only men I really trust to come through are Rod, and maybe Luke.

December 11, 1977 (Written in the waiting room while the valium took effect)

The Ladies Center does an excellent job counseling and preparing the women. But the men should be counseled too. They should understand all of this. The women as a whole are so young and seem flippant, slightly, about the abortion. I'm scared, but will do okay.

December 12, 1977

Tim came home Friday night at 3:00 a.m. Rod had soothed and comforted me, and most of the tears had gone. In bed at night, I was angry and distanced. He should have called earlier and found out. He doesn't face up to things sometimes. (A trait I share).

But the next morning, the doctor's office called: there had been a cancellation. So off we trooped, Tim not really knowing what to do. The clinic personnel were wonderful—much counseling—but it took so very long, from 11:00 a.m. to 5:00 p.m. The actual abortion was not too bad. The cramps afterwards, however, were almost unbearable. All the pain concentrated in my right ovary. It still cramps me as I write. I thought that half hour in recovery would never end. Tim and Sheila met me. At home Tim had brought me daisies and chocolates and bath crystals.

Late that night, alone, the tears streamed down my face. What had we done? Losses swirled around me.

December 26, 1977 (Austin)

Christmas at home with my family was truly delightful. Mother and Daddy danced to old time music; I caught a glimpse of the affection, deep-felt between them. No one could have a richer, warmer feeling.

Tim and I are civilly saying goodbye, but trying oh-so-hard to make it a sweet ending, and prolonged. Strange how I know this is so, but don't want to make a clean break. There's no room in his life for a woman who won't conform to his political needs and lifestyle. Lately I've begun to think that essentially I'm a loner, in a secret, private way. My life is lived on so many levels internally and I no longer even care to try to take another person with me to most of those levels. The internal aloneness is my strength, but also my isolation.

A woman of no faults! The ludicrous idea whistles laughingly through the dark caverns in my mind, bouncing drunkenly off the dark, ugly places, the fear holes, the screaming selfishness, the utter demandingness of my being. How little one human being really knows or understands of another.

I need to stay in touch with the words: this paper, this concrete black ink, it's important. To physically control the mind/message connection is important. Though as yet I'm not sure why or how.

Thinking back over this past month, there has been more pain than joy associated with Tim. I feel trapped yet uncertain all at once. The distancing has begun. Is it reversible?

December 28, 1977

Oh, but the mornings are so filled with warmth and the joy of his affection! Curled sleep/warmed bodies stretch around and through open arms and legs. Light kisses on my neck erase the lin-

gering sadness of the night's dreams. In the dream I was alone, at Hothorpe Hall in England. And no one could help me, but me.
Tim: "But people aren't meant to be that way, doing it alone."
Later after lunch with Ray:

Ray gives me strength. He listens to my Mexico plans of six months to read and write and says, "Hmm, sounds like a good idea." His point, well-taken, is that nothing publishable need come out of the experience. I'll learn though.

It's important to walk, not run, away from all this.

December 30, 1977

From a speech by Ernest L. Boyer, U. S. Commissioner of Education, given in Minneapolis, October 5, 1977, on Arts and Education:

"The educated heart means to me a deep respect for excellence wherever it is found. The educated heart means an expectation of beauty, a tolerance of others, a reaching for beauty without arrogance, a courtesy toward opposing views, a dedication to fairness and social justice, precision in speech and thought, and a love for graceful expression and audacious intellect."

January 1, 1978

The year ended, I suppose on a characteristic note: tremendous emotional upheaval. This is the year of endings—with Luke, with Cliff, and of beginnings, of me, maybe Tim, Susan. I'm learning to understand myself better, but it's a long, difficult process.

January 4, 1978

JLH asked Tim this morning if he were contemplating marriage to me; perhaps that's why his work seemed affected lately. Two thoughts: One, I'm not clear what Tim answered; and two, JLH and Bitsy were more perceptive than I'd thought. Tim's comment about deciding to give it one hundred percent and reevaluate later leads me to believe he plans to campaign first and worry about me later. I always assume the worst, and that's not healthy.

Lately the old quote from the Alexandria Quartet haunts me. In love, the partners are never equal: one always loves more than the other. Perhaps I am a lover rather than a lovee. It seems I am most happy when able to give a lot, and I don't handle someone being in love outwardly with me. Thought: maybe that's the fundamental reason Luke and I wouldn't make it. And with Rod, he's a lover and he loves me; I count on him.

One needs more goals in life than only personal development. Lunch with Sharon when she so remarked. But adopting an outside framework and structure to infuse life with meaning won't work for me either. That's my conflict with politics. Not that I don't like it, but I don't find it more meaningful than other human endeavors. I think I just don't perceive it as being an effective tool for *good* change the way Tim does.

How to win Tim: Such terminology, but at 12:30 a.m., it's the best I can muster:

1. Have more fun together.
2. Run, take walks, be outside—our best times are with nature.
3. Spend time apart while he's in town; this one is difficult, but important.
4. Don't discuss our "future together." We both get uncomfortable. If it happens, it will be okay.
5. Share doubts and fears, but not only those relating to our relationship.
6. Share joys, funny office tales. I need to discuss my work with somebody too!
7. Be direct as much as possible. Especially say what I want and if I don't care, practice picking something out anyway; usually I have a preference.
8. Be more accepting of our relationship. Tim's in my life. He's not going to change dramatically so enjoy the good parts, and put the rest on hold for awhile.
9. Meanwhile, on my own, I'm going to try to examine what I really want from myself, Tim, my work.

Unfortunately, where loving people is concerned, being realistic is not my long suit!

A value crisis has sneaked up on me.

Things I like doing:

1. Running outside on a good day.
2. Hot showers after running on any day.
3. Writing in my diary.
4. Finishing a task at work when it's well done and involves organization of ideas and people.
5. Talking with Diane.
6. Taking pictures, or rather looking at them when processed.
7. Reading, absorbing books; either with good plots or interesting philosophy.
8. Playing guitar with friends.

January 5, 1978

Paul suggested I think about a two week "vacation" from Tim. "The first week you'll be lonely. By the second week's end, you'll know whether you want to begin seeing him in the same way." Why am I so fearful of a separation? Afraid of being lonely, afraid of reverting to old behavior patterns. Paul said the latter certainly wasn't a good enough reason to stay in a relationship. Also, we've been ambivalent for quite some time now, and at least we'll break the pattern. I said I was so afraid of an ending and couldn't go through one. But that's not a good reason to stay either, and besides, apart we might get some perspective and find out what's really troubling us—each other or ourselves.

January 9, 1978

Driving Sheila from her hole in the wall (she'd gotten angry and kicked the wall, taken valium to calm down and fearful of taking too many had forced herself to throw up, and then I arrived!) I realized that any "roving eye" feelings I had were normal, and did not mean the end of my relationship with Tim.

January 15, 1978

In an Austin laundromat. Super Bowl Day. Truth: I do not get what I need from Tim. Truth: I probably never will. Truth: We drag each other down now. Truth: I should quit seeing him for a couple of weeks.

Why does it take the heart so long to learn what the head already knows?

January 17, 1978

Day two of the two-week "vacation" from Tim. Visit with Paul. He suggested the mistress role is not fulfilling. I've got a lot to learn about negotiating.

Paul says I'm overly romantic about relationships. But on the way home I felt as if everyone is out to squelch the romanticism. Reminds me of my father's talks on idealism versus contacts and how the world *really* works.

I've learned to control much of my life. The physical comings and goings; now I must try to control more of the way I meet my needs (that is, if I can ever figure out what they are . . .)

January 17, 1978

Sheila remark: "If it's true that the law is a jealous mistress, then I'm a lesbian!"

January 20, 1978

Query: Absent financial considerations, would you spend your time in the same manner, work-wise? Sheila answers yes. Me? I don't know.

January 21, 1978

Working on the Gulf illegal campaign contributions case. Ironic to think of me curled up on this cold, cold, ugly Saturday, wrapped up in the SEC report, while across town, Dorsey, the ousted President, must be going about his business. I have a mental image of his building a roaring fire in some elegant home contrasted with me and the gas heater and bundles of blankets!

January 27, 1978

Gulf was easy! There was only one lawyer on the other side and I actually enjoyed sparring with him and the witness. The next day

I sat in a West Texas ginner's office. I really do have a fascinating job.

GOMA (Governor's Office of Migrant Affairs), Gulf, and the cottonseed investigation all point out the problem of institutions out of control. They're not serving or helping the people they're supposed to. The fifty-five farmers in Morton, Texas, know something basic about independence of life style and the value of an honest day's work. They don't understand the marketing structure, and that's what's killing them.

January 30, 1978

I'm losing weight, so I won't be a snow rabbit amongst snow bunnies.

Paul says to remember I'm just as important as Tim. I'm remembering. The weekend went well as I did some distancing. But the problem is that I can't keep Tim and me separate in my mind. Do I really want him or do I just want him to want me? For that matter, I'm not sure I really want anyone. Or perhaps a better word is *need* anyone. If I'd had a month of not seeing Tim, I suspect I'd be even more level-headed and probably could have walked away with imperviousness. I hope my seeing him once a week won't keep me confined in hopeless addiction.

January 31, 1978

The trick is to maintain my own independence. Why is that so difficult? I get caught up in Tim instead of my own life. He can't give me meaning. This is a pattern with my life—giving men too much prominence, except when I was married to Rod. Part of the problem currently is the damn politics. Because it is a twenty-four-hour-a-day-job, I get jealous.

I've not really begun to think in power terms with Tim, merely transferred the romanticism to a different level. Now I think of us in a long-term "interesting" way. A different kind of love. As a matter of fact, I'm not in love right now, I'm "in possession." How strange to realize that as I'm writing.

Every once in a while I glimpse through to something very important about life, my life. It's *my* time; how I spend it is important; to feel value in actions. It has to come from my own movements in this world. When I read junk, or am unproductive, I'm conscious of waste, but am unsure how to fix it.

Reading *Daniel Martin*. It is the relationships we form so early in adulthood which color our lives: Debbie, Linda, Neal, Martha haunted me for years. Then David.

February 4, 1978

The University of Texas Student Union chandeliers are layered— lights like wedding cakes. Listening to Joe Krier give a speech at the University of Texas.

Slowly, I feel the aloneness once more of the human condition. And recognize the eternal seeking to connect.

Leadership is a larger concept than politics. But maybe politics is the quickest way to put leadership into public life. Good speeches have a balance of the personal and ideas! I'm surprised Krier is better at the former.

(I feel pretentious. Am I trying to play Doris Lessing of the *Golden Notebook*? Why, once written does it not seem so bad? Another way of being direct: first with other people, now at times maybe with myself! Hooray. Quietly.)

February 7, 1978

After an excruciating day: Paul says being okay seems off balance rather than on.

My mental/emotional life reminds me of my physical life right now: in better shape overall than ever before, but wanting to *do* something! Not merely be in shape to run, but to dance: not to just exist without depression/anxiety, but to live love relationships. Part of me is doing that.

Tonight I was to have dinner with Luke, but preferred to be alone in my house and write. So I did. A lesson: eight months ago I would have made Luke's invitation the highlight of my day and never would have cancelled. Oh, the imp of romantic imagination.

Tonight I finally wrote the first paragraph. A story (maybe) about the farm experience. The trick is to say something worthwhile.

February 8, 1978

When forced to decide whether to go to Houston on the spur of the moment to meet with two hundred plaintiff lawyers on the box case, or let Roger go (who had done some work on the case), I let Roger go. And was angry, upset, jealous, etc. Thoughts:

1. My boss should not have forced me to make that decision. I've now learned not to do that to underlings.

2. I maybe don't have enough cut-throat in me to get to the top. Being a "good person" is not always consistent with success.

3. A really good administrator knows there is enough glory to go around, if she does the job right. And good work from those who work for you reflects upward, too. The problem with that analysis however, is that I'm not at the top to be reflected upon.

Later:

Dinner with Tom: L: "How do you and Susan do it?" T: "Remember the scene from 'The Turning Point' where McLaine's husband says he wants her to go to N.Y., not because he wants to be rid of her, but because he wants to keep her?"

Tom swung me around in the hall. It was nice to feel small!

February 12, 1978

Last night, in front of me, Tim picked up a political groupie. He spent the night with her, then showed up at my house at 5:30 a.m. I was still in shock.

To tell Tim:

1. What you did was one of shittiest, ugliest things that anyone, much less someone who claims he cares for me, has ever done. I know it's hard for you to imagine the hurt part of what I feel, since you apparently can't become involved enough with someone to be that vulnerable. But try imagining at least the embarrassment you'd feel.

2. I'm also angry and furious right through my insides. I hate you. The deliberateness with which you hurt me is inexcusable. As I un-

derstood the rules, you were going to devote yourself one hundred percent to the campaign and try not to kill the piece of our relationship with potential and a pleasant past. You've effectively killed that. But you changed the rules in the middle: suddenly the game included (a) other people and (b) deliberate flaunting of it. That is not only unfair, it is absolutely inexcusable. I realize it would have been difficult for you to approach me with that topic, but not doing it reflects an inability to confront hard situations that I think, along with your ambitions, will cause you problems.

3. Your decision to commit to your career above all else forecloses meaningful relationships with people like me. And I sincerely question the judgment of politicians who are unable to develop personal relationships and who make decisions like yours last night.

4. As I understand your actions, you were not willing to face me as an adult human being with feelings and dignity and tell me straight on you wanted out of our relationship, or at the very least wanted it significantly altered to include outside sex. Your handling of this has made me lose a lot of respect for you.

5. I wish I had broken the picture of you before I handed it over.

6. Unfortunately your actions confirm all too well some of my negative feelings about politics and politicians. Deliberately seeking what you want at the cost of anything and anyone. Somehow I thought you were above taking advantage of political groupies.

7. Naked ambition tied to no "people" roots provides the most fertile ground for misuse of power. And Tim, if you can treat me like that, I question your ability to make good judgment calls on government.

8. Introducing me during the day as your girlfriend, and running around on me that same night are, at best, duplicitous.

9. On a masochistic level, I want to know how long you've been doing this. But I'm not sure I'll ask.

10. If I could hurt you, I'd do it any way I could. You had best watch the kind of behavior that leads me, a relatively quiet person, to think in violent terms.

11. You're absolutely right. I shouldn't love—and I shan't.
Later:

I called Lee in Dallas. He said to fly up. I did. It was storming. Lee gave me shelter, a sense of calm between the sobs and two important ideas: (1) I needn't feel like a fool, and (2) don't eat more shit. When I called tonight to let him know I was okay and say a meager thanks (oh, Sheila, so much more than a nice note is in order!) he said it was nice to have me for a whole day, and the day was not counted as lost. I am lucky to have him as a friend.

Patterns and lessons.

Too involved too soon—hold back a piece.

February 13, 1978

I told Tim about hurt and anger. He doesn't really understand. He perceives his actions as only stupid and selfish. Certainly, but so much more.

Now I see why Cliff hates me so much. He thinks I did to him what Tim did to me. And perhaps I can now understand what Tim feels, which must be close to what I felt about Cliff, why not be friends, etc. Tim doesn't understand any more than I understood with Cliff, why I don't want to see him or even have him in my life. Cliff, you'll never know that I now understand some of your hurt and anger. I'm sorry.

February 14, 1978 (Valentine's Day)

As usual, I will be beau-less on V.D. Last night had dinner at Lowell's—lots of dishes (I was watching George very carefully for the extra silverware I wasn't sure of, etc.!) During dinner (for ten) I had a flashback to an evening Rod and I spent with the English gentry. At Lowell's over cheese they discussed breeding dogs in rather graphic terms; in England it was sheep or horses. Once again Luke opens doors for me; but once in, I'm my own woman.

Two delightful women were present. Mrs. Packard, about seventy, was visiting from Philadelphia. She had bright blue, hard (in the sense of tough) but warm eyes. A hint of a blue-eyed old Susan! She manned a hotline in Philadelphia for drugs, teenage pregnancies, etc. Because "no one would talk face to face with an old grey haired lady." Her daughter started the Head Start program in Baltimore. I want to invite Diane and all have lunch. Maybe Ruth Denny. Ruth founded the Houston High School for the Performing Arts and now tells raucous tales of artsy teenagers who know it all. A couple of them did. For example, Tommy Tune. Ruth's as feisty as Mrs. Packard.

Told Luke at home about Tim. Typical Luke—worried about my fear of public reaction, and said it's a comment on him, not me. He understood (he said) Tim's sense of conquest. But women feel it too! Only we control it. Or at least I've worked hard at it. Over the past year I've learned how to relate to men in a feminine, sensual way, but not to have that alone be the conquest tool. Rather than seduce Lowell, I have learned to seduce his dinner party! Conquest by asking questions of people and hopefully being myself. (I still can't quite believe people will like me for exactly what I am without trying "to be nice, witty, and charming." Or maybe I really am more of those things than I imagined.)

Tim left a note on my door to inform me, "Contrary to my behavior, I think you are wonderful." It amazes me that he can so miss the point. I've no doubt he thinks me terrific. But he doesn't *treat* me that way, so it really doesn't matter what he thinks. A shade of Rod at one time in our relationship.

Later: All this analysis of Tim is BS. What the whole incident boils down to is that he wanted to screw other women, didn't have the guts to tell me to my face, so when presented a good opportunity, screwed someone, and then threw it in my face. The remarkable thing is that although I am home very sick, I am happy tonight. And for the first time in the breakup of a relationship, have no desire to find another man soon. I suspect that's a good sign.

From a book review of Pasternak: "Yuri Zhivago in the horror of inhumanity surrounding him remained sane through the shared realities of nature and personal feeling."

I think I've gone beyond my need for revenge. Maybe.

February 15, 1978

The "click" is happening again. Reading *Clout: Women, Power and Politics*, it occurs to me that Tim's betrayal has pointed out the male sexism I so despise. But politics is such an ugly life. If I thought lawyering could make one a cold, "bad" person due to the environment, politics is one hundred percent more that way. The only reason I have been okay in that world so far, is that I've been playing in it. Since I honestly don't have an appointment in mind for myself, I don't have to claw for the power. Oh, I feel so silly and naive!

Later: Despair at any sense of progress in the world. On the news, coal miners on strike, farmers telling their butane horror stories, abuse of elderly people, and arms sales to both sides in the Mid-East crisis based on some logic that it would help peace efforts. (This mystifies me; don't sell to either side and the ratio would remain the same, it appears to me.)

February 19, 1978

Reflecting on Tom and Susan: Why is it that the measure of how well one person knows another is the extent to which you're privy to the other's insecurities? It's almost as if we equate intimacy with knowing the "bad" rather than the good about a person.

February 20, 1978

The reality of my life has never matched up with the "reality" of lives as presented in books, movies and TV. Consequently, I expect my life to be off-center somehow and different, and I like that. Not only can I *not* be, but I also don't really *want* to be, Mark and Diane!

Just when I think I've categorized my parents and their relationship, Mother calls to say she and Daddy just built a six-foot-tall snowman complete with coal eyes, scarf and broom. Oh, Daddy, you are not the ogre!

Later: A momentous understanding! I don't have to like to cook! All these years I've felt vaguely that there was some "ought" associated with cooking. And while I've forged ahead in career, divorce etc., I always felt the "oughtness" in the small things a woman is expected to do, or feel. But I've never felt awkward (in this sense) or guilty about not liking football so it *is* those "female" things. What a relief!

Paul said I assume that everyone close to me has the capability to feel as deeply as I. Not true, he says. Hmm. Somehow, I have never thought of emotional depth as being different in different people, more like intelligence than education. I always assumed everyone *could* feel that deeply if they chose to do so.

March 2, 1978 (Vail, Colorado)

Skiing is wonderful! I've just begun to get the hang of it. When I have a good run, it's heaven! But disco night life is not my style.

March 6, 1978

Skiing taught me I could leave Austin and Texas. China looms more realistically on the horizon.

March 7, 1978

Paul said what he had to offer was caring. I can't believe he really cares for me because I don't give him anything. Is it possible just being *me* is enough to have someone care for me?

Sometimes all this talk of competency confuses the issue. I don't feel like a "bad" or "valueless" or "unworthy" person at all. I just feel lonely. If I've lost the dream, what will replace it?

March 9, 1978

The rejuvenation of my ficus tree never ceases to amaze me! Given the slightest hint of water and some faded sunlight filtered through the silver-papered windows of my office and voilá—new leaves lick hungrily forth from the dried up old branches. Old Ben (as in Benjamin ficus) is like me. Given half a chance and a bit of encouragement, we both bloom. In the midst of personal trauma (yesterday's tears all through lunch after seeing Tim), professional chaos (JLH has gone crazy over the farmers—our meeting this morning verged on the absurd) and intellectual frustration (goddamned marketing figures in this memo I'm trying to write tonight!), the beauty of the cycles of life's rebirth fill me momentarily with awe.

March 12, 1978

I finished my first quarter-marathon! 63.40. Had to walk three times for a few yards, but that's not bad since I hadn't run regularly in several weeks. I'm proud of myself, but really tired!

Sadat on TV, having spent eighteen months in solitary confinement: two places where one really gets to know oneself—prison and war. I hope there are more places. But some solitariness is the key.

I dream of being creative with these painful times. This diary, or beginning with my soap opera existence those last years with Rod, could serve as a story line. No visions of being a "real" author. But an autobiographical writer, perhaps.

Anger at work Friday. Cliff and Matt might settle the steel case without me. Matt: "That's part of the risk you take when you date someone in the office." Bullshit. Later, Lee cancelled his trip down for the weekend. I concluded all men were bastards. Without men, my world is larger—except when I have a very steady man/relationship. It would be fun to live with someone I could talk to.

I want to think through "power."

March 13, 1978

Are all men on the make? Maybe there really are some fundamental differences in men's and women's sexuality in that regard. At night I go to sleep alone and do not mind. Independence is returning.

March 14, 1978

Finished the cottonseed report today after a very long and hectic day. When I delivered it to Tim, he was jogging down the street. I kissed him from the car. My first kiss in two months. It was strange. And natural all at once. I know in my mind that I'll feel in love and glad again for another man's company, but it seems far away. Tim's actions have produced a deep mistrust in me. The jolt may have plunged me over the edge into maturity; finally I am wary of people, of their motivations.

Sometimes I feel totally separate from everyone I know. As if I live life in a different plane of existence that parallels everyone else, but is not quite touching. Does everyone feel this way—looking for ways to jump the gap between the parallel lines? Am I to the stage again where I enjoy the analysis of the relationship more than the reality of it?

Lately I've been bored with large groups of people. Can't seem to get the energy to move outside myself to be genuinely interested in them. My inwardness consumes my thoughts, leaving little to give. I'm also becoming self-conscious at work again. Do people like me, etc. I don't want to fall back into that pattern. One of the fallout lessons I've learned from the Tim experience is that the world, even my own private world, is not always fair. I'd never owned up to my having enemies. Am I growing too tough?

Remember the Taj Mahal at twilight!

March 18, 1978
1. Ben Bradlee remembered me!
2. A press person called me a power fucker. Feeling hurt and shock. Must get harder.
3. The farmers in Plainview gave me an American Agriculture strike cap. I was proud!

March 19, 1978
Pachelbel's Canon in D Major may be the most beautiful music I've experienced.

Strength returns, in solitude and quiet; each day a victory to live alone in step with myself. Tentatively I grope for other human beings, to renew the connection, perhaps this time more whole than before. Today I ate with friends (Mark and Diane), painted a card, took pictures of kite flyers, read, smiled at music and contrasted my life with those of people with children. I may be moving away from that goal/dream.

I'm smiling again on my own! Can watch shadows shifting across this page and grin, not needing to share it, or have wistful feelings. I'm happy alone again, and revel in it! Quietly glorious on my little couch! Mary said she envied my freedom, and knew I didn't envy her her children and Phil.

March 24, 1978

Bud came into town. Called me "refreshing." Although I'm centered better, the words from people you care about still mean a lot.

Easter Sunday, 1978

Stan, Sharon, Tim and I talked long and deep. We were hard on Tim. Stan still smarting from Tim's betrayal of me. Tim will get the power he asked us for and get the help to use it. (Aside: Long ago Lee and I talked under a third rate velvet painting about the necessity of knowing what you'd do with power if you had it.)

Later: "Women on the Hill" side literature arrived. I could get excited about the possibility of women getting included in power structures. (If John Hill wins the governorship, we'd be more included in Texas politics than since Ma Ferguson's time.) But it's harder than I thought to put into practice these ideals of equality. We need to include blacks and Chicanos *now* in the Aransas group. But who?

March 28, 1978

CREATE YOUR OWN DREAMS!

March 29, 1978

At the baseball game tonight, I realized what a wonderful group of people I know. Some of whom I love. And I want someone to share that part of my life, the everyday, ordinary. I have a good life these days. Perhaps the myth of marriage and children is just that for me. And the reality, though departing radically from the myth, is fine!

April 2, 1978

I think I'm happy/contented, notwithstanding horrendous sinuses. No sense of security about a man in my life, or what I'll do after June! Wonderful!

Last night at the Law Review banquet, I realized I'd made the right decision about Houston law firms. Comment made about Ray:

"He manages to be both an excellent lawyer and his own person." As if one couldn't do such a thing normally. What kind of profession am I a part of? In the room all the people have tried so hard to be successful. Now they must learn, and are in awe of, characteristics that for ordinary mortals come naturally: love of people, family etc.

On Brian: young, perhaps brilliant, maverick lawyer who opened up shop on his own. He shouldn't have to come hat in hand to "successful" law firm members. Please, Brian, don't have a broken spirit!

April 4, 1978

My most productive session with Paul in quite some time. Topic: Sex and Monogamy. Briefly, I'm coming to understand intimacy vs. sex. Not to take responsibility for more than my half of a relationship. Paul: "You're concentrating on the wrong issue of sex. It's honesty of relationships." I'm probably ready to leave Paul in one sense. But I'm beginning to learn so much!

April 6, 1978

Whirlwind times lately. Understandings have come in leaps and arrived often unbidden upon the threshold of my consciousness. Holding Tim last night as he slept, exhausted, on my body. I felt peace, connection. We've been through so much together. He's become less my lover than my brother. Women always do the nurturing. Is it instinctive, protection of our "young"?

Like Martha Quest, I'm in one of my "thin" stages.

The Priogine Nobel lectures are superb. Newtonian time was one dimensional movement of a body through space, wherein the originating or present conditions set both past and future. Under laws of complexity, entropy, each time/space is right and is different from all others. The system is open, with room for randomness.

Later, reading Jung. (Aside: sexist!) I understood the relatedness issue again. In his context, archetypes for dreams are only meaningful as they relate to a particular individual, e.g., "cross" to a child; "cross" to an old man. As I read the words, I *saw* "I-Thou" imprinted on the mind-page. There is a reality in the relation/connection. That's what I respond to seeing green along the lake while jogging, or passing stunned by the blueness of bluebonnets. That's the "magic" of really looking and seeing another person's eyes.

Why does the mind (spirit?) seek to synthesize all experience into a coherent whole? That's what I'm engaged in, although conscious at times. It's a delicate balance to retain the fire of commitment with the peace of "ordinariness." I take through giving.

April 7, 1978

With Tim in hospital after his surgery. Waiting, learning the nuances of silence.

Loving is a one way giving. Relationships go both ways, but today I understood that loving is giving without regard to response. The feeling I have toward Tim is like that of mothers' toward children. You can't possess them or expect return, but you just love them. It's a lesson I almost, but not quite, learned with Luke. I'm becoming more accepting. I don't know where Tim and I are heading, but we're going there as equals.

Relief flooded through me when I finally saw the doctor emerge and say everything was okay. Tim, after recovery, opened his eyes, spoke, and I was amazed at the fragility of life.

April 7, 1978

Reading Jung: Although I agree the unconscious side of man has been too little explored, I disagree with the dualism that appears in this book. I feel the self as a "center" and information/ knowledge radiates to and from it from several sources. While the idea of a collective unconscious appeals to me, I'm not sure I agree that dreams are our way through the doors of self to individuation. Or that they are the main source. (One of the truly amazing parts of being an adult is the ability to disagree with authority and not feel guilty.)

April 23, 1978

Life can be so sweet! In one sense I've achieved "the good life"; my material wants are met and friends abound. I've begun to find security in my profession. So I've found before thirty what so many strive longer for. The question then is how to live even more fully. What is really important to do with limited time?

At Mo-Ranch I watched ten-year-old boys throw rocks over a parapet. We give back to life by providing the web of experiences to "grow" and nurture the next generation. It's time soon in my life to contribute back to the world and replenish what I've taken—not necessarily through children.

April 24, 1978

I missed "alone time" these past two weeks. In my house yesterday for a few hours I relished the quiet. Worked in the yard, puttered, began reading Heilbronner's *The Human Prospect* (on negative attitudes; since the world is heading for disaster through critical choices.) For this reason Tim sees politics as essential and the most important way to avert the impending doom. On the way back from Mo-Ranch I said I saw artistic endeavors as the one way I was certain that contributions to the world are made and that it saddened me that my talents didn't lie in that area. Tim said he used to agree, but now thinks the world is so screwed up that we have to gain control first so there'll be a place for arts to flourish. Although I agree that decisions on social issues, division of wealth, etc. are important, I *feel* instinctively that in music, art and literature, there is lasting value. Perhaps the former is an intellectual conclusion born of empirical evidence; e.g., my welfare legal aid clients, while with regard to the latter, I have an inner certainty of its truth.

After talking with Ray, I decided to begin remembering dreams. For the past six to nine months, I hadn't been remembering them at all so gave myself a couple of weeks to become aware of dreaming again and later will begin a dream notebook. Amazingly, once I decided to remember, dreams started coming back. Maybe all this talk of the unconscious is more powerful than I'd thought!

May 3, 1978

To lead, one needs to be aware of both the grandness of the dream and the large world that is the stage, and also the small and ordinary things that make up our lives. Bitsy's concern for the Linden woman whose banquet speech Bitsy had to cancel is an example of recognizing both. The trick is to think on a grand scale—beyond nationalism, individualism, as a world citizen—but to live daily in the ordinary and with passion and compassion. Live each day with feet planted passionately in the ordinary.

May 9, 1978

Tim went to Acapulco and I feel totally disoriented. I felt hurt, angry because he disavowed me to JLH. When bringing in John and Bitsy's tickets, JLH said: "There's only two, where's yours?" T: "I'm not going." JLH: "What were you going to do?" T: "I thought I'd spend some time alone." JLH: "Please fly down and help with transition, then you can go off." T: "Okay." All he had to say was that he'd planned to do something with me, but would cancel it. Just acknowledge me. It's not important that Tim understand why he's not good for me, just that I understand. There *is* a middle road to politics.

I need to center again. Why am I so off balance? Sheila says the reason the "power-fucker" remark hurt me is because I feel guilty that it might be true, and she is right. I need to get there on my own. Then it's mine and no one can take it away. I feel bad it's taken me so long to understand this. Now it will be even longer to set the mess right. Ugh! I hope I haven't done my career too much damage.

May 13, 1978 (County Democratic Convention)

One giant step tonight! I came home after seeing Tim! Slowly I'm learning about me! I can do it on my own. Yes, now I even prefer that. I'll make my world myself.

May 14, 1978

Thinking about my career; things I want in life. Mostly independence,
a. in a work sense—to run my own show;
b. financial—maybe—but I'm not sure I want to pay the price;
c. emotional—I want to control my life, its ups and downs.

That's the main problem with politics; you're never really free.

Paul put me on to something when he asked if Rod were a happy person. Happy people I know: Joe Bill (one side of him at least), Matt, Ray.

Later—wasting energy, I swing my emotions again. Finally, (overused and untrue word!) I realize that no one else can make me happy. I'm not pleased with my sense of direction or accomplishments in life. I'm drifting; that's why I pick up on men—just an activity for me to do.

I still don't know what I want to do when I grow up. Yet, I *am* grown and my life slips away. One reason I'm angry with Tim is that I'm jealous he's found what activity gives his life meaning and allows him to act out and act on what's important. Whereas I can't seem to get that figured out.

It's scary to be an almost-autonomous, responsible person. According to the book *Adjusted American*, I should just work harder, admit my own ambition and get on with this business of living. One possibility is that I'll never find something career-wise that I'm really committed to. Then what? My stomach churns.

May 19, 1978 (Middle of the night)

A great gift from Paul was the idea that if I can't sleep for some reason, get up and do something rather than lie in bed worrying about sleeping. Since it's Friday night with no grievance meeting in sight I have the luxury of being awake between 2:00 and 4:00 a.m.

I came closer than ever to resigning my job today. JLH canceled for the third time our AMPI case meeting. And without even a call to me and Matt. We caught him at 6:15 after a reception; he made the necessary decisions, but publicly got that mean gleam in his eye and said, "Linda always pushes her business first." Even Matt was shocked at the snide tone.

May 21, 1978

Texas teeters with violence. In Austin, a cop/friend of Sheila's was killed by a passenger during a routine traffic ticket case. Fifteen shots and a grenade were aimed at another friend/cop Joe; it's a miracle he's alive. On the same day, George Christian's thirteen-year-old son walked into his English class and killed his teacher with a rifle. Will the Christians ever be able to feel life is sweet again? I ache for them as well as the teacher's family. And tonight, the news reported the collapse of the roof of a Garland church during services, killing at least one child. What does it mean?

Tom and I went to a party Saturday night, drank beer and danced. He's one of the most non-sexist men I've ever known. Sunday morning, we ran and ate breakfast. All afternoon I luxuriated in bed reading the running book. Then off to run with Ray. R: "You've changed in that you don't seem to be looking for a man in your life for meaning." As he said it, I realized it was true. Right now my life is leveling out. I enjoy knowing that each night I'll sleep in my own bed. As long as I have male friends to spend time with, like Tom, Mark or Stan, and have occasional lovers, I'm satisfied. In fact, right now, I don't want a serious male relationship in my life. I need a breather from taking any responsibility for another.

On the track I thought that instead of concentrating on the other person in a relationship, I should concentrate on what I feel like when I'm with someone. If being with someone makes me feel good and like myself (learning about the tire gauges with Tom), then that's a relationship to nurture. Not the ones where I feel nervous or insecure.

From the newspaper: "Moral" is what you feel good after. If true, I'm most moral when running!

May 25, 1978   I'm 29 yrs old – an antitrust lawyer w/ AC's often –

A day! 9:00 AMPI meeting with JLH, who lectured Matt on losing his temper. At 11:00 I did my first TV interview on the West Texas Coffee case, then flew to Dallas for meeting about Oldsmobile Dealers, advertising.

Standing in line to board a plane to come home, I realized I was trying to "stand" attractively; that is, even exhausted, utterly spent, I was trying to get complete strangers to "like" me. How absurd! With men particularly, I try to make them like me, rather than see if any of *them* are pleasing to *me*! Balance of course is the key. But for a while, I'll see if they (the world) will come to me a little rather than stumble over myself to please others.

On the TV I witnessed a curious thing; I'm really not pretty, but I am competent! What I said was fine, even passably articulate. I looked terrible, stringy hair, pimply. Somehow I had convinced myself I was pretty—and I'm not (not that I'm ugly, but nothing spectacular or twice-lookable). But that gives a measure of anonymity.

Finished Heilbronner's *The Human Prospect*. Scary. Do we really need to reach way beyond ourselves? Is it utterly decadent to think of going to Nepal with Outward Bound rather than being responsible and producing for society?

May 28, 1978 (At Enchanted Rock near Fredericksburg, Texas)

Alone on the far edge of pink and green rock, my body flat against the hardness, I felt the wind and rock and me as one. Similar to the canyon/wind Outward Bound feeling when I stood naked and became one with the wind, only this was horizontal. Then a lizard ran out, scared me, and I knew I had a long way to go before I was no intruder.

I love the Texas land. Yellow flowered fields between Johnson City and Willow City.

What is wind? Today I could feel it *and* feel its absence. And hear it across the chasm, rustling leaves and rocks before my skin tingled with its touch.

May 29, 1978

"Any path is only a path, and there is no affront, to oneself or to others, in dropping it if that is what your heart tells you . . . . Look at every path closely and deliberately. Try it as many times as you think necessary. Then ask yourself and yourself alone, one question . . .'Does this path have a heart?'If it does, the path is good. If it doesn't, it is of no use." Carlos Castenada, *The Teachings of Don Juan*.

Reading the *Tao of Physics*. The author explains the Buddhist concept of "seeing." But it's the *feeling* on the trail of seeing *green*! A shock of recognition!

I wrote Outward Bound about the Himalayan trip; decided not to buy a house. Both for financial and simplistic reasons. It's important to keep my material life small, if not spartan. No one person needs more space than I have, although it would be convenient. Eventually, we of this earth of limited resources will have to recognize this and come to personal grips with it. It is a luxury to live alone as I do even now.

To successfully take my Eastern trip, I must work at simplifying my self and my life. In concrete terms:
1. Lose weight. I'll climb better, and chances are there won't be an abundance of food. There must be less of me at an optimum weight. Probably around 110–108. (Ugh—I'm one hundred sixteen pounds and have rediscovered ice cream. Sigh!)
2. Run and swim to get in shape. Be able to run five to ten miles and swim one mile in forty minutes. (I might cheat on the swimming.)
3. Clean out closets and extra stuff in my house. An exercise in deciding what's important.

This process has been beginning over the last few months, only now I'm conscious of it.

June 4, 1978

Last night I sat alone on my patio, slightly high on beer and Mexican food, and watched the stars and listened to music and passing cars. And was in touch with me. And alone. And felt that aloneness was fine.

Copied thoughts from last night's drunken, moonlit ramblings:
1. On Rod's brother's book: He maintained two-hour sleep schedule to write it. To create something tangible is important. I understand men building businesses and dynasties. But I feel it is "less" somehow to build a Division at the Attorney General's Office than it is to write a book.
2. Wise warriors pick their battles; e.g. I wear lawyer clothes and don't swear in front of opposing counsel, in the context of women's rights.
3. I remember a time when stars were fuzzy. And clouds had hazy edges fading into blue skies. Now I see sharply through my glasses.

4. Each day alone is one of strength. So much of single people's emotional energy is devoted to finding someone. To pretend that the truly together person wouldn't do that seems off balance. There must be an innate or universal longing of all humans to find a connection point. Thought: it's a bit like rediscovering the solace of your parents.

5. I'm almost strong enough to truly give. There is a solid "me" to share.

6. I've created my own mainstream of life. It's just that swimming in it is more difficult than I'd envisioned!

June 6, 1978 (Middle of the night)

The koans make sense to me: to stay in Austin, one must be able to leave it. To be truly a leader and powerful, one has to be able to need to lead no one, and have little inclination for power alone.

Finally tonight I cried. The loneliness welled up and spilled over. I needed the release. I want to see my sisters' children, Karina and David.

June 2, 1978

Daddy and Mother in town. As we left lunch today: Daddy: "You are a most impressive young woman. And thank you for calling your mother to talk. You know, I never talked to my father or my mother either. One of the things I've done wrong in my life, among many, was not to talk with you. Guess I always thought you should do things on your own by yourself and not ask for help. I still feel that way for me, although I realize for others that's not true." I was touched.

June 11, 1978 (On airplane Houston–Washington)

Clouds lie in cultivated rows beneath me. Alone, I'm not in the least lonely!

Next to the Concorde, the 727s look pregnant.

I want to become lean—in spirit and body. To seek the essential and start a process of fine-tuning.

It's important that I've begun to wear my hair pulled back with clips.

Like Matthiesson (*Snow Leopard*), finding himself fighting the Tibetan mastiff with his staff within hours of creating it, I find the timing of my reading the *Tao of Physics*, listening to the Priogine lectures and reading the *Snow Leopard* significant. My mind/spirit is also being prepared/armed.

June 13, 1978

High on spirits!

There is a timelessness to these days. Another level. Alone I must reach it. But the closeness of connection makes me scared. To *feel* with another, does the vulnerability in the end make one strong?

I'm close to breaking out again. Why eat and drink and overload the body and heart/spirit? Fear of change, of growth and challenge. Strength of "alone" please return! Let my soul give, flow with all being. Let no separateness divide me from the oneness, the everyday, or the grandness of green.

To read this someone might think I were mad. No. On the brink of breakthrough.

June 20, 1978 (Minneapolis at a National Association of Attorneys General convention)

Sandee, Jackie, Elizabeth. Old friends seem real. I'm centering more and more. When the pressure gets great, I just imagine myself on center—almost a meditational tool.

Last night, dinner with JLH, John and Mary Beth, General Burch and Burch's campaign manager. JLH has grown and matured. He wears the mantle of governance now. Perhaps the crazy campaign process does temper one for public office. He is calmly assured. And he still speaks convincingly of right and justice. But there is a "packaged" quality about him now. Before, he was rough-edged and quite real. Now he's more polished, urbane, a winner, less outwardly scrappy, but sleek.

Three comments about women have really gotten to me:

June 28, 1979 (Minneapolis at a Nat. Assoc. of Attorneys General conventn.)
3 comments about women have really gotten to me.

68　　　　　　　　　　*A Woman's Odyssey: Journals, 1976–1992*

1. The Louisiana Attorney General stopped me and asked me to bring him a pencil. He apparently thinks I'm someone's girlfriend. I brought it, hoping he'd later be embarrassed. He wasn't.

2. On the elevator, an Assistant AG made some crack about why I wasn't being more extensively lobbied, because he'd do so. Damn it, and my badge even had my title on it!

3. Last night prior to dinner, as we were all waiting for a table, JLH told Burch that we would all have dinner together, then the "women" would leave and they could get down to hard politics. In fairness to JLH, neither Mary Beth nor I are at the same level as everyone else there and in fact we didn't leave. But the rage came up. At dinner they discussed abortion. JLH is personally against it: "Every woman would carry her child to term, I'd hope." But he'll live with the Supreme Court decision. On the issue of state funds for poor women and abortion, JLH appears to be okay, but has trouble because it leaves the impression he's *for* abortion. I listened to the men discuss the right of women to control their bodies, and coldly noted that when we have fifty percent of the power, I only hope we have compassion for those who for so damn long have screwed us around.

June 17, 1978 (On plane Dallas–Minneapolis)

Fundamental truth: We spend our time the way we want to.

Before airplanes, people must not have had the vision of rivers as ribbons, sensually lazying, slinking their way through lush green fields of the Midwest. On mountain tops perhaps, they could gaze down and *see* the perspective. So technology has helped the *seeing*. What other breakthroughs, ways of seeing are around the corner for us? Astronauts were the first to *see* the totality of earth. What more?

June 17, 1978

From Grievance Committee. A black woman's complaint against a rude lawyer. Cadence of speech, rich in color against the sterile language of the law: "fiduciary" duty or "seduciary" act. White background and shades of coffee/black, nuances of character. Her white hair a silver hue against the blank white of the walls.

June 20, 1978 (Minneapolis at a Japanese art exhibit)

In front of a statue/head of Buddha. In exhaustion more mental/emotional than physical, I closed my eyes, became my eyes and still *saw* through the eyelids. The room was faint and shadowy. The red velvet curtain behind the Buddha was green. Slowing my breathing down, I melted—was *with* the wooden floor. I experienced no sense of loss of self, no lack. The connection is a process with the natural world; I have not yet achieved it on a personal basis. Slight feelings of fear. I'm not going crazy, but I'm off somewhere where few tread. Center me, O' Lord.

With regard to Mary Beth: I don't need others' approval. I've tried. They can come to me too.

June 25, 1978

Quietly, this morning I was ready to meditate. On a daisy covered pillowcase, half-lotused, I sat on the floor and focused on the breath at the end of my nostrils. Thoughts came, and I tried to let them flow by. Beginning lines of the Lord's Prayer, unbidden, became my mantra. From "Our Father who are in Heaven," the words compressed to "Our Father thou art." Even as a child those words "worked." In crisis times, on the silent retreat when Rod and I decided to marry. In the many churches I've entered on my travels, into the rich darkness of "holy," in the hospital chapel most recently while Tim was being operated on, always the prayer words fill my mind and the cadence calms.

On becoming lean: I'm learning to take small steps. One nuance of nurturing is the leanness. Also a beginning patience. I'm reminded of Lessing's admonishment to read books when you're ready. I've read the Nepal information, circling concepts slowly. For example, upon reading of Buddhist meditation, I didn't (as would have been my pattern earlier) immediately try it. My timing is balancing better, at least on an inner plane. I'm curious to see if it will be evidenced at work.

Friday, at a party for Nancy and Dean, I arrived in blue jeans in the midst of casual chic. So, undaunted, I returned home for a long dress. Walking into the Gatsbyish crowd, alone, I had a moment of panic, self-pity, then "centered" and it worked!! It's easy to do it at Enchanted Rock. To do it in that context or at the conference table is significant. Hooray!!!

June 27, 1978

I want to learn to fly and to take pictures. But that too complicates my life right now. "One" pointedness is difficult and I don't need any more activity. But I'm becoming ready to fly.

I worried about the "evenness," the loss of the highs and lows. But tonight, and all of today, I felt the plateau of joy infusing the moments. Washing my hands for the last few weeks has been an exercise in presentness. Clasping them, squishing the soapsuds against the skin of opposing flesh and tendon and fingerbone, I am totally aware of just washing hands. And this was before meditation.

My tongue made love to a single peanut today!

I know I shouldn't throw all my career away carelessly, but I don't want to only be an antitrust lawyer.

June 30, 1978

Meditating, my eyes began REM. I couldn't control my thoughts and empty them to a quiet mind. But I'll be patient. Just the doing counts. And an inner calmness is beginning.

The women are wonderful! We put on a hospitality room and breakfast at the State Bar convention. Working beautifully together, we all did our share without effort at coordination. I need them for support, and to be effective we need each other. There is an acceptance of each woman's totality of personhood and each woman's personal competitiveness.

July 2, 1978

Weekend in Corpus with Luke at Tim's party. Everyone was nice to me and I think not out of pity. Seeing Tim with Debbie was fine. I just didn't want to watch them, so moved when I was in the line of vision. Scene: Barbara throwing a one-hundred-dollar bill to Richard when he asked her to bring him some money for poker! She's beautiful, bright and has class. Beside her I felt like a chunky blond peasant, but satisfied with being me.

This weekend I was quite easily and naturally one of the guys— *and* girls. When one least expects it. I've been "even" lately and enjoying it! When asked by people how I was, I could honestly say, "Quite well" and mean it.

Good talk with Jorge about value choices in a limited world. We need to examine the criteria for deciding: (1) who decides (2) what they decide. Elitist vs. democratic. My total certainty that women are equal to men and willingness to impose that view on others regardless of their views gives me pause. Since I know others violently disagree, I wonder how many issues are around about which *I* feel that unerring, undoubting sureness—while others feel diametrically opposite. In that case, who decides?

Jorge: on democracy and equality: "We must understand the difference between what is and what ought to be. For example, we all ought to be equal, but we're not so long as some are educated, others are not, some are rich, some are poor. Society in a 'democratic' country then proceeds to let these equal-but-not-equal people have equal say in government through voting."

I'm confused about elitism. Equally scared of rule by "the Masses" (Phyllis Schlafly's folks) and by the "few" who think they are superior. I'd buy the idea of a philosopher/king but no one I know has the humility along with the potential power. C'est impossible.

Once again, late at night, I can't sleep. This has been going on for a week now and I'm slightly confused.

Concentrating on my breath at nostril's edge while meditating, I suddenly realized that the very air itself connected us all! The molecules flow in and out of each living person/thing and we are all part of some whole.

July 5, 1978
1. "Relationships are the ends of life, not the means!"
2. "Power entraps even if it is used to do good."

Running, the wind whistles between my legs if I go fast and there is enough space between legs on a stride. Meditating this morning, the breath through my nose was the *same* feeling as the air between my running legs!

July 7, 1978

Running with Ray I had no rhythm or "feel" for the run; was merely trying to keep up and go fast, eight-minute mile maybe. Rounding the corner after the old railroad bridge, I thought that at times endurance is grace.

July 9, 1978

I don't have enough alone time again. Thinking about flying lessons puts me in a decision quandary. Tonight I think I shall wait until next spring. I have plenty to learn and explore in the next three and a half months before Nepal without stretching myself too thin. (Mother didn't like the idea of flying. Wonder how much that influenced me?)

Paul on meditating: "It's not so important what occurs during the meditation time, rather the doing."

July 14, 1978

Dinner with Ruth Denny and Sheila. R: "I've accomplished most things in the last fifteen years." (She is at least fifty-five, probably closer to sixty.) LA: "Why then?" R: "Before, I didn't really set goals."

July 16, 1978 (In the laundromat)

The accomplishment of everyday tasks of living gives me pleasure. Yesterday, I polished silver and watched the tarnish vanish like magic after applying Tarnox. I wonder if women who stay home all the time marvel at cleaning the way I do. Probably they have too much to do.

Last night after a full day of Grievance and politics (I helped organize a $25,000 fundraising effort for the arts people), I went to

Scholz's to join Tim, et al. I fell into an ego trap. Drinking beer with everyone, I knew they all liked me. And I wasn't sure whether I liked being "partner-less" or not. It's socially awkward at times, but ever so free. And I didn't want to be Mrs. Tim *at all.*

I came home early and sat outside, almost meditating on the moon. Watching the moon, I realized how caught up in ego I was. And how drinking really clouds my emotion. I wanted to be held. A year ago I would have continued carousing, made eyes at Joe Bill, and appeared drunk at Cliff's door at 3:00 a.m. Instead, I came home at 9:30 to gaze at the moon. Progress takes many forms!

The reason the fat stuff is important is because body and mind and soul are connected somehow. I know that, but can't quite get it together. People like me who've dieted, instinctively understand that mass equals energy; otherwise where would all the "me" go when I lose weight. The pounds become energy that connects up with the rest of the world. Consider the possibility that what *leaves* contains consciousness!

July 17, 1978 (At Deep Eddy swimming pool)

The concept of "unity" is not foreign to me. As a child I envisioned what it would be like if each pebble were "really" a world or earth like the one I knew. And assumed that there was a "bigger" world in which our world was merely a pebble. Stories of Albert Schweitzer's not stepping on an ant made infinitely good sense to me, not wanting to be the victim of a big "stepper" from the sky!

Now when I'm upset or angry with someone, I perceive a part of them connected to me. And yet there is a distancing process too that allows me to gain better control. A koan: the perception of connection grants distance.

A lifeguard here has a perfect willowy, sloping hipped body. The sheen of tanned, sunlotioned skin was beautiful. I admired her and suddenly thought/realized it was without jealousy or uneasiness. You don't have to acquire things you like. I hope the important men in my life will look at youthful bodies admiringly *with* me and feel no need to acquire them. Is that wishful thinking? Will I be able to do so myself? At least I'm moving in the right direction to be able to enjoy the visual feast and not covet. They too are part of the whole.

How does acceptance of unity fit with my notion of the necessity to fight for right? Injustice isn't changed through acceptance.

July 18, 1978

Random thoughts:

On reading books, from an article: Good books should be interesting, memorable and re-readable.

I've learned to control my body, am conquering words, but have great trouble controlling my thoughts. And the latter is of utmost importance. But perhaps I just need to take small steps and it will come. (Written with a smile!)

Significant time: Paul Horn's "Inside" album of flute music played in the Taj Mahal filled my living room. Finally after weeks of sitting on my table, the Sayings of Buddha were in my hands. I read and some came into my consciousness. *Timing.*

I don't really want to let go of sensuality. Reading the Buddha sayings I could *feel* my mind wince as a thought jarred and either (1) I wasn't ready for it or (2) it wasn't right for me. My mind isn't developed enough yet for me to be wholly comfortable trusting its judgment on such things. But right instincts are there. Trust myself; listen.

Paul session—unsettling: "You won't need a 'best friend.' You'll be your own."

July 19, 1978 (El Paso)

Working with Katie today was fun. She is going to explode one of these days. What an incredible potential. I'm proud to know her. I enjoy these numbered days when I can teach and show her things about lawyering. She'll pass me soon enough. For now I revel in showing off and sharing.

July 22, 1978 (Taos)

The mountains are their own reward.

July 25, 1978

On decisions: In the office we have begun to get very busy. Our decisions impact more folks now and are carried out in the public limelight, e.g., Gulf and Phillips illegal campaign contribution case; the extent of representation of state commissions by the AG; antitrust hearings on nuclear plants; AMPI; a merger program. The buck stops here. I'm not worried or unnecessarily anxious anymore, realizing that I'd rather I made the decisions than someone else, but I'm not yet totally comfortable with all the responsibility. Even so, it's fun. And I'm calm although tired. I talked with Susan about all this after work; she doesn't think of her legal work like I do. She perceives her job to be *enforcing* the laws, with little discretion. If a legal argument can be made for the constitutionality of a statute, she makes it, rather than substituting her judgment for the legislature's. In plaintiff's practice, which is essentially what I do, discretion in how to solve a particular problem is essential and the whole key to what I do. To borrow a phrase, I'm still learning to figure out what all the equities are and having to balance them at the same time! I wonder if one just grows into the decisional process and begins to have fun.

Notes for thoughts on men/women:
1. The *possibility* of sex totally colors male/female relationships.
2. Looking back, I think how men have preoccupied my life, and then later they go away and I am no longer interested in their daily lives. We establish an intimacy of a different kind than that of Sheila and me. But so strange is the ultimate tenuous nature of that connection.

July 27, 1978 (Early Austin summer morning; 6:00 a.m.)

I'm working well again. Matt did an excellent job with the peanut folks. I was proud and bought him a beer, even though we had words over his comment that he wouldn't hire Margaret as a lawyer because she didn't shave her legs!

I am settling in to being assistant chief for real, instead of acting chief in practice, as Matt has become a better leader. I worry/am concerned with (1) occasional feelings of professional jealousy evidencing a selfish lack of generosity (if there's enough luck, there is certainly enough credit to go around), (2) a lack of ambition or sense of moving myself rather than responding. Writing this down, I'm not sure it's as true right now. It doesn't "touch" me.

I'm scared about having the IUD put in. Damn, I'm such a physical pain coward. I'll try to recite the "fear" litany from *Dune*.

August 6, 1978 (Sunday)

Alone running at the stadium; utter aloneness in the pre-dawn. It was about 5:00 a.m., dark still, and I was scared.

Reality doesn't have to be shared. Maybe I don't have to communicate the feelings, insights, etc., to anyone, or write them down. Maybe it will be okay just to feel/experience them. In other words, the "secret to living is life." Where does this fit in with the reality of relationship? Somehow, experiencing life alone seems like hearing a tree fall when no one is around to hear it. While running, I thought that it really wasn't "alone," but rather a relationship on a larger plane, to nature, to energy, to "world," to Tao. This is one of the most "foreign" thoughts I've had.

August 11, 1978 (Austin)

To write the date I glance at my new watch and smile. My world begins to move too swiftly. Montana, then home to Wanda (my high school friend visiting me from her new home in Scotland) and a desk crowded with difficult decisions, then off again to D. C. in three days. I love the pace, but seek interstices of alone/thought time. It was wonderful to read *Zen and the Art of Motorcycle Maintenance* on the plane.

Montana: Words like "majestic" and "splendor" have new meaning to me. Each mountain stood alone with an individuality and singularity that reached out and shocked me breathless. Other mountains I've seen almost in "clumps," or more properly, ranges. Glacier lakes, cold and clear, let me touch my hand to them, melt into the green/blue and be a part. An alpine meadow was seamless, dotted color. For the first time I had a sense of Seurat's paintings. And waterfalls. Someday I will return, backpack, and earn the views.

At the conference there were excellent people and a good exchange of ideas, much to Matt's and my surprise. We had conflicts. He baits me, Paul says in an "older brother" way. Most of the time I handle it okay. But once, I just got up and moved. He was looking for women to sleep with and commented that I really couldn't do that because the men would think less "professionally" of me. I mumbled something about picking men who would feel as I do, and he launched into a lecture on how naive I was, that women just fell for all this "meaningful relationship" buzz word stuff. Suddenly, my rage over his anti-ERA stance merged into my feelings about his attitude towards women and I felt the complete gap between men and women. Over-generalization, but I was totally shook. Do all men have sex as such a different aspect of their character that we really are objects to that extent? I walked off, stood apart from the Assistant AGs, breathed deeply and tried to face my feelings. I knew Paul and Rod, to name only two men, would violently object to being categorized like that, and indeed shouldn't be. But I felt so alone in a room of all men (except one other woman lawyer). Later, calm, perspective returned. How easily I went off balance! And how fragile is my trust of men. Life, please be gentle with me for just a little while longer. I'm flying with rather new wings, still damp and stiff!

I had to work hard to make myself stop worrying about what other people thought of me—was I smart enough, did I make good contributing remarks, etc.? It was wearing to try to just be me and let that be enough. When I explained this to Paul he said that it took effort at first to be "authentic" and that some people never even try. I was *amazed*. It honestly never occurred to me that other people didn't just have it all together on that issue.

Jobs, career decisions, confuse and unsettle me. Paul said he wanted a "yes" or "no" to the question: "Do you want to be a politician?" When pressed, I said yes, but not necessarily an elected one. We discussed what policy matters I wanted to affect and why I'm too general in my concerns right now (my words, not his), and need to do some serious thinking about governance, community. The ideas evolve slowly, but a responsibility to "give back" to the world and thereby of course gain, grows large in my mind. Things I listed for P:

1. Environment—but on a non-state, non-national level. Clean air knows no national borders.

2. Women's involvement in government—not just on women's issues, but at all levels. For right now, until or *if* cultural and educational patterns change, we have a particular perspective on problem solving that I want to see injected into the decision making system. Overly generalized, but it's a sense of compassion, of balance. Does the possibility of conception give women as a group an ever present sense of alternatives, of a balance to life plans?

3. Redistribution of wealth/services—this is tied into honesty in government for me. For example, telling me social security is taking my money to give to someone else is fine. But don't pretend it's still "mine" and that I'll get it back someday. Expectations placed on the system because of false information only lead to frustration for everyone.

August 12, 1978

The end of this particular diary. It will be filed away. A long record of twists and turns along my life-path. Sitting in the Texas sun I so love, I feel strong, slightly sad to pack away an old friend, frayed at the edges (real?), but ready to move, grow, live.

Hello.

August 16, 1978

Getting started is sometimes harder than doing. A new volume, a new era, a same me. An astounding realization hit me full face this afternoon while reading *Zen and Motorcycle*: I've never questioned the assumption that what is reasonable is good. Example: the most *reasonable* way to handle X situation, has always translated for me into a value judgment that it's the "best" way to handle X. In my personal life, however, I've not always chosen the most reasonable way, so perhaps there is an intuitive sense of value that overrides the reasonable button at certain times. If reason isn't the highest good, what does that mean?

The *Passages* precis described 43–50 as being a time when one understands that one is alone, in that no one can understand everything about another or be all things. But I'm learning that now. Not easily, but the notion sits better these days.

While in D. C. I ate lunch at the White House. Awesome. Scott Burnett showed me through. The door to the Oval Office was closed because President Carter was behind it. I was stunned. So close to the institution that survives. "Success is survival." But more than that; not just of the fittest, but of some of the ideals. I never expected to be so moved. The atmosphere was loose, non-authoritarian. Vice President Mondale passed me in the mess, Hamilton Jordan at the next table, Tim Kraft (lovely brown eyes) hugged me, and I liked him. Jody Powell didn't remember me. Someone pointed out where Haldeman's office had been. A chill passed over me; the flashback vision of the closed Oval Office door had new meaning.

Tom Reston said the U. S. can no longer expect its allies to do whatever we want. But people don't realize it and give Carter a hard time for some things he can't help. We're no longer a super power in the sense we can dictate to other countries. As he explained that, I realized how parochial in my thinking I too had become.

August 20, 1978

Wanda teaches where children are taught to be non-competitive in their understanding of themselves. W: "These children know they are each unique and have a place right inside that is purely theirs. They exist and affirm that existence without envy of others. So each can feel secure."

Over pizza Debbie, Wanda and I talked of writing. Wanda doesn't think discipline is the key, rather having something to say. I'd always assumed my problem was just not being able to write well enough, therefore couldn't write. But if I have something to say, then maybe I can write just to say it, even if it's not great literature.

From *Zen*: You are never dedicated to something you have complete confidence in. No one is fanatically shouting, "The sun is going to rise tomorrow."

August 22, 1978

Decisions about job. Yesterday I visited with JLH. He was pleased with my steel case memo. What to do next? Washington? Fed-State Relations office? But then I wonder about work. Do I want to leave the public sector? Can I play happily on a smaller stage? Seeing JLH made me again want independence in my work. It's not good to be tied this closely to politics for job security. And one of these days I must face being alone and needing to plan for the future, financially as well as emotionally.

Options:

1. Ask White (the Democratic candidate for Attorney General who ought to win easily in November) if I can stay as staff attorney, then try some cases and save money for an eventual six months' time off to write.

2. Bargain to remain Assistant Chief.

3. Find something on Governor's staff and ask JLH; e.g. Washington, Federal-State relations.

These are the decision times when I miss having someone *share* with me.

August 23, 1978

My would-be nine year anniversary, El Paso, oh, Rod. . . .

I'm in a serious stage again. Not thinking of funny stories to relate about my day at work. I want to be better about seeing through to the humor, to laugh with/at myself. Politics makes me uptight, in a different way than lawyering does. That should tell me something. Somehow I think it would be good for me to settle down in Austin next year at the AG's office, stay out of politics on a formal level, put a lot of energy into lawyering, save money, learn to fly and begin the outline of the book.

August 24, 1978

A productive day. Almost careened into anxiety attack at work, but instead *worked*! I need to learn to be more outwardly calm with the staff. I get excited and it's infectious, but it gets too hectic and I suspect does not inspire confidence. Also, I want to learn how to

outwardly slow down when a law clerk or someone wants to talk
or explain or ask questions. I want to cultivate that aura of calm and
evenness and not show external agitation so much. It would also
help me to listen with full attention; I get bored and jump ahead
otherwise. And often miss some good points when I jump!

August 27, 1978

Scattered. Hard times at work. Lost Rule 12(b)(6) motion in the
vending machine case. Immediately negotiated part of a settlement
and felt exhausted and over my head. Thoughts: I always assume
someone else could do all this so much better than I, yet maybe
that's not true and I'm doing fine and shouldn't expect myself to
feel great and up and non-worried/non-hassled.

August 30, 1978 (On plane to Lubbock, rough weather, hard to write!)

Lost the motion for summary judgment in the Vending Commission case. I *hate* losing!

At Grievance committee meeting last night: harsh faces bathed
in harsh light. A woman said she couldn't speak up, but as the vitu-
perative words gushed out, the voice rang harsh. She has a harsh
soul.

Scene to remember: A young man sentenced to ten years for
aggravated rape by a ten-woman/two-man jury in Lubbock in the
middle of our taking a Section 15.14 antitrust statement. The final-
ity, the power of the system is awesome.

Talked with Mary Beth about the women in town having meetings.

August 31, 1978

Talked with JLH about Gulf, Phillips and vending cases. He's
got his priorities all confused. He considers the oil cases important
cases and the vending case not. The difference is that the oil cases
are political, while the vending case involves an issue for the A.G.'s
office on tough policy.

Sometimes you just have to leave JLH alone. So off I'll go and
try to solve all this stuff on my own. Once again, it's a good lesson

in doing a job for its own sake and in doing my job well because I feel better that way, and not relying on strokes from someone else. Actually I'm probably lucky to have learned or be learning that lesson now. To have abruptly been on my own, as I have been most of the past year in lawyering, sort of pushed me out of the nest.

JLH's problem *is* that he's lost sight of the fact that politics is like lawyering—only a tool to use to accomplish things. It's not good enough to be Governor if all that happens is a lot of political intrigue.

I want to be a good public servant. JLH doesn't want anything to rock the boat now. Unfortunately, antitrust work always rocks someone's boat. I'll have to figure out how to keep everyone excited and working steadily when I know JLH doesn't really want suits filed, etc. This is hard. The public's best interest and his don't coincide right now. Although I try to understand political realities, the bottom line has to be that you first do the job the people elect you to do, or pay you to do. I'm uncomfortable with all this. And I'm losing some respect for JLH. If he's not going to be AG, the least he can do is designate people who will run the show. It's sad when our marching orders are to be non-controversial rather than to be right.

Mary Beth keeps a diary too. It was good and bad to see hers. Good connecting, feelings. Bad in the sense of recognizing again that I'm not unique, that although all of the writing is important to me, it's not a particularly big deal beyond that. (Bringing home once again the idea that my life must be lived the best I can for me; be the best person I can according to my own values.)

September 3, 1978
Played in the pool with Nancy, Dean and children. I'm not really interested in kids suddenly, at least very young ones. Another phase of the mother instinct. Dean was old, but experienced. As he leaped out of the pool to get a stray ball, I wondered what he felt like faced with children he may not see grow to marriageable age. I suspect he keeps his own counsel well. Nancy spoke of needing unstructured time with the kids. Time when doing something wasn't

just added to the list of things to do for the day. When Nancy smiles, her face crinkles and the harsh lines around her mouth melt. Dean and Gregory twinkle. Her other son, like her, is thoughtful.

Nancy is worried about not being considered a real lawyer. As she talked, I remembered all my fears of the same sort. But the next ten years are growing years for the boys and important ones for Dean. She's torn because she wants to be there with them, yet doesn't want to throw away her career.

Glimpses into Nancy's soul: She keeps two diaries, one for her and one for the boys. "Of course, sometimes if I'm too tired, or there isn't enough time, I'll write in theirs first." Having children teaches unselfishness. I'm not sure I could do it.

As I drove back home, I tried to be rational, think of what I really wanted. Right now I'd settle for a back rub. I drove past Tim's house. He was moving Debbie's furniture in. Life changes. I want someone's arms to run to tonight. I can make it alone, but every once in a while I'd like to just let someone else take care of me.

I'll never be taken seriously as a lawyer. So be it. It's my life and I sense going to Nepal is important. So—I'll trade that for other rewards.

Before settling down (in the sense of children-type commitments, maybe even before a permanent person), I've wanted to (1) do the Eastern trip and (2) go to Mexico for six months, learn Spanish and write. Number one looks like it will happen.
Middle of the night: 4:15 a.m.

Troubled sleep lately. Thoughts rushing through my head about leaving the AG's office. Who will try the steel case? Can Kathie or Kay come with me? But if they do, will anyone be left who knows the files well enough? Katie will be left with enormous responsibility, the vending case. She's awfully young to handle it, but I'm sure she'll do fine.

It's time to move on. But I wonder if some day I won't look back at my years at the AG's office as some of the best professionally. I sense that I'll never be such a "big wig" again, with my own "fiefdom"! Can I handle that? Not jetting off to D. C., etc., practically whenever I want to? Can I learn to work again as part of a team, and not be the leader? And as much as I like all the people I'll be with, somehow when politics enters in, I don't quite trust them. But it's exciting to think about learning a whole new area, new issues, and maybe having an impact on legislation.

I'm having difficulty defining what substantive areas I want to work with. First thoughts: environmental and economic issues. Environmental issues because I'm personally interested and concerned, economic issues because in the shorter run (as compared to the ultimate importance of environmental issues) that's where the power is that makes things run; antitrust work has convinced me of that. If there is ever to be any real change, it must come about as a coalition effort. Attitude changes are what concern me, because from them grow actions to implement ideas in longstanding ways. Equality for women won't really exist until business accepts and integrates us fully into the work force, which means an acceptance of shared jobs, day care facilities, flexible working schedules. Although some of those things can be legislated (indeed, legislation is foundational to the attitude changes), most of the changes will come only through negotiation efforts with individual companies. That's one reason it's so important for each woman to be the very best person (Buddha-like) she can be.

A wave of scaredness went over me. Leaving lawyering, a safe cocoon, is a little frightening. Ah, jealous thoughts—will Sheila get ahead, etc.! Damn, will I ever learn to just accept my path when I find it and stop comparisons with others' paths?

At Deep Eddy pool, two six-year-old girls sat facing each other cross legged on the bank playing a sophisticated version of patty-cake. The rhyme was something about a mother giving her daughter a "dolly," but the girl wanting a "soldier," telling her mother that now instead of "toys" she wanted "boys." Comments from the women. "We haven't really taught them anything about women's lib." I disagreed and rolled over on the towel with a new verse:

And now I'm older
And quite a bit bolder
But just as then
I'm mainly interested in men!

Nancy said to figure out what I want five years hence and then proceed the best way from now to then. Trouble is, when I envision five years hence, I have a blank screen.

September 6, 1978

Ugly scene with JLH concerning realtors. He questioned my loyalty and judgment. To hell with working in the Governor's office.

Bad hearing on the Gulf-Phillips case. Judge Mathews didn't listen; called me a "pretty young face"; all the heavies were there in the courtroom. Lost. I felt absolutely battered. Tired, embarrassed. My work seems totally incompetent and worthless. Guess I was just flying too high and was due a dose of reality.

It's these stolen quiet times between the maelstroms that allow centering.

September 10, 1978

I flew to Dallas. The look on Nana's face when I came through the door was worth all the hassles getting there for her eighty-ninth birthday, and more.

Arrangements with Mother about Nepal. The time has come to give back to my parents. I can hardly remember a time when I wasn't more at home with the "worldly" parts of living—driving downtown, arranging reservations, writing business letters, etc.—than Mother. Eighth grade maybe.

Ran and breakfasted with Luke. He went to Santa Fe alone. After running, he said I could shower at his house, that he could scrounge some clothes for me to wear to breakfast. It was not an invitation for any more than just that, but I declined and came home and met him later. I've finally learned not to create situations that could lead me astray.

JLH apologized formally to me and Matt. But you don't really get over those scenes. That's two now.

September 12, 1978

It's a rough work day. Lost the steel case direct purchases in the computer. I've been taking out on my staff my conflicting feelings about personal things. Not good. This afternoon I'll be better. Need to run; get calm. But in the midst of it all, I pretty much am *only tired*. Work is suffering. If I'd do more while here instead of mull around old decisions with Matt, it would be fine. *Enough*. Don't make decisions when you're tired and in the midst of emotional upheavals!

The steel case may be tried in December. If so, I may not go to Nepal. Part of the roller coaster feelings stem from making life decisions anew every other day. My only stability is myself.

After visiting with Lance about the arts issues in the campaign (aside: shirt unbuttoned way too low, but slightly sexy anyway): There are too many cadres of "bright young men" trying to make it in politics. Power games, ins and outs. Why do I try to be involved in a world like that? And the trade-offs, the knowing people. Although that's how the world works, I can't quite get used to not starting off trusting people. But over the past year in politics with JLH, that's the lesson.

September 15, 1978 (Holiday Inn, DFW)

Events race by. Matt and I are becoming seasoned, but it's a bit heavy. JLH vetoed Matt's previously agreed-to settlement of the peanut case. I held Matt's hand at the Graves, Dougherty law firm foyer before we went in to tell them the news. I'd never seen him so distraught before. Even detected a slight tear. In the midst of it all I had a minor wreck in the car. Sigh. Some days are just like that.

Room service. Breakfast at the table. That's probably only the third time I've had room service. Over the past years I've really changed in some things. While married to Rod, I couldn't imagine spending alone time and enjoying it. It took getting divorced for me to find out I could enjoy myself, my own company.

Sheila's been angry for two weeks about work. Lately I've really liked her a lot. We'll both have to work at our friendship, since we've both changed. Common bonds of misery won't do! She knows exactly what she feels when she feels it. I recognize the good feelings but refuse to immediately acknowledge the bad or hurt or angry ones. I think as a child I was taught not to feel or show those. An unfortunate spin-off from Mother's Pollyanna optimism and refusal to deal with Daddy's alcoholism. We were taught always to look on the bright side and think in Christian terms of a cross to bear. All this amazes Sheila. She identifies the feelings immediately.

Running with Katie yesterday, I tried to explain the basic players in the steel case. I want to pass on as much as I can to her.

From *Snow Leopard*, p. 93: On "chod," a Tantric discipline to overcome horror of death. Matthiesson performed a mild version of chod and looked over the precipice. Always, I've done that. As a child, climbing trees when the heights scared me. Jumping across streams on rocks or across gorges. Plunge into the heart of the matter; to get to the other side, this is necessary. Tiptoeing on the edge of life is not my style, or my destiny.

September 17, 1978

Matt, after talking to Joe L, determined that everyone else in the office was just going to coast for the next four months. JLH's problem is delegation. It was tough enough for him to do it when he was around, but now his campaign absences have made it virtually impossible to function effectively. So Matt intends to take off and look for a job. As I listened, I was disturbed. Matt used the example of Al's activities. But there are two problems with that analogy: Unlike Al, we are responsible for other people, not just ourselves. If you're going to be a leader, you have to give and lead your staff even when you don't feel like it. For example, the staff meeting I called Thursday before leaving to go to DFW. Matt and I were both exhausted, but the other lawyers needed to be told a little of what was going on, and to feel some sense of participation and direction. But it wasn't easy. More importantly, the people, the taxpayers, pay us to do a job. And as much as there is loyalty to JLH involved, we really aren't working for *him* ultimately, but for all the people. Therefore, even if JLH gives us a hard time, we still owe the office and the people good faith efforts at doing our jobs.

Stan and Sharon had their baby. Today I visited them, then Mark and Diane came by with Eric. Diane watched him until she requested that Mark watch him. Mixed feelings about a child. I really only want half the responsibility. Am slipping back to thinking I would be happy enough if I never had my own children. Who knows?

September 18, 1978 (Jimmy Carter Mideast Peace Night, written in a car at a gas station on a rural farm road)

Carter pulled the Mid-East together! Is world peace possible?

He has almost convinced me that public service and power politics can be done and done well with finesse by *good people*. He said Psalm 85: "Let them not return to folly. Blessed are the peacemakers." Carter's present to the nation. Listening to Carter on the radio I had glimpses of a world at peace, fragile and tenuous. And of people like him going beyond themselves to give and to help. I want to become that way.

Hey, the reason it's neat and good to be an "up" person, to be less serious, to see the humor and magic, is *not* to "catch" or impress anyone, but because it makes *me* feel better and enjoy my life's time more! Somewhere I got the idea that intimacy, with a man especially, was involved with serious matters and sharing doubts and fears rather than joys.

Work has become no less hectic, but I handle it better.

September 20, 1978

When I read of pollution and inflation and Rhodesia and Nicaragua, chills run down my body and I'm scared, thinking of the world to come, my own financial insecurity, and whether I really want to bring a child into this world. What will happen to me if I don't become more responsible? It's all fine to be a young "hippie-type" bureaucrat/lawyer. But will that be enough at fifty, and with the responsibility for another human being? Not giant worries, but sobering thoughts in the midst of my life-for-the-moment world. Matt is all concerned about life choices as represented in our next job moves. Lately, I'm calm about all that. Although important, the choices made and paths taken are not of as much importance as what we make of them.

September 21, 1978

LBJ's definition of a great lady: the kind of woman you'd like to have for a daughter or a sister, a wife or a mother, or the trustee of your estate. (Speaking of O. C. Hobby.)

September 24, 1978

Work thought: Dropping out isn't enough. There is more to "living" (not the right word; can't find it) than self-finding. But what? Not wealth (I'm certain of that); not power (I'm slowly learning); perhaps fame (?). So much for traditional answers. The only thing I'm sure of is that an essential richness and experience is to live and love one person. Children? I don't know. It will have to be different than most child raising.

Ironic: I write of work and its importance/non-importance, and prepare for an evening of stuffing envelopes for JLH!

September 25, 1978

Last day with Paul. He cried. I felt sad and joyous.

I'm cold tonight from ice cream and air-conditioning. Guess I'm not an alcoholic if I reach for the freezer rather than a beer late at night!

September 26, 1978 (On plane with Stan to D. C.)

Stan and I talked of politics and JLH and Governor's office structure.

Miscellaneous Paul thought from yesterday: We spoke of the importance of long-term relationships and I said I wanted one.
P: "You have those kind. Rod, Sheila."
L: "That's not what I want or mean. More like what I assume you and Denise have."
P: "We have a relationship *now*. It may not be the same or we may not be married forever, but it will always be long term and permanent."
L: "Is it on balance: good?"

P: "On balance, yes. It takes a lot of effort to have a good family life, and we're committed to it, but sometimes after a long day, I wonder."

(I felt he was telling me that having children and one person wasn't the only path.)

P: "How are you?"

L: (Big, quiet smile) "Free!"

September 27, 1978 (On plane from D. C. to DFW)

Serendipitous or maybe just "foreseeing" events: Diane Stanley in Kathmandu was born in Guatemala. When Pat Bailey told me that, I felt almost eerie. The two far out places in the world I had picked to travel, and with my mother! Should I arrange my affairs in Austin in case I stay over there longer?

On this plane are a number of older women who were members of WASP, the Women's Auxiliary Service Pilots, who flew BIG planes in World War II. They're heading for a reunion at the Air Force Academy. My God, women are terrific! Yesterday, walking on Capitol Hill, I passed women lobbying for ERA extension. I wondered how it would be to lobby for that instead of antitrust issues. Perhaps the emotional commitment I have to women's issues would render me a less effective lobbyist on those. But it would be fun to have my heart involved in everyday work again.

Bentsen shook my hand, his eyes opened a bit wider and he said, "You have a good firm handshake." I was tempted to say, "Yes, just right for a budding politician," but, of course, just smiled.

At the reception, I drank too much beer and wanted to be with someone, feel "pretty" and desired. Finally called Sheila. When we all went out to eat, I talked with Stan and his brother Tex and knew I had done right in staying with them. It's important to stay in my own world, with my peers. The important Washington politicians travel in another system.

Stan takes care of me in public. Makes introductions, feeds me lines, etc. He tries to let me show off the way I do for Sheila. I just now understand that.

I'm moving away from my world slowly, but I don't yet know where I'm going. On this airplane, tired, I sense an independence, a centering. But I feel fat. Will that ever stop? Will I ever learn weight moderation? That is crucially important now. Because I can handle upsets if I'm thin but fall apart if they're coupled with being fat.

How interconnected is the human condition! The other side of separateness. I left the plane in Nashville to make a phone call. I trudged back into the plane and came upon the pilot visiting with the WASP pilots. He'd bumped a wheel on his landing and the women were gigging him. I laughed with them and my spirits soared. Later, I asked for tales. We talked of women's lib. They think my generation too serious. Query: I think they assume I'm about eighteen, so am unsure which generation is referenced. But they are the women who made it in a man's world and most never helped other women, like their secretaries, to also achieve more. When I mentioned that, one said that now there was not enough ambition. Things were too easy and women nowadays just wanted things given to them and were rude about things like men opening doors. Another lectured me before I could respond, on how she liked men and wanted to have them whistle, etc. So do I, but not from the judicial bench! Damn. The women's movement has lost more credibility over ridiculous behavior by a few over-ardent and rude women who can't graciously say thank you when the door is opened!

From the *Snow Leopard*, page 113: "The absurdity of a life that may well end before one understands it does not relieve one of the duty (to that self which is inseparable from others) to live it through as bravely and as generously as possible."

P said of my proposed trip: "I hope it's fine." Just that. (Was he saying the same thing Matthiesson's guru said about the *Snow Leopard* trip? "Expect nothing.") What is therapy? Honest friendship. Not confusing objectivity with caring.

Notes from last session with P:
Traps:
1. Letting someone else define my identity, or losing it in an authority figure.

2. Idealizing therapy.
3. Marriage/family is "good" but not everything.
P: "Can you stand to live in a world where everyone isn't like you?"

September 29, 1978

On the plane to Austin, over and over I looked at the clouds and *felt* the Nepal flight happening simultaneously. Am I crazy to take my fifty-six-year-old mother to a strange and perhaps harsh land? I must begin to learn again from her, to respect her personhood more.

The current struggle is to really live without someone to report to or who will "approve."

October 2, 1978

Lunch with Nancy. Now there is a remarkable woman. She almost cried (indeed, a few tears fell) as she spoke of leaving law practice for a while. Dean lives life at a fast pace, good humoredly, and always seeing the good, not the bad or the problems. It makes it difficult for Nancy to let him know how she feels when it's not wonderful. As she says, he comes from a generation where people in love didn't admit to non-perfection.

Nancy is boxed in by the Superwoman complex. Ironic that our men respect us and want us to be "lady lawyers" and partners and still want almost total access to our lives. In my case, it works fairly well because I have no children and therefore no divided time or emotional loyalties, and because I have a much less vested identity interest in my career than Nancy does. Her entire life has turned upside down in the last year. No wonder she feels lack of closure.

Dean doesn't want her to quit work. Echoing my thought from the other day: Would a man love me the same if I took off time to have a child? For men, work is the fundamental identification point, I think. There must be a middle ground of understanding the work/life relationship. Wish I could find it. Children are the changing point. Nancy doesn't want someone else to do the everyday living with them; how else can she find out what happened at school? But if I do that I want one half of the time and responsibility. I have a feeling that if I think equal relationships require effort and time between two adults, adding children is more than doubling the challenge. Somehow, I have a hard time envisioning most men changing half the diapers!

Nancy worries about what will happen to her lawyering five years from now if she quits. One response is "Who cares?" in the sense that five years is a long time. But on another level she's right. I don't ever want to get myself in a position with a man so that I'm really financially dependent and without marketable skills.

On leadership: If it's true that great leaders must be synergistic with their followers, then I'm often not sure I want to be a leader. And I suppose, if one questions that, then she isn't really cut out to lead. It gets back to Lee's old question of knowing what one would lead about or to what end the energy is directed. On days like today, I'm bored with the power plays, disillusioned with JLH, and I question lawyering. Perhaps another reason I'm not cut out to be a leader is my needing to be alone at times. I don't want to be responsible for others even though I like having the authority. Yet the gregarious side of me balks at the thought of a solitary existence such as writing.

A Houston law firm partner is taking time off. The thirty-nine-year-old itch. Although I applaud the decisions of Ray and Nancy concerning work, I have enough of a work ethic to feel vague discomfort as we all turn inward. There is more fundamental change in society occurring in those actions and decisions than any marching ever produced. Will the productivity structure survive a professional class which sees beyond the work ethic carrot and seeks more personal satisfaction at an early age? Are we shirking some responsibility beyond ourselves? I don't understand what all this means.

Thought: In structuring my work life, I need periods of intense activity involved with people and ideas, followed by stretches of mountain-type time. But with moderation being the key to their successful integration.

Lately, antitrust is not enough. The giving back I do of any meaning has been in one-on-one conversations.

I wish I could put aside my "serious" thoughts. I'm more fun to be with, for me as well as others. Why do I seem to think that real sharing is serious rather than humorous? Sheila has that wonderful gift of making people laugh. I do it at work and entertain. Sheila would be surprised, I think. I'd like to expand it. However, a comedienne, I ain't!

Advertising shots with JLH: He stood apart from the rest of us, fearful of being mauled by requests, questions. I felt sorry for him in his isolation. But a real leader must do more interacting with her followers, not just dart out with pronouncements and then shrink back into the king-trappings. Part of a leader's job is to *lead* and make decisions based on open and honest input from staff.

October 3, 1978

When I first went to Outward Bound the summer after my college freshman year, I smoked and had never performed any physical feats. (In the 60s in Texas, we high school girls changed clothes during gym period and sat on the floor so our hair wouldn't wilt—then redressed!) My fears of the program were for the physical side. We were to swim a mile in boots, canoe into uncharted whitewater, and survive alone for three days in the Canadian wilderness. But the physical part was just a window to the mental/spiritual. My most vivid memory is watching a brilliant sunset while I was on my solo. It was the second night alone in the woods. Seeing the beauty, I ached for another human being to share it with. Even my worst enemy, or my discarded boyfriends, or my parents, would have made the sunset's beauty bearable.

The Outward Bound spirit is returning to me. Calm exhilaration about living. Becoming basic and wrestling with life and love, not to overcome it, but to be with and through it. What people will I meet in the mountains of Nepal? What places and visions of this world and this self? Will the poverty be too much to see past?

October 4, 1978

JLH changed his mind once again on peanuts.

Politics makes strange bedfellows I'd heard, but watching Mary Jane dance with Hugh at her fundraiser was almost disgusting. That man has caused as much harm as almost anyone I know in public service in Texas.

At lunch, Mary Beth discussed mentors, or more accurately, the lack thereof for women. Later we talked of children. In three years she'll be "free." Her word. It seems women are less apt to say they would to it again when questioned about parenthood and answering honestly. Men think its terrific, important, etc., because they're not restricted in the same personal and emotional ways mothers are.

She loves to eat Wheat Thins too!

October 10, 1978 (On plane from Lubbock to Austin)

On boarding I watched a spastic man maneuver his walking cart to the plane, and prayed a thank you for the four miles I ran this morning.

Weekend party at the Tobin ranch for arts people fundraiser for JLH. Nana and Mother flew in. Quite a crew of three generations of Norwegian women. At the party Nana sat in all her ninety-one years of glory in the enormous O'Neill Ford designed livingroom/library. A woman walked up to her: "And how long have you been interested in the arts?" Nana: (not hearing too well) "I just flew in from California." A perfect non-sequitur!

Tonight at the airport between planes, Nana told me that she and Mrs. Tobin had visited at the party. Mrs. Tobin at age seventy-five said she hoped she'd be in as good shape as Nana at her age. Nana: "She's not in as good a shape as I am right now!"
What a marvelously feisty grand lady! The trip down here did us all good. I'm happy.

What a wonderful day in West Texas today! Matt and I got along, the farmers were supportive, Gene Bloys gave us a terrific agricultural lecture. I really like learning about the land and farming now. We looked at soybeans and I ate some raw in the field. Then got a tour of a cotton gin. For this I'm paid.

October 5, 1978 (At the Al Mustin Lecture at the Community Center)

Eye contact and modulation of voice together with almost too perfect silver hair; the message overpowered by technique. He talks of the Path to the One: I disagree. I think there are many paths to many ones. But all the paths leading to all the ones comprise the One. (Thus each person, each wind molecule on her path has significance through merely existing. This to me is the source of the concept of the dignity of each person and the respect one must have for the world's beings.)

Why do I have such a reaction to this group of people? They all look alike. Leftover feelings of all those years of Wednesday night choir practices. I have a healthy (I think) skepticism for easy answers. Charismatic leaders are hard to swallow. There is a difference, to me a crucial one, between Zen acceptance and "religion." People don't really examine their priorities.

Where do thoughts come from? Good question. When you slow down your thoughts, there is something between thoughts.

I learned a lot of this through a long and difficult process with P. And remembering the tears and pain, I am jealous in guarding access to that knowledge and refuse to be open to the idea that there may be an "easier" path, *just as valid* for someone else. Well kid, you haven't come very far on the generosity of spirit.

In the East, the conscious mind is called a "drunken monkey." Good analogy. Descriptions of meditation sound like loving.

Mustin's thesis is that crisis times are the motivating factor toward growth. I grew up in that atmosphere.

Yes we all believe in death.

October 12, 1978
Girl *friends* with Sheila, Katie and Sharon.

October 20, 1978
I just counted the weeks I'll be gone. Seven and a half. I'm scared of being lonely.

October 21, 1978
When in the mountains, I want my spirit to be calm and accepting of the moment, like the cheerful Sherpas.

October 25, 1978

Sometimes this diary seems superficial. I can't capture the thoughts and feelings of depth. Writing too much in case someone will read it. When will I learn that honesty of self is ultimate?

October 26, 1978

I wanted to capture profound thoughts this evening. Not capturable; maybe a good sign; life is for living wholly, not for writing about.

Main feelings upon turning thirty:

1. Satisfaction—these have been good years.
2. Need for structure of quality and recognition of limited time.
3. How to reconcile number two with Zen.

October 28, 1978

For a moment at Sheila's today, I envied the lightness and space and smart investment she made in "Mondo Condo." And questioned my judgment in spending all this money to go to Nepal. But tonight, I luxuriate in aloneness and am aware that this little space is sufficient. Oh, the alone feels good! And I need the silence.

I'm afraid of the cold in Nepal. Of the dirt, of the poverty, of being alone in the midst of twelve people. Of not having enough humor and spiritual generosity to make a cheerful trekker.

Just finished the *Snow Leopard*. Sometimes life has more meaning than I can apprehend.

October 31, 1978 (Halloween)

Had a terrible gut anxiety attack today precipitated by problems with the accounting office regarding a leave of absence. I feel rootless and scared about not controlling my future. No one seems to understand that I don't want to be a lawyer anymore. Maybe not even me. That's why the Governor's office is important to me. I want a way out of lawyering that's acceptable.

Suddenly I feel very much the Catch-30 and want to quit working, stay home and have a baby. There's a terrible confusion that most of the time I can deal with rationally and with a sense of humor, but sometimes just can't. How much of wanting a baby is really just not wanting to work for awhile? I'm not comfortable sharing this crazy side with anyone. Maybe because I'm not comfortable with it either.

Looking at myself in the mirror, I have a delayed turning-thirty feeling. Giant bump on my head, dark curly hair on my inside thigh. Hey, I just realized I'm in an old-fashioned attack, and it's probably best to just leave it alone and figure out later. Will I ever learn?

After flipping through some old diary entries, I decided I was okay, bumps and introspection notwithstanding. At my birthday party at Luke's, I felt rich with friends, and can't quite believe I'm equal to them, but they must like me or they wouldn't have come. I vacillate between extremes of utter arrogant egotism and incredulous insecurity. It's been a long road to be able to stand centered and like myself well enough to assume others will, too. And to drop the games geared to get ego reinforcement entirely through others' perceptions. Yet this is crucial to my life as just me and to any meaningful relationships.

Do it, don't stew it! The last person I need to spend time and energy justifying myself to is me!

November 1, 1978

Matt just convinced me we'd screwed up royally for two years and not done enough. As usual, he's partly correct and I've managed to hear and feel guilty about all of it. But it's not altogether true! We've done some good things.

I just don't have enough "drive to be first" to put in the energy. Too scattered in my world endeavors. Maybe I really am not cut out for leadership and professionalism.

I feel physically bad—sore throat, sinus, physical weakness. I feel as if I have to fight all this to feel good about myself. It's a waste of energy to cry over past lacks. If I've not been a good assistant chief, there's nothing I can do now to change it. *Except be better in the future.*

November 5, 1978

Good conversation with my sister:

Janet: "I can tell you this, the one love that doesn't change is for your children. If something happened to Bruce, I'd go on. If something happened to one of the kids, I'd manage to go on because I'd have to care for the other one. If something happened to both, I'd go insane."

November 9, 1978

John Hill lost. The people of Texas lost. I lost.

Yesterday (a million years ago) I numbly ached for the state, the cosmic sense of the unseen bad, the Yantis the public never perceives. For JLH and Bitsy. (They're fine. JLH: "I feel like a kid who's worked real hard to get ready to take a test and now they won't let me take it." Bitsy: "Guess I'll have to go back and get a Masters of something.")

Today I awoke to the radio announcing "the first Republican Governor in one hundred and five years." All day my insides ached. For me as well.

But a curious freedom; no reason to come back from Nepal. Too early to determine what it means. Why:

1. Tim: "John Rogers says we didn't hit hard enough and spent too much time preparing to govern."

2. Siff: "Clements direct mail."

3. Maybe best simplistic analysis, Mariotti: "People elected and voted like they've always done: Dolph Clements."

Pasts like mine, however, are tremendous preparation for election losses. Scorpio regeneration. Rising from ashes, but the problem with the Phoenix analogy is that it does require ashes from which to rise!

When I almost allowed the tears this afternoon, Matt came in to tell me women friends of mine really weren't friends and had said, "You can always tell when Linda is between men, she then does women's issue work, and she's a star-fucker." I hurt. Divisive women are ineffective. Men who promote divisiveness I have no need for.

Having done a lot before now, I feel no need to be powerful or authoritative. Being a private citizen appeals to me. I sense major outside changes coming on, perhaps that will integrate with the inside ones. Today I thought it would be good to spend some time working and learning about the land, how to grow things and to once again teach young children. To be more directly productive.

Losing an election is nothing compared to getting divorced from Rod. Perspective.

It will be good to be in Nepal and not worry *at all* about how I look. To care not a whit if a bump arises, or if mascara runs. To seek no one's approval but my own. It's a strangely freeing experience to differ with Paul and with Sheila. Trusting my own judgment.

I'm still reeling from the shock. Maybe more than I fully comprehend. Tonight on the phone with Cliff, I thought that well, if things are unbearable, one can always commit suicide. Not out of desperation, but calm recognition of the choice. That's one of the ultimate differences that being alone rather than having a family makes. Tonight I feel alone without tears. Losing the election was like losing Tim; more than loss of the particular, more significantly, loss of a dream.

November 12, 1978 (Middle of the night, 4:30 a.m.)

Since 3:00 a.m., I've been in a full blown, old fashioned anxiety attack. Ugh! The old blood racing, heart pounding kind. Calm down, body. Nothing is worth wasting heartbeats. Today I've just been zinging all over. Manic high with Nancy at lunch, almost in tears at work as I cleaned out my desk, actual tears over beer with Rod, politics *everywhere*. So many lives rearranged! For me personally, it's probably good. Learn to land on your feet. I don't want to fight anymore. If I can choose my life, I want more peace in my daily surroundings. Will these feelings go away after six weeks and will I be rejuvenated? The world stretches before me. Healthy, intelligent, a little battered but seasoned. I can create and choose how, where and with whom I live. A quiet wow.

New thought: In general, people have become more three dimensional to me. I glimpse my sisters as women.

November 15, 1978

Last day at work yesterday. Sad, emptyish feelings. JLH gave me a huge hug, but he was broken. Mumblings about the party and helping the people. It seemed as if my saying goodbye and being in his office didn't register. There was a veil or wall between him and the world. Perhaps understandable given the election, I left four and a half years of working with him with a sense that I was glad to leave. Does Texas politics necessarily create two personality types at that rarified level? Dolph went soft and paranoid/ineffective and got slightly crazy. JLH put his ego on the line as all candidates must, and the king complex struck.

That is only one part of JLH though. Tonight I miss the generous man willing to give young lawyers a chance; the new Attorney General who fought for justice and fairness and made us so proud to be a part of his office. I remember drafting my first controversial opinion. It held that women could use their own names on drivers' licenses; they didn't lose the right to use whatever name they chose just because they got married. JLH had to be convinced, but once he was, he stood with us.

Politics makes things sad and confusing.

❦ *Nepal Journal:*

November 18, 1978 (On plane to Dallas—the beginning)

Tears at the airport have numbed my mind. The swift takeoff of the jet was so fast, yet so removed from the immediacy of flying in the *air* that the small plane glories in. Sheila's body was thin through her hug; finally, we broke the barriers of physical touching. At the stoplight at 38th, she turned to me in the car and on *her* motion, hugged. We laughed as cars honked.

Later: London to Bombay—on plane

I can't get over the graciousness of the Air India people. Half the population of the plane is under age five or over seventy-five, necessitating lots of diapers, bottles and special attention. Most Americans I know would go crazy, but here people seem to accept this teeming mass of old/young humanity with remarkable equanimity.

We're all eating like idiots. A quick perusal of the community gear revealed a suspiciously camp-like diet of powdered eggs and vanilla pudding, so we are wolfing down chicken curry and beef whenever offered. Word is out that ninety-five percent of us have done an Outward Bound program previously. A flicker of anxiety— I haven't done much hiking and hope I can keep up.

One of the trekkers, a shrink named Joe, teaches at the medical school and split his ticket to vote for Governor Clements. Ugh. I wanted to ask why; he volunteered it was a protest vote. Protesting what? Politics prejudices me too much. Here on a plane to Bombay [I still can't believe this is real!], I don't want to argue. But I look at him with different eyes. How defined and how limited we are by our prejudices! The mountains will show/teach me more on this.

One section in *My Mother, Myself* discusses how much more readily boys are prepared and pushed for separation from mother. "Don't baby him," etc. This, of course, later teaches him all accidents are not fatal, rejections are lived through and the self goes on. I'm a product of a very traditional childhood in those respects. Only in swimming that first mile did it dawn on me that I could do things. Even as close in time as Tim's and my waterfall walk at Pedernales

Falls, I remember his striding off the creekbed path and onto the hill at the end of the property. I followed him up a not particularly steep path, but was surprised momentarily when he didn't offer me a hand. Obviously, he assumed I was capable of negotiating the steps he'd taken. Of course, I was. But I've been conditioned *to assume I can't without help.* And even now, when my intellect revels in self-independence, emotionally I slip back looking for the outstretched hand.

November 20, 1978 (At Delhi Airport)

India's humanity is overwhelming. I watched Delhi's streets this morning and although I expected poverty, was still unprepared. Children and dirt everywhere. No sanitation system. People drinking and washing from fountains that almost looked more like cesspools. A Communist parade held tens of thousands of people. Red banners everywhere. Tents made of rags pitched three feet from automobile roundabouts. Half naked children beg with large bellies and blackened feet. The earth seems worn out, dusty, as if it can't produce anymore. Horses and cows are bones covered with skin sores. We walk the streets draped with camera equipment. The contrast aches, and I (like every other tourist, I suspect), am caught in ethnocentricity and want to take a child home. Which is worse— what we see, or the relative ease with which we avert our hearts if not our eyes?

Connections with our travel agent and OB leaders were unsuccessful in Delhi, so we improvised and managed to get all eighteen of us and luggage to the hotel. A not insubstantial feat! A young woman named Chris was my roommate. It was her birthday, so at 4:00 a.m. we sat in a Delhi hotel room drinking beer.

What do these people think about? Subsistence only? Hindu religious beliefs? In a complete way, I feel totally separate and apart from the Indians—I can't imagine their hopes or dreams. It's unlike being in Mexico, or even among the Indians in Guatemala. This lack of sympathy—is that the word—not empathy? must be one of the building blocks of colonialism and early slavery. Is this what some people feel about blacks? And some men, about women?

In Kathmandu:

The day was awfully long getting here, late plane connections, etc. Finally, the exhaustion set in as I gazed around our cheap hotel room, trying not to look too closely at the cot coverings. I felt so alone, and lonely.

November 21, 1978

Today we explored Kathmandu on bicycle. It's an interesting old city, surrounded by the mountains in the distance. Although the people are poor and diet is endemic, the natural beauty and lack of industry makes it seem totally different from Delhi. We went to a Hindu then a Buddhist temple. At the latter was an enormous red prayer wheel, and pilgrims in from the mountains for a festival. Monkeys are everywhere, but people do not take kindly to our photographing the animals. Haven't discovered the reason yet.

Our trek route has changed. We're going to almost double the distance and cross Thrang-La Pass at 17,700 feet. In the snow. They told those of us who didn't bring down parkas to buy a heavy wool sweater. Why did I throw out sweaters? Ugh. But while the climbing looks pretty tough, the rest of the trek experience almost qualifies as decadence. We'll have thirteen students, two leaders, six Sherpas and twenty-one porters. Apparently the Sherpas and porters will do all the cooking, carrying and cleaning. We all looked at one another in disbelief when they told us. Doesn't sound very Outward Bound-like.

Tonight we have a meeting to go over the route, etc. Tomorrow is reserved for logistics, buying sweaters, etc., then on Thanksgiving we go to Pokhara. I'm finally getting excited and am ready for the mountains. Today, when the haze lifted and I glimpsed them, it was as if my soul were freed up again. I'd been feeling slow.
Late at night:

We divided into groups. Chris and I and two older women from Hawaii (pretty gutsy—both about fifty-five and traveled here on their own and plan to stay a month afterward). One of them looks pretty frail, but she'll probably put us to shame. The men seem okay. Hal, an executive at Montgomery Wards with a daughter my age, is clearly going to have trouble accepting OB's rather Zen approach. He always wants to know every logistical detail three days ahead of time. Two very nice, very young guys, students, and the rest I haven't sorted out yet. We didn't get Joe, the shrink. Too bad, I'd gotten to like him. Our leaders lacked a lot of enthusiasm tonight, and Chris and I were both looking longingly at the other group that seemed a bit more lively. But one of the key tenets of OB is that it's much what you make of it, so here goes! The other group also got the two guys who were smoking dope at the London airport. Suits me fine not to be with them. (Hash is almost free here. I'm just not interested before I go to the mountains. Some vague feeling of purity more than legality.)

So we begin. I'm not sure whether I fear it will be too easy, or too difficult. I sense it will be quite solitary, which is fine.

November 22, 1978

This morning while shopping I was charged by an elephant! An amazing experience—I was so shocked, I forgot to snap the shutter. Also took my first rickshaw ride, for thirty-six cents. Succumbing to jet lag and a long morning of picture taking and explorings, I decided it was okay to be carried. Gold temples are next to vegetable markets, and bicycle bells warning unwary pedestrians filled the air.

November 23, 1978 (Thanksgiving Day)

Day one of the trek. Our Sherpa Sardar (leader) is named Dawa. After a huge dinner tonight, he let me sit by him at the fire and offered me some local whiskey. The mountains are beautiful, the Valley lush, green and filed with rivulets flowing to turquoise rivers. Joe and I talked at length.

November 24, 1978

We made camp last night beside a roaring stream, in a large canyon. The sun came up between the mountains in pink glory. The women camped together for the first and probably only time. I slept so well, and feel peaceful this morning. Yesterday at dinner I said Thanksgiving grace, "Bless this food, thank you for safe journeys, grant us open hearts and souls in the mountains and bless those who love and care for us at home."

It's nice to be alone in a group.

Writing will be difficult as we camp almost at dark, early at 6:00–7:00 p.m. Tea is brought to our tents in the morning with a smile. Yesterday, we approached the camp, found a large blue tarp spread out with a cloth over a hump in the middle. With Sherpa flair, Dawa yanked the cloth off like a magician to reveal tea and biscuits!

Lunchtime: We had an easy morning. The trek was level. Dawa gave me Nepali instruction, and we were accosted by Nepali children singing a song about climbing Mt. Everest. "How can they make such a climb? How can they climb Mt. Everest?" Mountains loom in the distance, snow-covered, stately in their white majesty, and reminding us of the challenge to come. The villages are picturesque, brown-thatched roofs. And people smile a lot.

We stopped for lunch on a hill. It's still strange to be waited on—hot tea prepared for us.

My first try at a backbend! Pat is teaching me. A delightful wholesome twenty-three-year-old California kid.

At Camp—Day two: The snow-covered mountains define us. Today, I hiked with Pat. A calm, steady pace up hills and learning about his life, gymnasts, etc. Meditated facing a valley and hills. It rained and the new coat was nice. Evenings are long and nights longer. Sun goes down around 7:00 and doesn't come up until 6:00.

I have few profound thoughts. The OB spirit of just doing what's at hand has infused my spirit. No big thoughts. The smell of wood burning is the normal background, along with dung.

For a next trip, I'll bring a small foam pad as a sit-upon.

After Dinner: Camp sounds fill the night. Our newly extended family coughs and talks. "Where's my notebook?" Huddled on the tarp next to one another for warmth, to write in the lantern's meager light, we begin the process of coming together, molding a kinship group. Sharing is important here. Jean gave me her extra pair of tights; I reciprocated by giving John my extra notebook.

Thirty years of teaching make Jean delightful with the Nepali children. At sunset, she played volleyball with them and taught them how to count. The schoolmarm voice rang out over the valley. Pat turned to us: "I'm in love with that old lady." She and Jean have been traveling around the world together since September. What a pair! Jean: "I'm afraid I'm losing my courage and daring." LA: "Unless you have a very different definition of courage and daring, I'd say you have a lot of both!" Jean's laugh is rich and deep. A nature book writer and calligrapher. I'm going to commission a picture of me in the sleeping bag on a mountain with the bubble. Sort of like *The Little Prince* drawings.

Like St. Exupery's little prince, I fear that without labeling, grownups might mistake it for a smashed hat.

Jared can sit quietly. Most of these people can handle long silences. Thank goodness.

I must write while I can. The warmth already goes quickly. Soon, we'll be so high that mittens prevent nighttime writing.

Today was our first *real* trekking day, and it was fairly easy. We went from 3,500 to 5,400 feet and camped atop a ridge overlooking a green valley with snow-covered mountains in the distance. The mountains loom majestic and infuse everything with their presence. In our case, we all seem entranced by the beauty, but apprehensive about the climb. I fear the cold. Reminiscent of my solo time at Minnesota OB school eleven years ago when I desperately feared being afraid of the dark, now I try not to be afraid of the coming cold. During the day, we strip to shorts and T-shirts that get sweat-soaked from our day packs. But early, we switch to vests, etc.

The daily routine is that we awake (really, get up, we're all awake by 4:00 a.m.) at 6:00 when the porters hand us cups of tea at the tent opening. After a breakfast of oatmeal and biscuits (English-type cookies, not gravy-type), we walk for a couple hours until lunch, then again afterwards till about 4:00. Tea is served and we talk, play frisbee, wash, etc., till dinner at 6:00. It gets dark by 6:30–7:00 and cold by 5:00. So daylight time is precious. In the evening we're huddled together on a tarp around a lantern (the Sherpas have the only fire—for cooking) telling tales and reading and writing.

The head Sherpa, Dawa, appears to have taken a fancy to me. Last night I wandered up to his fire. He promptly pulled up a flat rock, said, "Sit down" and offered me some local whisky made from millet. We talked and smiled a lot. His English is very good, and a hell of a lot better than my Nepali!

We have four tents for fourteen of us and "sleep around." Even were one to want privacy, it would be nigh impossible to have it. We share the trails with animals—goats; long-snouted, heavy-bellied pigs; water buffalo.

November 25, 1978

We climbed down a long, very steep gorge, hard on knees, but I'm learning the quick shuffle step. Sort of like skiing down rocks. This morning, I read "The Waking" as my turn at inspiration. We had an incredible view of Anapurna and Maachapuchare. Around a corner and we would have missed viewing the ledge tucked away in the Nepali village but for Dawa, shepherding us as always and pointing it out to us.

This afternoon was really rough. A long, slow, steady ascent to 5,400. Dawa walked part-way with me and said he'd help arrange a trek for my mother. About 3:00 I thought I'd not make it, so stopped in a tea house for two lemon drinks and biscuits. There, in a dirty Nepali home with chickens running around at my feet and small dirty children, I was happy to just sit down.

One lady was pushed off the trail by a herd of horses laden with goods. We share the trails.

Chris is a steady delight on the trail. Constant good humor and ready to share her expertise about all sorts of hiking matters.

At lunch, we stopped at a waterfall and washed hair and swam in the icy waters. After watching the men climb up a rock cliff, I decided I would try to conquer my height fear. Going up was frightening, but I made it, heart and thighs quaking. Jared, one of the instructors, helped me down. Outward Bound spirit!

It gets very cold at night; I'm glad I opted for the warmer sleeping bag. This morning, we climbed 2,500 feet up to 7,300. The calves feel it, but I'm getting the rhythm down. Tomorrow it's all *down*—

the old body can't win. Last night Dawa and the two instructors and I went to the house of the local medical man and drank rakshi. The scene was just like Dersu Ursalu—oiled faces, firelight, silver drinking vessels lining the dirt walls. The doctor didn't drink and explained rakshi (millet alcohol) was like the Communists—at first very good, then later "fight with guns." An interesting explanation of alcoholism. For a short time this morning, I was all alive on the trail—about a half-hour. It was eerie and wonderful. Green, incredibly steep valleys with the snow mountains looming on the horizon. Profound thoughts are rare. Just being. Basics dominate our existence—sleep, food, peeing and shitting.

November 27, 1978 (Tatopani)

An exhausting but beautiful, incredible day. We hiked from 10,000 feet to 3,500 feet over about eight-ten miles. My knees hurt even though as I ran down the rocks I felt I was skiing the mountains. Beauty is sometimes reserved for those who make the effort. Today, I first got into the walking like Sherpas. Each step deliberate and putting one farther along the path. Like life, there is always an ache somewhere, but we learn to exist and find joy in it. For hours, I was nothing but my legs. This morning we hiked to a spot where I felt we were on top of the world. The mountains surrounded us. Tonight I had a beer while some folks had a toke of dope. Hash is everywhere. But we're staying in a town camped in the backyard of a tavern and there is light and a table to write on, so I feel I should take advantage of it. Last night was very cold, even in my bag in a tent. Today I have hiked with cramps and a cold—why me? I'm finally getting the hang of the small camera and plan to hike with it in hand. Someone had a guitar in the tavern, so I played a bit.

November 28, 1978

People are beginning to get tired; even Chris looks a little down. My goals are modest. Yesterday, I was content just to make it. I had a very difficult day. Throat is sore and the knee hurt badly. At one point this afternoon, I didn't want to go on but of course I did, and eventually climbed off the path onto a rock in the middle of the Kali

Gandaki River. I watched the clouds through the gorge. The proportions are immense and hard to capture either in words or in pictures. As the white of the clouds drifted past, I hurt, and was tired.

The trail is good, on occasion quite narrow. One misstep and that would be all. I watch in utter amazement as the porters and local people run the trail, barefoot, carrying sixty-pound loads. We can barely make it sometimes.

Dawa continues to watch out for us at every turn. He's like a guardian angel, aware of each of us, guiding us along as he very unassumingly arranges everything for forty people. Just when I thought I could not go another step, there he was, offering me an orange.

The food has been good—almost all local produce, squash, rice, etc. Tonight we're having buffalo. Dawa bought a live water buffalo so we walked our dinner up the trail.

Because of the gorge, light and warmth are even more precious than before. There's only about an hour of light at the end of the day and by 8:00 we're all in bed, exhausted.

November 29, 1978

We walk toward white mountains. The joy is in the process, the trek, not the result. Soon bodies will wear out. Let us simplify—be one with the vastness of the Kali Gandaki. Each step in the same direction. Crystalline mountaintop lines—lovely in the distance, slope in a giant swoop towards the next hill.

Last night the community pulled me through. Mind puzzles, scratched in the dirt, entertained cold bodies.

Larjung: Today, the scenery changed radically. Green trees and huge rhododendron forests that were jungle-like have been replaced by pine trees, vast cold distances and the roaring Kali Gandaki. We walked up part of the river bed. Eerie snowscape. I watched as people trekked ahead of me like ants. Pictures can't capture it. Imagine the mountains 19,000 feet straight above. Today, I felt much better although I'm having trouble with the knee. The memory of my quick springy steps down the other day at Goripani is bright in my mind.

Wonder if I'll ever feel that again? Something always hurts when you hike, I guess. We heard today that a porter died at the pass last week. So the night we go over the pass, we'll give the porters our tents and sleep out at 14,500. As I write this, it occurs to me that this trek probably sounds much more difficult than it is. What saves us is that we do actual hiking only about six–seven hours a day.

I hiked alone today. Staring up at the snow majesty of the mountains, it seemed simple to want to find one person to love. Basic things seem essential—food, warmth, shelter—someone to love and be loved by.

Tonight it's my turn to stay in a local tea house instead of with the group. A good night's choice since my dorm room is much more sheltered than the tents. The latrine here is situated directly over the river, so I watched my pee go into the water. Normal for men, but a new experience for me.

November 30, 1978 (Jomosom)

What is beauty? This is a windswept, cold, dusty military town. People are dirty, clothes are dark colored. There is little outwardly to recommend the place. Yet there is a certain beauty in its very coldness. And we were brought together as a group. Around the tea table, cold, slightly restless from a short day but tired, we read poetry aloud. Andy's voice on "Fern Hill" will remain in my memory.

I feel centered. I think I'm more accepting of myself than I knew. On the trip, I've little desire to show off, or to be anything other than what I am. So I don't feel guilty if I don't join in card games. I participate in my own way sitting outside the mainstream, reading and writing letters. Perhaps time to list the people:

1. Chris—twenty-eight, bright blue eyes, Ph.D. candidate in leisure studies; reserved, outgoing on the surface, but very uptight and straight underneath. But a delight to camp with—always willing to help another without becoming saccharine.

2. Jean—fiftyish, from Hawaii, a retired school teacher who keeps up well and seems full of common sense and good camaraderie.

3. Jan—her traveling companion, forty-nine, writer, hiker. Her con-

stant exclamations of "how cute" or "how darling" have begun to
wear thin. She seems to still enjoy sneaking off to smoke hash with
the younger people.
4. Pat—twenty, gymnastics teacher, half Indian. One of my favor-
ites. He has a nice air about him for one so young. We hike together
often. He showed me a poem he'd written. P: "Well, I'm not Robert
Frost." LA: "How do you know?"
5. Andy—twenty-seven, the leader of the group. Quiet, command-
ing respect from his silent stance. Inscrutable.

December 1, 1978
    A relatively easy day, my cold improving and with it my hu-
mor! The scenery changed from pine forests to barren hills. Fierce
winds whipped dust up against our backs and for a moment apprehension filled my being. Then I remembered I could do nothing
about it anyway, so best be glad it was behind me and just see what
comes. Lessons in Zen acceptance come in handy these days.
    The poetry book has also come in handy. Tonight we all huddled
round in the tea house and read aloud. The trek is difficult mentally
for a few people who seem unable to entertain themselves for the
long afternoon and evening hours. One man especially, a business
executive about fifty, does fine physically (he personally worked
with Dr. Cooper, etc. and was sure we all knew!) but can't handle
silences and just quiet sitting.
    Now that I'm feeling better, I've become more part of the group.
Before, I've been withdrawn and spending all of my energy on the
physical, merely getting through each day. Tonight, I even insti-
gated a group story. There is a certain laid back quality to my
existence; instead of hurrying from spot to spot, I go slowly and
many times alone. But I don't feel lonely. Dawa more and more
becomes like Dersu Ursula. This afternoon he appeared as I was
trekking and, as usual, I walked in his footsteps. I learn from him
things he doesn't even know he teaches.
    The animals change also. Now we see yaks, sturdier ponies
[Mustang is the name of this province] and occasionally men riding

horses. The Tibetan culture is more in evidence. Many prayer mounds dot the trail and we carefully walk to the right.

The constant smell of woodburning smoke, people sniffling, murmurs of Nepalese from the Sherpas' fire and the slap of cards as the rest of the group plays hearts, form a background music that has become home.

December 3, 1978 (Muktinath, 9,000 feet)

It's hard to write about yesterday. Almost a dream. But we really attempted the same Himalaya pass that the Mongolian hordes had to come through when they invaded India.

We started at 6:00 a.m. and went 4,500 feet up to almost 17,500 feet, then weather caught us and we had to climb back down. Cherryann got hypothermia and had to be carried. I've never felt such complete and total exhaustion. We got back to our camp at 5:15; many quite sick. I was lucky, and other than being tired, with a mild headache and nausea, was okay. High on the mountain, when the pass was in sight, I didn't mind turning back. It was a white, cold nightmare. The only reason I was never afraid was because I had blind faith in Dawa that we would be okay. Frankly, looking back, I think I was totally naive to how dangerous the whole expedition was. I did, however, fall in love—with my boots! At the last minute before we left, Dawa made me change into them from tennis shoes. If I hadn't, I suspect I'd have been a case like Cherryann. Jared was incredible on the mountain. His patience with Jan was remarkable; I was about to tell her off. She doesn't think much of others.

I'm not sure I ever want to climb that high again, at least not in weather like that. Lots of people were upset about not making it over, but we still had two hours to go at 1:00 p.m. and were facing a four-hour down hike in heavy snow to a high camp at 14,000 feet without tents. The challenge for me was always the *trying*, so not making it over didn't devastate me.

Today is a rest day—much needed. Clean (well, sort of) hands and face made me feel immensely better. I have no idea what I really look like. Suspect I've lost weight, but it's hard to tell since I brought large pants. I have on occasion been lonesome. Maybe what I'm really learning on this trip is a kind of inner self-reliance. I've resisted the urge, except for once when I asked Andy for a hug in his blanket, to turn to men for physical affection when I wanted reassurance. I'm learning to find that in other places. The night before the climb, instead of finding Joe to curl up with, I went to my sleeping bag and talked and sang with Chris and Pat—the group providing what previously I only got from one man.

This morning I climbed up to Muktinath Temple. A little fifteen-minute climb and I was beat. Afterwards, I hiked up to a rock, sat in the sun (I'd questioned whether I'd ever be warm again), and was glad to be alive. These days are strangely solitary, although not lonely. Dahligari and surrounding peaks form a white snow mountain bowl around this holy place. Here where the fire and water flow together from the natural gas and springs, come pilgrims as far away as Bombay, walking *seven* months. An old, very dirty, semi-toothless Tibetan woman guards the entrance and extracts your ruble. Dawa said that to drink from the fountain brings long life. Not being sure which fountain, I tasted a little from two sources. This may be one of the most beautiful places in the world.

December 5, 1978 (Marjong)

Excitement is sitting at this clean table waiting for a hot bath! We're having another rest day after hiking eight hours down from Muktinath yesterday. We're all pretty tired and are still recuperating from the Pass. Chris and I left camp this morning and came to this high class hotel for a hot bath and breakfast. We feel decadent, but deserving. She hiked all day yesterday with tendonitis in her shin and I've now developed an allergy on my hands that is blistering and beginning to puff up with blood. C'est la vie. Guess there's always something. Unfortunately, I looked in a mirror and discovered a big new wrinkle on my forehead. Somehow I had hoped to be through with building outward signs of character for a while.

Each night I gaze at the stars. They are truly incredible here. So close you feel like touching them. The moon, while new, has had the aura of the whole moon backlighting it. Joe (the shrink from S.A.) and I meet almost every other night and compare notes on our experiences with our two different groups. He divorced his wife and left his six kids two years ago and has a girlfriend named Linda. His last name is Lee, and apparently she wants very much to be Linda Lee. As I write, I realize how remote sex is from this life. None of us has any sexual feelings, as far as I can tell. Those are "luxury" feelings and, contrary to accepted psychological theory, sex is a far distant third to food and shelter.

Last night, everyone really got loose. The group had lots of tension to release. We all had some rum and sang and told jokes. For once, we had an enclosed place to eat and a table and a candle. Even the businessman loosened up. On the mountain, he thought he was going to have a heart attack and had to be talked up. Group dynamics are changing. One set of people spend most of the day and all night smoking hash and drinking. I feel a bit like a prude—somehow, I figure I can get stoned and drunk *anywhere*—and here, I want to be aware. One thing I've tried to do anyway is get away from the idea that at the end of a hard day, the reward is a beer.

The dangerousness of the trip is beginning to dawn on us. Or rather on some of us. I don't think some of the people who put the group in considerable jeopardy realize it. One older woman has totally fallen apart. It's almost like a movie. As we go higher, she gets stoned and drunk every night and babbles during the day. There is a raw quality to us these days. [As I write this, we're having a discussion on women's lib—I'm not participating.]

Dawa and I had a beer today and a talk. He said Cherryann would have died on the mountain had we not turned back. And lots of us would be sick.

December 6, 1978 (Larjung—lunch)

Yesterday's rest day did us all well, although some folks are incapable of entertaining themselves for very long.

Last night was warm for sleeping! After dinner, I went to the other camp and drank rum and talked with Joe, Tom and the instructor Jimbo.

December 7, 1978 (Ghasa—lunch—Pearl Harbor Day)

We all partied around the campfire last night and danced with the Sherpas. The setting was like the Swiss Alps. We've traded white, snow covered ground for green pine trees and majestic views of Anapurna and Dahligari. I'm still awed by the dimensions. To have lunch seated in the gorge between the sixth and tenth highest mountains in the world, over three miles above me, is heavy. Rakshi (rice wine) flowed profusely, and the scene grew primitive. Porters and campers beat rhythm—on rocks with sticks. The Sherpas chanted songs for their dances; we didn't do as well trying to sing pop and rock songs for dancing. Everyone got high, and although I joined in, I didn't drink much.

This morning I walked with Chris. It's nice, in the midst of some of the raucous crew constantly doped up, to have someone so stable and straight, even if terribly conservative. We talked about jobs and work. Politics and law still seem very far away. It's been so long since I've heard about what's happening in the world. Half of it could be blown up and I'd not know. Pearl Harbor thoughts.

December 8, 1978 (Lunch, outside Tatopani)

I walked with Dawa this morning and jumped from rock to rock. *Finally*, I had a wonderful run! We stopped for a long bath at Tatopani—clean hair!

Last night Andy wrapped his blanket around me at dinner. A fun, high school infatuation feeling. Later, I lay alone outside and looked at the stars. I'm so at peace these days. No real thoughts. Think I'll sit and sun. Not write.

December 9, 1978 (Lunch—somewhere north of Beni)

Slept outside last night on a hill looking at stars and a half moon. Got wet, but was worth it.

December 11, 1978

The last two days were tough. I woke up one night throwing up—ate something bad and was up all night before a long day's trek. For the first time, I was ready to go home—sleep in sheets, etc.

However, today, after a good night's sleep and a bowl of porridge for breakfast, things look better.

Two more days. What mail awaits me? I begin to think of home, work, etc.

We chased our dinner the other night. Water buffalo with adrenalin! He got loose and we all chased him round the camp. Tasted a bit tough.

December 12, 1978 (Outside Pokhara Lake)

Andy read us this quotation from Rilke:

"That is at bottom the only courage that is demanded of us: to have courage for the most strange, the most singular and the most inexplicable that we may encounter. That mankind has in this sense been cowardly, has done life endless harm; the experiences that are called 'visions,' the whole so-called 'spirit-world,' death, all those things that are so closely akin to us, have by daily parrying been so crowded out of life that the senses with which we could have grasped them are atrophied. To say nothing of God."

One of the best-paying professions is getting ahold of pieces of country in your mind, learning their smells and their moods, sorting out the pieces of a view, deciding what grows there and why, how many steps that hill will take, where this creek winds and where it meets the other one below, what elevation timberline is now, whether you can walk this reef at low-tide or have to climb around, which contour lines on a map mean better cliffs or mountains. This is the best kind of ownership and the most permanent. It feels good to say, "I know the Sierras" or "I know Point Reyes." But, of course, you don't. What you know better is yourself, and Point Reyes and the Sierras have helped.

What have I learned on the trek? I'm whole, alive, stable and have developed more inner balance than I'd realized. Being only myself—no pretenses or at least no obvious ones—was fine. Some people liked me; some didn't. I liked some, not all. The mountains are clean, demand respect, respect competence. Beauty changes—outwardly in snow-capped majestic peaks, to pine trees, to immense gorges and vast plains of jutting stones—and inwardly in the eyes of each of us. My body is more connected to my mind. Awareness of aches and pains has taught me to listen, to feel what strengths these frail vessels we're blessed (or cursed) with possess, and to live with the weaknesses.

A genuine "I'm tired" between friends is worth infinitely more than a fake "It's beautiful." Subtler emotions than love make a smile or a hug on a cold night shine warmth.

December 13, 1978 (Back in Kathmandu)
1. Just as I finished reading mail from home, word came that one of the group OD'ed on some bad heroin and was rushed to the emergency room. Poor Joe has had his hands full. I'm a little in shock.
2. It's good to be somewhat clean, even if with a cold shower.
3. I may never touch drugs, or even drink excessively, after this trip.
4. I'm off to our "final feast." Tomorrow almost everyone goes home. I have one day alone, then Mother comes. It will be good to see her.

December 15, 1978 (Kathmandu, sitting in a Sherpa tea shop with Dawa as we arrange a mini-trek for Mom and me)
Carrying scraps of paper on me has proven fortuitous for writing.

My immediate predicament is how to gracefully refuse to eat any more of the dish set before me. We've been in this place for about an hour as Dawa visits with friends and arranges details with the Sherpa, Lockpassubu, who will trek with Mom and me for four days—22nd–26th. He ordered this dish called Moo-moo [transliterated] which appears to be semi-raw buffalo or goat meat wrapped ravioli style in rather raw dough and covered with a hot pepper sauce. Given the somewhat tenuous state of my stomach these days, it's not exactly what I had in mind.

For the last two days, I've been running around Kathmandu like crazy making arrangements—bureaucratic stuff, permits, etc. It's good to feel at home here now as compared to four weeks ago. Amazing what a little experience can do for you.

Later: Mother arrived. Early—she had quite a harrowing Delhi experience, but came through it terrifically. Ah, the Norwegian Lee women.

Surprise! Daddy bought an eight-millimeter movie camera and sent it over with Mother. So if I can learn how to operate it, I'll have a movie of us. (Ain't modern technology sum'thin?)

Mother is sleeping now, and for the first time in days, I feel quiet and able to write in peace. So much to record. The man who almost died from heroin really affected me. Anger at the prevalence of hard drugs and dope and a tinge of fear at how little one really knows about the people in one's everyday life. Joe thinks Dan probably did it deliberately as a suicide attempt. That night for the first time, I was scared about being here alone and was glad that as things turned out, one of the guys stayed over an extra day so I shared a room with him last night. The point was that although I've lived alone in Austin for years, I was sincerely concerned about spending one night alone here. That's how Dan's trip affected me. I wanted to go home, but in truth, I didn't want to go home and sleep alone.

Yesterday afternoon, Jared and I went to get a massage. A first for me! Strange experience—there I was lying nude on a pad in this slightly seedy place [everything in Kathmandu looks like that] with an old woman who knew what she was doing, and a young girl who didn't, as the first touchings from another human being I'd had in a month. I really crave some physical affection, not particularly sex, although I miss it now that life doesn't revolve around staying warm. I want to feel close to another person, to have arms around me and sleep. Truth: I wanted to sleep, just that, no more, with any of the guys still here, but didn't because I figured it would be setting up a difficult situation. I'm not ready to sleep with anyone right now.

December 17, 1978 (Tiger Tops)

Diane S. was delightful. We ate dinner last night and discussed politics, women's issues, while listening to Willie Nelson's "Stardust" album. It was the first time in weeks I'd really talked with anyone about semi-intellectual topics. Also got news, e.g.,

Carter's China move. It was interesting to hear her news about D. C. and State Department and Public Information Agency politics.

Today has been rather amazing. We flew in a non-pressurized plane (seated about eighteen), then rode the elephants two hours to Tiger Tops. Crackling through jungle foliage that was taller than we are, perched (rather precariously) atop these beasts, is sort of like sailing through large waves—only here it's tall grasses. Right now we're sitting before a fire in the lodge area, having a beer and waiting for a slide show on the National Chitwan Forest. It's incredibly luxurious (should be at $90/night) compared to my first four weeks. Mother loves it—so do I! Hot water is terrific! Saw myself in a full mirror for the first time since Austin. One forgets one's body image. I'm thinner from being ill the last week of the trek, but am sure it won't last (lack of willpower).

Late in the evening, we sat in the dining room over coffee. The guides appeared and led us on a mad dash to view a tiger at night eating his kill. We piled into a Landrover for a mile, then walked in darkness down a trail for a quarter of a mile, then went barefoot the last one-eighth to the blind.

December 18, 1978 (Lying on our own private beach—Tiger Tops)

No one else is here. Quiet. Unable to write much again. Just being. Thoughts of the beauty I've experienced. Occasional home thoughts.

Elephants' tails have a brush-like thing on the end. The elephant walked like Nana—knees bent outward. Tall grasses—can't capture scale—one would hate to get lost or fall off the elephant.

I've been chatting tonight with the only other guest at the tented camp—the Assistant Game Warden for Nepal. Conservation efforts here are recent, and with a country so diverse—Everest to jungle—little coordination is maintained. Chitwan National Park, where Tiger Tops is located, is the oldest of four Nepali parks. Primary game are the tigers (only two thousand in the world, two hundred in Nepal, forty in Tiger Tops); the one-horned rhinoceros (huge mothers! we saw five this morning; probably the only time in my life I'll chase rhinoceros by elephant-back); a fish-eating crocodile;

and three hundred species of birds. Today, I finally began to get the hang of using binoculars. This morning, we rode elephants for two hours looking for wildlife. The Nepali elephant/trainer was delighted with my meager attempts at Nepalese and away we went, crashing through grasses two-elephants tall. This land would support GIANT COWS. It's quite awesome. If you fell off the elephant, the grasses would totally obscure any vantage point to see where you were. Paths are few; the elephants go crashing through the jungle creating their own. After a month of controlling my own transportation (by foot), it has been psychologically uncomfortable to be at the mercy of the elephant.

This afternoon we came up to another portion of the park via landrover, boat and thirty-minute walk. We're a bit remote. But the camp itself is superb. Tents with beds, hot water bottles put in them each evening. For my mother's first night *ever* in a tent, it's a civilized introduction. After setting up, we walked through jungle areas looking for some rare crocodiles, fish eating type, but didn't spot them. Try again tomorrow. This is the first time I've ever used the binoculars to bird watch—and I love it.

Mother and I are talking a lot. She had a difficult experience in Kathmandu when kids in the next room had a drug party and began hallucinating, making weird noises, throwing up, etc. She was worried that I was doing that, too. After discussing it, I explained that although I certainly drank and had smoked dope occasionally at college, there were no major vices, other than my sexual morality, for her to worry about. Guess she's grateful I'm not OD'ing on heroin. We talked. She tried to explain how draining it is to be a parent sometimes, when you love and worry about your kids.

Late this afternoon, the mist finally faded and I glimpsed the Himalayas in the distance. I had missed the mountains. It's nice to be generally warm, the jungle is interesting and I'm enjoying it, but my soul yearns for the mountains. Something has happened between me and the mountains. Beginning in New Mexico. Hard to believe I spent the first thirty years of my life without them. Now I feel tenuous, like a beginning of a love affair, since I know so little, have so much to learn about and from them. I still fear the cold.

The personnel here are well-educated and knowledgeable. Our guide yesterday was a young woman archeologist who worked eight years with Dr. Leakey, then spent one year working with Jane Goodall and some hyenas in Kenya. Apparently, we were extremely lucky to see a tiger last night. They are elusive creatures. Tiger Tops keeps extensive data on sightings, etc. By measuring the cat tracks, they can tell which tiger is in the vicinity, what the breeding patterns are, etc.

December 19, 1978 (Thaka)

I had trouble reading yesterday's entry, so must try to be more legible. This morning, we took a two-hour walk (saw barking deer, spotted deer, monkeys, egrets) and a boat ride deep into the jungle to visit a Thaku village. Until about the last twenty years, the only inhabitants of this area were a few villagers who had developed an immunity to the malaria strain native to the region. Government inoculation and DDT programs have virtually eradicated the disease now, but few people choose to live here anyway. The villagers were cleaner and looked much more prosperous than any I'd seen in the north. Two-story houses line one side of the path, and stores of rice seem plentiful.

The two-hour walk was an excellent introduction for Mother; she did very well. It's fun to watch her learn about what to take with her, how to carry things, etc. We had to wade a small stream and, standing on one leg to put shoes and socks back on, she was determined not to have help.

Three women were fascinated by Mother's camera and requested a picture. Quite a production—they all dolled themselves out in their finest apparel and stood at rigid attention. People are amazed at the Polaroid film process. New folks arrived at the camp to share "our" wilderness. The director (and his wife) of the American School at Dacca. He had camera equipment of his own and showed me how to work Daddy's. Took some shots of M and me.

The food is great here—lots of curries—and I'm still eating as if I were trekking eight hours a day. Hmm. The weight will catch me if I'm not careful. Mother has also developed a taste for beer so we drink before dinner. More calories. GROAN! I was really looking lean immediately after the big trek, but dining in Kathmandu has replenished the old carbohydrates. Sigh. The never-ending battle.

December 20, 1978 (While waiting for the plane to fly from Tiger Tops to Kathmandu)

The American School/Dacca guy taught photography at one point, so we now have some "professional" footage of Mother and me atop an elephant!

One kind of duck here mates for life—if one is killed, the other pines away and dies. They fly in pairs—in the same direction. Will I ever find a soulmate?

December 21, 1978 (Kathmandu—misty morning, damp and cold)

Having breakfast coffee with Mother—outside a small Buddhist shrine bedecked with marigolds—two puppies of undetermined origin frolic with their mother.

December 22, 1978 (On top of a hill at 5,800' overlooking Kathmandu Valley with a view of the Himalayas just around the mountainside. Warm sun, cool wind, evening fast approaching)

This is my mother's and my first trekking (as opposed to just walking) day together. Unfortunately, we drove by taxi out of town and immediately began a three-hour hike straight up. Actually, it's probably about one hour, forty-five minutes at a normal pace, but Mother nearly died. Not literally, but it was a bit much. Went from 4,500 feet to 5,800 feet in about two miles. Not difficult in the least, but no respite from constantly going up. I'm ecstatic to be back on the trail and away from the city. It doesn't bother me at all to go slowly and wait for Mother. I take pictures and drink in the countryside. We walked from 10:30 to 1:30, then camped for the day. I put out an ensolite pad and sleeping bag for a pillow and Mother rested and appears revived. I'm really proud of her. Thank God she jogged before she came. Otherwise, she'd never have made it. She is simultaneously enormously proud of herself and filled with apprehension about the morrow. We go to 8,000' in about one and a half miles. She'll do fine, although it may take a while. Our Sherpa Lockpa has sized up the situation and smiles with me a lot. He took Mother's daypack for her (it couldn't weigh more than three-four pounds). We've been sitting in the sun providing entertainment for the local village children as she sketches.

Yesterday, in Kathmandu, we went to the Tibetan Refugee Center and bought Tibetan rugs to be shipped back to the States. I bought two for the little house, one in blues, the other in natural wool colors, beige-type. Mother bought one for herself.

The trip has made me question lifestyles, lawyering. Time in the mountains is so real, so full and so peaceful. Strange to think of folks at home madly buying Christmas presents.

December 23, 1978 (Second day trekking with Mother)

Chisapani is beautiful. One-hundred-eighty-degree view of the Himalayas. Mother did *much* better and was helped immensely by the fact that we only trekked two hours. We are camped on a hillside with the third best view I've seen of the mountains. Ringed by snow peaks. This afternoon we've lain around. I shared helpful hints on how to pee downhill, then hiked some nearby hills while Mother sketched. The scabs on my hand blisters are healing. What a relief. In the cold weather, they've hurt a bit. Today, for a while, I was really ready to come home. My thoughts are moving away from here and slowly returning to the other world, work, etc. Gradual reentry. But, I've enjoyed it. I've enjoyed fiddling with camera equipment, lying in the sun, letting thoughts drift like the clouds.

Trekking with Mom is a lazy, slow-paced endeavor, so I'll try to write down some images to remember about Mom and me in the Himalayas. Maybe I can use them some day in "Travels with Mom":

It was the slowest mile that had ever been run in Dallas. But she did run it. And that was all that was required to be able to go with me to the Himalayas. One year before I had given my mother a pair of running shoes. (Actually, I had given her a pair of athletic socks into which had been stuffed a check with the admonition written on a Christmas card that the money was for the purchase of such a pair.)

"IF I go to the Himalayas, and IF no one else can come with me, and IF you can run a mile, then you can join me there." On our last journey, she had huffed and puffed up a Guatemalan volcano. I had no intention of the same thing happening halfway around the world. Besides, she was fifty-seven and a regular mother; I didn't want to be responsible for her too much.

Now I raced through the streets of Kathmandu to meet her plane from New Delhi. I shuddered to imagine her escapades in negotiating an overnight stop in New Delhi, my mom who had hardly been out of the states to Mexico. The taxi driver was interminably slow. When we arrived, I frantically raced around the empty terminal looking for a short redheaded grandmother. There she was. Perched atop her luggage in a long deserted waiting room calmly reading *The Thorn Birds*. (She believed in thick books for traveling.) I was four hours late. I guess mothers have to have a lot of faith.

"What happened?"

"They put the wrong time on my ticket and I couldn't find you to let you know, so I've just waited. I was getting ready to call the Embassy if you didn't come soon."

Pretty good thinking for a kindergarten teacher. Actually, she was one of the best special ed teachers in Dallas. Worked wonders with kids no one else could touch. But years of dinner table conversations where her work was considered "baby work" had made me less aware of her prominence.

We explored Kathmandu, that city of the mystical name from the Guest House, a $2.50-a-night establishment that she adapted to quite fine. Yogurt, vegetables, Buddhist shrines, child labor, feces in the street, mountains in the background—she viewed them all and drank in the mixture of this crossroads city. At night, we wandered the old part of town on cobbled streets with hash sold at every corner and shy, sly faces peeking from doorways covered with cloth hung to let the breeze in. We went shopping. For pockets.

"There aren't any pockets on your blue jeans."

"You're right. What do I do? Why do I need them?"

"For your knife, and money and string and things you want to carry."

For $1.25, an old man down the street added deep pockets to the designer jeans. In purple over the denim color. Mother sauntered down the main drag, hands in pockets.

Nepal has only one road. It goes from Kathmandu to Pokara. All other traffic, both people and goods, move along trails that wind through villages and fields, along streams and beside rivers, and eventually through the mountains to Tibet. Most trails end up in Kathmandu where the mountain people come to sell their wares and purchase what little they can for the winter. To see the country, one needs to walk, or trek, these trails. Some are wide, like groomed English country lanes, while some are boulders that barely are marked through deep river valleys. Some parts are steps carved into sheer cliffs and some are pleasant meandering paths with flowers growing wild alongside.

"I've arranged for us to take a short trek. About four days' walk from Kathmandu. We'll sleep in tents and have a Sherpa guide, Lockpa, and two porters."

"Fine, but you know I've never camped. For that matter, I've never slept in a sleeping bag."

And so began the ritual of "The Evening's Entertainment." Mother entering her sleeping bag. First she struggled out of the famous pocketed jeans, and into a too large pair of my dad's long underwear. A sweater and woolen cap completed her nighttime ensemble. Thus attired, she attempted to stuff all the clothes with her body beneath them into the bag. We laughed till the Sherpa came to ask if we were okay.

Later: 7:00 p.m.—Chisapani—a cold, damp night. After huddling by our small fire, we've climbed into sleeping bags in the tent. This is written by flashlight.

I've had enough of this kind of independence. It's been a growing, learning and good experience. But I want to go and grow *with* someone. As I walk each day, I've thought how people really are meant—in a basic sense—to be paired. Will I ever experience that?

December 24, 1978 (Christmas Eve—5:00 p.m.—in a wet fir forest somewhere south of Shepouri)

What a Christmas Eve day! Frost covered the ground when we awoke. After breakfast, Mother and I went on ahead and proceeded to get lost with the woman porter in the woods. We laughed—what a bunch of ninnies. Next, we went for about three hours to what was to be our camping place, arriving about 12:45. Mother was doing terrific considering everything. The views were fantastic. We were walking along a ridge from which you can see an entire range of the mountains. But it contained difficult and confusing trails. After arriving at Shepouri—about 9,000 feet, with a Buddhist prayer place and flags (no settlement, however)—we changed and prepared to laze the rest of the day. Spectacular views. I shot some movie film even though it was too bright. After about an hour, Lockpa returned saying there was no water available, so we repacked and headed down. Mother's first experience with downhill trekking. Lockpa went ahead looking for water and camping spots. We followed with the three porters—and promptly got lost a second time. I can't believe it! Trekked twenty days and never got lost—here even the porters were baffled. At one point Mother was tired and so was I, so the five of us just plunked down and started laughing. Mother had one hell of a daughter who'd lead her thirsty and lost on Christmas Eve to a damp Himalayan forest. But it was rather funny. Lockpa eventually found us, a bedraggled brood, and off we went for another hour. So here we sit, opening some mixed nuts Mother brought from the States and having our tea. As Mother said, she has some adventures to tell. I'm really tired. She must be exhausted. Her only comment was, "If you tell people back in Kathmandu that we went on a mini or baby trek, I may shoot you!" Aha, soup's arrived!

December 25, 1978

Christmas Day! Soup last night turned into a chicken dinner, the chicken being the same one we watched suffocate in Lockpa's pack during the day. Then Mother and I drank a flask of rum, the Sherpas began to dance and we had all-in-all a fun Christmas Eve. Today was four hours downhill. Rough stuff for Mother. At one point, a Buddhist monk was leading the way down this huge

mountain. I chuckled at our parade. Lockpa had to practically hand
Mother down the mountain. We got back here about 2:00 p.m.
Mother gave me red socks for Christmas.

December 27, 1978 (Kathmandu—Anapurna Hotel—Sunny!)
    Mother and I are having an expensive breakfast at a fancy hotel
celebrating our feeling better. I contracted a bad sinus infection while
trekking. Fever, etc. I wanted to come home early. Then I felt so bad
I didn't care. Moved us over to a better hotel room with bath, etc.,
so we'd be warm. Popped some antibiotics and am substantially
better. Hooray! We've had fun anyway. Mother has not been hungry, slightly sick. So has lost five-six pounds and keeps exclaiming
about her thin state. Last night the electricity went out and we lay
in bed two-three hours talking family, friends, etc. As I went to sleep,
I wondered if I'd have a kid who'd do things like this with me when
I am fifty-six. But as Mother says, it takes more than a year—more
like thirty—to build that relationship.
    Yesterday, we went wild shopping. I bought a Thanka painting
I really like, and a bunch of presents. Mother had had her eye on a
yak wool jacket, so on the spur of the moment after dinner, we each
had one made. For $20, figured it was fun. The first time she'd ever
had a tailor take her measurements and have something custom-
made. (For that matter, other than bridesmaid dresses, my first time,
too.)At times like that, it's nice not to have been rich all one's life
because it is such fun to experience something for the first time.
    Lockpa had Mother and me over to his room the other night for
some thang-pa (a drink you can't buy—have to be invited to a Sherpa
house). Real honor. There we were seated on the floor in a dark
candlelit room around a box covered with rags. The thang-pa is
millet pellets fermented and put in a large (two-cup size) container.
Hot water is poured into the millet and then you drink the water/
millet through a long plastic straw, leaving the millet in the glass.
    We splurged and celebrated our last night in Kathmandu by
going to the most expensive, neatest restaurant in town. Sat around
a huge fire and drank Bloody Marys. I wonder what it will be like
going home.

We leave tomorrow for Delhi, arrive at night, then plan to go to Agra and try to leave for London the 31st. We're having trouble getting reservations out of Delhi to London, but will try again in Delhi. Mother has never seen London and wants to spend a few days there. Only costs $50 more for a stopover charge. If we can find a place to stay—London on New Year's Eve could be tough. And *if* we can get tickets to some ballets/plays, I'll be happy. If all fails, we can always take a train up to Hothorpe (where I worked with Rod) and I'm sure we could stay somewhere in the Hall.

It's almost sad leaving Nepal. Mixed feelings, ready to go home but not ready to leave. A sense of unfinished business/living. Maybe because I didn't see Everest. And I want to see China/Tibet.

December 29, 1978 (Ashton Hotel-Delhi)

Travel comes in three stages or types of experience for me: the physical beauty (mountains, rivers, sunsets); the people I meet, grow, learn and love with (Dawa, Joe, Chris, Jared); the cultural (museums, the Red Fort, Hindu Temple). Of these three, the trip has given me the first in a new perspective. People and art I've long responded to, but to commune alone with natural beauty has been a slowly growing process over the past several years.

Yet I learned also that no matter how splendid the setting, ordinary living demands may force one to look solely at one's feet on the ground, thereby missing the majesty above. It's an art to appreciate beauty when living conditions are harsh. We Americans are literally so insulated from weather, we barely feel the seasons.

Strange dreams since reaching India. Vivid colors. Also have been anxious for the first time about luggage, travel details, etc. I realize now how pleasant it was to have OB provide all that, so I was free to just be me.

December 31, 1978 (Leaving Delhi—Hooray!)

Horrible day at Agra—nightmare taxi ride back after mini bus, hotel too expensive, etc. I felt terrifyingly alone. But on a dirty Indian road, I realized that having a partner and stability are worth the trade-off. That although people care about me in my life, there was no one *now* like Rod who used to *find* me if I were lost and be there for me. I wonder if I have experienced my last round of magic— if I have become resigned to life without it.

We are "puddle jumping"—from Delhi to Moscow, Paris, then London. It's about forty degrees below zero and a blizzard in Moscow, so 100 miles out we are diverting to Amsterdam. Comfort and security are so relative. Here on board Air India, I'm perfectly content, even though it's a twelve-hour trip. Just to be *out* of India and heading homeward.

What will I do for work upon returning? Lawyer for a while, earn money, enjoy the routine aspect of my life. I am reminded of my initial feeling about law school—having worked as a secretary in a plumbing supply office, school was delightful—even *law*. Now, having "adventured" for a while, ordinary life seems just fine.

The writing may return. Very little on this trip. Next time I must make myself take short daily notes—just to later use as reminders for writing.

Last night in the fog driving from Agra, I reminisced about the incredible moments of sensuality I've experienced in my life. Indelible in my consciousness is kissing D, forbidden territory for the first time. Blue eyes rich in his dark face. Alfredo touching my hair by firelight at Aquas Horinas. Both moments of innocence in a passionate/sexual sense, but with a pervasive and sweet/vibrant sensuality that memories can evoke at will. Sleeping with G was similar. Born of a deeper need than sex—a human need for touch, for connection. Strangely, none of those three times has been with people who—at the time at least—I really loved. There have been intensely passionate moments with others, but those are different, not characterized by this poignant sensuality I now recall.

In Agra, I stood before the Taj Mahal almost in tears, feeling totally dejected and crushed by the responsibility of traveling. I wanted help, decisions made by someone else.

New Year's Eve (Amsterdam Airport)
There's something about airports that gets to my feet. After twelve hours of travel from Delhi, the foot is cold and lonesome.

We've been here six hours—hell of a way to celebrate New Year's Eve! But I'm at last moving in the right direction. Home to Texas.

January 3, 1979 (On plane from DFW to Austin)
    Finally—going home! Jotted thoughts for future entries:
1. Westminister Abbey in the snow—NY Day at noon, everyone stopped and prayed for world peace, political leaders.
2. Parliament shining over the Thames at night in the snow.
3. Macbeth—Albert Finney—fantastic. Thoughts about political ambition. What it does to one.
4. Too tired to know what's happening. Matt was fired by the new Attorney General, Mark White. Me, too? Need to think about jobs, etc. Later.

January 7, 1979 (Austin, Texas)
    Quiet Sunday morning in my little white house. It feels a palace to me! Jumbled thoughts about work, being home. Where to begin?

January 8, 1979
    First day to go back to work. Early morning thoughts, dressing carefully like long ago I packed for the first exciting day of each elementary school year.

January 9, 1979
    Job decisions, work. I'm tired, need exercise, need a little peace. Meeting with Hartley, strange. Okayed the Kirby case, said litigate steel. The Trentlemen job offer sparked rethinking.

January 10, 1979
    Early morning Texas sun rises exactly at 34th Street and Speedway and creates a golden tunnel of glistening along a rain-soaked street. Texas skies are home for my soul. Watching the display of clouds over the Capitol, I smiled at nature's homecoming program.

January 11, 1979
    If I'm going to try to write this spring, I'm going to have to

become more disciplined.

January 16, 1979 (Inauguration Day)
   Quick Thoughts:
1. Bitter pill.
2. Republicans flocked to the capitol grounds in mink and ultrasuede. There were no "people" at the inauguration.
3. Sunshine? Yes, but my sentiments are more accurately reflected in the "glamour and clamor poem," i.e., "there's not one inauguration worth a good, slow two-inch rain."
4. It's not that I disagree with the essence of Clements' speech, but his emphasis in government and the methods he'll use to accomplish getting government "back to the people" bother me.
5. It made my stomach hurt to listen. Perhaps only then did the JLH loss hit.
6. Rethink what government *can* and *should* do.
7. Have I stayed too long in the bureaucracy?
   Work—I feel good about being more efficient and decisive, but uncertain about my ability. I miss having Matt to talk to about cases and decisions. Katie said she felt "ethical" problems representing our defendants in the vending case and was not getting enough experience and not enough guidance from me. Hard conversation for both of us. I tried to reassure her and said I'd help more and would, of course, stay lead counsel, all the while knowing I wasn't much better experienced than she.

January 17, 1979
   Harsh words about Carter from Jan and Diana. "He doesn't really believe in the ERA. We've not gotten anything from him." And this from women who were pissed at Abzug, too. 1980 will be tough. If Carter loses, I sense the political climate shifting so rapidly, ever rightward.
   Matt called about jobs, work, etc. People have quizzed him about why he stayed so long at the AG's office. I need to leave the office, but really don't know what I want to do. If I stay lawyering, it's

imperative I develop better work habits. (Although since I've been back, they could hardly be any better!) It's difficult to get all this career stuff together. My first priority should probably be to write some short stories this spring just to see if I enjoy writing. I pull back from the contentiousness of law and politics, since the trip. Not sure that I want to spend life's limited time doing that.

January 18, 1979

On plane back from El Paso with Katie: A good day. Productive work. Interesting revelations about political favors and politicians' involvement, etc.

January 22, 1979

On plane from Reno-Austin. Sometimes I think Clements may be doing a better job than JLH would have done, on little things. Heretical thought.

January 29, 1979

I can't get the writing together. Maybe I should just hold off a while. I've wasted thirty years. Another month is okay. Or is that laziness and fear of failure?

January 30, 1979

Started to wake up early and write. Good!

Good talk with Diane. She says the last year is the hardest she's had. New baby and no time to herself. Men don't understand. The father should take an entire week of child care to see what it's like.

January 31, 1979

Jimmy Carter jogs. And has learned to quit work at 4:30. The arts will miss Rockefeller. Zest for life is the common denominator of the people I've admired, from Rocky to Dawa.

Long talk on the phone with the new Attorney General, Mark White. He was personable. I was nervous, but orchestrated a neat coup: MW speaking before the Kennedy committee and our division. Also got the okay on the Gulf-Phillips and Vending machine case. A long half hour. Then worked until 9:00 getting a packet together for him. Tired.

February 5, 1979 (Sunday morning)
The slide show of the Himalayan Outward Bound trek was fun, but too long. I had a good talk with Joe, the doctor on the Nepal trip. Joe: "I came up because I think you are a beautiful person." It matters to me that he thinks so. Joe was the nicest I'd seen him, not drinking, seemed gentler. We're easy together. There is no pressure on the relationship and neither of us wants anything more from the other. It seems I'm getting stronger and stronger. Good, I'll need it.

Tim asked me to take pictures at his wedding. I said I would. Sheila was outraged that he'd ask me. We really think differently.

February 7, 1979
The pace is almost overwhelming. Work is tough, although I've become more efficient, and a better leader. Yesterday, Katie told me the staff was afraid to talk with me because I was so busy. Don't want to become unapproachable. Also must watch ego-tripping and showing off. Katie was more formal with the witnesses. I played "good old boy." I let her take too many of the notes, etc. Also, must stop talking to her quite the same as David B. One problem with pushing state employees past 5:00 is that they didn't sign on for those kind of job hours and aren't paid to do it.

February 9, 1979 (At the El Paso Hilton)
Sheila called me today. Crying in her office, she couldn't get everything done. I understand her fears and frustrations. After work I traced her to the Veranda to have a quick drink although it was really hectic to get ready to come. Something is wrong with the pace if there's no time to have a drink with a friend who's crying.

It seems unfair that mere timing dictates that M. White will get a chance to walk into the Governor's office. Query: whether one should continue operating in the world as if fairness occurred and was a factor. Hinges on one's religious beliefs and sense of good and evil in the world.

At the Veranda tonight, Sheila and her friends discussed Racehorse Haynes' brilliant bar lunch talk. They both admire him, yet believe he cuts it too close to the edge ethically. I said nothing but thought of the discussion I'd just had in my office about David's witness and how he couldn't threaten to sue him if he didn't testify truthfully at a Section 15.14 sworn statement. Am I so naive?

Both Joe's are possible people in my life and probably available now that I'm not looking. Maybe if I look less hard for a permanent connection, it will happen.

Sheila feels unconnected and alone. I worry about her fling with the "lustee." In so many ways I'm tougher than she.

February 16, 1979

Middle of the night. Feeling sick. Hard night the 13th. Called Jackie at 3:00 a.m. crying. Tonight, work anxieties. Need to get on a more regular schedule. Talked to Joe: "YOU work too hard." Never sure if I really do. Not as hard as Sheila. Scared and tired. Just want to feel better physically and get the steel brief off. Don't like this part of lawyering, i.e., the writing.

February 18, 1979

At work I'm becoming autocratic. In slight ways I try to assert my authority, my "boss-ness." In so doing, I often repress rather than encourage people. This must stop. I want to be the kind of leader who cultivates an atmosphere conducive to each person's performing his best and most creatively. How to do this?
1. Listen better and *all the way through* to staff ideas.
2. Act calmer (be free to be calm).
3. Think a moment before putting someone's ideas down; maybe there's a way to say no firmly but with grace.
4. Be as honest as possible with praise *and* criticism.
"Personal action can either open out possibilities of enriched experience or it can shut off possibilities. Personal action is either

predominately validating, confirming, encouraging, supportive, en-
hancing, or it is invalidating, disconfirming, discouraging,
undermining and constricting. It can be creative or destructive."—
from *Politics of Experience* p. 29

February 19, 1979
    El Rancho night. Hard day in Houston: the Light Taylor Townsend
case. The opposing counsel threw a fit, threatened to stomp out of the
deposition twice; Katie's eyes grew big. (Mine did too, inside. But I'm
supposed to know better.)

February 25, 1979 (8:00 a.m. Sunday morning)
    I should be working on the Clements letter, but have writer's
block. Work is getting out of hand—too much—but I'm learning
better how to handle it and enjoy being in charge.
    On commitment: The lobbyists once more run the Lege, not-
withstanding the old Reform movement's clean up-job. Seems that
maybe keeping the system operating honestly and effectively takes
the same kind of renewable commitment that a relationship does.
Once is not enough. Periodically we must review the situation and
again try to keep it moving and growing in the desired direction.
    Why, oh why does it take so long to understand the essential
concept of life's not being static? One key must be to learn joy in the
growth and change, rather than fearfulness of change. I think that
arriving at X is only a stopping off point for X+1, X+2, etc. But to
fully live wondrously in that realization takes self-confidence that
life's dealings will be at least fifty percent good and that what isn't
good is at least manageable. I'm learning. Things to tell Attorney
General White if I get a second chance.
1. Office is tired of politics, needs lawyering.
2. Leadership is vision of goal. No point to power without purpose
to use it. What are his (my) purposes? We have the same problems
with being understaffed, and so become crisis oriented rather than
having a plan for solving problems.

February 28, 1979

11:30 p.m. Long days. Survived the Incredible Monday. General White argued the steel hearing okay, then I took a witness's deposition from 2:00-7:15. He was a *huge* black man (6' 4" maybe) who arrived for his deposition wearing BLOOD-SPATTERED SPATS! The old-fashioned white things that fit over shoes. His language was unintelligible. And people think antitrust law is dull. But he wasn't very helpful as a witness. The next day's conference with Federal Judge Bue was good. Trial set for March 20. Here we go.

March 4, 1979

From Beth's poster: "A ship in the harbor is safe, but that's not what ships were built for."

March 5, 1979

Settled Phillips case for a reasonable amount. Then tried to get Margaret a raise. From Jim Nelson's reaction, I think it's the first time anyone on the seventh floor realized we were doing six people's work with four lawyers.

When I took the car to be washed, the front seats weren't vacuumed properly. So I drove back around, told the attendant and asked if they could re-vacuum. A surly looking black guy with big gaps between his teeth was eating potato chips and a sandwich for lunch. He grunted at me as I explained the problem and pushed half-eaten potato chips through his teeth as he ate with an open mouth. I was intimidated, almost scared (would have been had it been dark). As I stood there feeling scared, awkward, etc., he asked which lane I came through: L: "The right one. Look. I don't want to get anyone in trouble, I just want the car vacuumed."

He got another guy and began to vigorously spray the inside carpets with soap solution. I was worried they were angry and were going to get everything too wet. Noticed that the one guy sat directly on some legal papers on the seat, without bothering to move them. When they finished, the gap-toothed man turned to me and said, "We just did your car up real good. Not many white girls would have *not* snitched. Next time you look for my lane at the car wash."

And suddenly I understood the surliness and the great gaps people have between them that can be bridged with a little risk and courtesy. How many white women had put him down? And how many black men had frightened me at dusk with mean glances? Color and sex, what a combination to overcome. Yet for a brief moment, we did. Amazing.

Katie has become open, smilingfaced, quite gorgeous in her letting-go. I wonder if she'll remember me when years from now she's highly successful on a professional level. Being with her is analogous to being with Beth on a personal level. Needing a mentor myself, I've nonetheless become sort of one to a few others. Strange world.

March 10, 1979

Wanted to see "Days of Heaven." Wrestled with wanting to wait and see/share it with a date. Finally realized I was kidding myself about any real dates on the horizon. Couldn't find anyone to go with me, but on a whim, stopped at Dr. Bullard's, my eighty-year-old landlord, and asked him. He hesitated, then agreed, said he hadn't seen a movie in ten years. Afterwards we went to his house for grapefruit and coffee. When I left he said he'd like to go again sometime. I really like him. He's interesting. His world is volcanos. He's a retired geology professor who was consulted when Mount St. Helens erupted, and flew in a helicopter over the destruction. When he was young, he led mapping expeditions to then uncharted Alaska wilderness. The huge ships dropped anchor, then opened the decks and men on horses swam ashore with compasses and tents. This is *my* country—America.

March 11, 1979

On TV, Mr. Baldwin, the ninety-five-year-old founder of the ACLU, quoted R. L. Stevenson: "To travel hopefully is better than to arrive." I want to be like that.

March 28, 1979

Last night after work I drank beer with Susan. At one point she said she knew I'd gotten the Phillips case from Cliff because I'd dated him. It was like a smack in the face. Recoiling, I tried to figure out how much of that was true. More than I care to admit, I suppose.

March 29, 1979 (At Planned Parenthood Clinic)

Nervous first time pelvic-exam women (girls?) fill the waiting room. It's good to do this, although I need to learn patience to understand waiting. I'm going on the Planned Parenthood Board so want to see how it feels to get services here. No one knows who I am, but the staff was kind and full of information.

Work goals are hazy these days. Don't really want to lawyer much, but want the prestige and ability to fly around and be flexible at hours. Watching Planned Parenthood operate, I was reminded of my year as a secretary, ugh! Don't want that. Slowly am formulating a month or six on Mexico/Colorado trip. Maybe.

April 4, 1979

Strange conversation with Daddy about drinking. He denied he was addicted. I was astounded.

Later: Women are wonderful. Went to the women's luncheon and had marvelous time, then talked with Diane about love and life.

"How we perform as individuals will determine how we perform as a nation." Lately, I don't feel very productive. But the fault lies in myself, not in the system, Mark White, etc.

April 6, 1979

Before work: Decided yesterday at lunch to take the summer off from work (which has been non-productive) and try seriously to write. Actually, decided to see if I still feel that way by May 1. Considered asking Mary Beth if she needed a helper. Of course, after thinking about leaving, everything at work in the afternoon seemed so sweet. Each time I was able to make a decision or give advice, I thought how much I'd miss it.

All areas of my life are unsettled and uneasy. And the knowledge that just fixing one won't fix all makes the inertia worse. Think I'm having a "meaning" crisis. In Nepal I finally understood the importance of one person. Now I can't match up with one.

April 12, 1979

Tough Planned Parenthood meeting. Lots of work.

Parents in town. Daddy drives me crazy. He and Mother don't talk to each other. I don't want a relationship like that. After my outlining all the possibilities for lawyering, writing, etc., Daddy asked, "What would you do if you could do anything you wanted?" "Get married and have a baby." We were all a little stunned.

April 14, 1979

Made an appointment with Paul. Hope he can help me.

Lee S. is running for city council in Dallas. He's in town for the weekend. When he talked of his campaign and walking the precincts, I fantasized momentarily about walking them with him and just calculated vote-wise how much more territory he could cover. This morning, upon reflection, I realized how much of a typical traditional woman I was. Never really thinking I could do it, as the candidate, but only in a secondary role. When will I ever learn?

My body is too big. Clothes don't fit and I feel lumbering and awkward. Important to stop the eating.

April 15, 1979

Unless I take control, I'll be the ultimate dilettante.

April 17, 1979

At Ricco's alone, eating dinner: I wonder how many people in the world really choose each other. Or is it just the thing to do at a particular time? Grown-ups get married, have children. Otherwise— monstrous thought—they'll be alone in a restaurant.

April 18, 1979

"To write, first find pen and paper." So I pulled off the cover to the typewriter, inserted a sheet, and pounded a few words. Maybe I don't have to do a traditional series of stories. But so far I think of them as an overall outline of a larger endeavor. Now I must break each one into smaller components and tackle it in manageable sections. Initial step is to decide which one to write first. This sounds an awful lot like writing a brief. It's the first sentence that's so hard. What I need is a book of first lines.

Whenever I do something on my projects, I feel better about myself. It's like being thinner. I ought to have learned that by now.

April 22, 1979

Early Sunday morning. These cool end-of-spring rainwashed mornings are calming. Deep purple (from the mulberries harvested earlier) splotches my fingers. Squatting on the little plot of earth in front of the cottage, I hurried to pluck the wind-fallen fruit before the birds and ants got there first.

Cool winds make my one hundred percent cotton nightgown feel warm and sweet against my skin. I remember vividly awaking in the Concordia house one summer morning when Rod had gone for a month. Sunlight streamed into the breakfast area and the blistering sun was only a pale glowing precursor of the day's ultimate discomfort. Orange curtains intensified the warm glow in the room. Satisfied, I looked round and realized I was alone and could do whatever I wished for the next few hours' time. The quiet was luxurious. Cat-like, my soul stretched in it.

Today the wind blows. The connected wind of the lower canyons and the Himalayas. Wind on my face *is* my face. Hey. When running maybe it will help if I think about being a part of the ground and air, moving with it, throughout it, not against it.

Met George Dale, my flight instructor. Glasses, old, v e r y s l o w talker.

L: "Mr. Dale, I want to learn to fly."

GD: (with just the merest suggestion of a twinkle) "W e l l,
l e t′s t a l k."
Excellent run last night. Big loop at Town Lake.

April 26, 1979

Diary writing has been lost in fast-paced living. Yesterday, my
first .8-hour flight time. It felt good. George is an excellent teacher,
but inflexible. I like him. The day was perfect, a bright pink sunset
to fly into.

Mark White on the failure to hire personnel for Medicaid Fraud:
"Haste makes waste."

Am trying to become more efficient at work. Control paranoia.
Don't want to write. Need to read flight manual.

May 1, 1979

Quick morning entry. Made it through the work crisis. Never
cried. And I'm pleased with myself. Recognized the anxiety symp-
toms and rode it through. Really don't like that zinging feeling
through my veins. Don't want to lose the insights though.
1. Make a job situation where I can control things. Eventually.
2. Figure out how to get out of rat-race pace, or how better to live
calmly in it.

May 9, 1979

Flew my first tentative landings.

May 12, 1979

Today was nice. A whole day without meetings. Did errands;
ran; ate hot dogs; rode the bicycle. I like the feeling of accomplishing household tasks. Went to Pecan Street with Dr. Bullard. We
walked through a street dance and I wondered how he felt. The old
and young are perhaps too solicitous and, out of being polite, don't
communicate. We ate together and I think he really enjoyed it. I
did.

May 15, 1979

Yesterday was heavy. Negotiated with steel defendants. Sometimes I can't believe I'm actually discussing *millions* of dollars. Attorney General White did quite well, although Hartley had the best line. In an after-discussion concerning the difficulty some men had with treating women as lawyers and as people, "You've got to know when to hold 'em."

Later, however, it got tough. The Master Key checks were sent to private as well as to public colleges and hospitals. I was in shock and it took me too long to recognize the problem. I wanted it to disappear rather than have to fix it. A real mess. Also I am scared by the management study, but again guess what I must do is just the best job I can and if that's not good enough, learn to do something else. All the work stuff is tough.

Flying, on the other hand, is fun, challenging and interesting. We did touch-and-go's the other day and at the end I'd finally gotten the hang of it a little. But during the lesson, I screwed up a takeoff. Ugh. Can't seem to separate out messing up on a skill and my self-worth, or some one else's perception of my self-worth. An insight: whether I screw up flying or skiing, or even lawyering sometimes, does not reflect on my personhood. When that happens, I need to just correct the error and go on, not mix it up with whether someone will still love me, etc.

May 16, 1979

"I am only one. But I am one. I cannot do everything. But I can do something. And what I can do, I should do; and what I should do, with God's help, I will do."

June 1, 1979

A crosswind prevented my soloing.

June 9, 1979

Alone, sunning for a moment. It's too hectic. This week I did

D. C., then flew back for the Governor's Energy meeting. Need to control my own life more.

June 16, 1979

Midnight, having just flown back from Snyder/Lubbock. The pace hastens. My speech was about a B+ tonight at the Agriculture meeting. Good mike voice, but need more inflection. The faces looked a little confused.

Good talk with Marge Toombs, then her son Patrick, on the way back. He discussed his trips to Russia with 4-H. An incredibly polite, clean-cut, straight kid. One I'd want on my side.

June 17, 1979

At the grocery store, I briefly glanced up from my shopping list to see a couple entering the store together. Suddenly and with a pang, I realized how long it had been since I'd had a partner to shop with. No longer do I plan a week's menu with someone. I'm lonely.

June 19, 1979

Today I have the blahs. I'm worn out from the steel case. All the second guessing. Pissed at Lynn. I don't see any break in the work cycle. I don't want to live like this. But what else can I do? Work causes my stomach to hurt. The job may well be too big for me to handle. Each day I come home feeling as if a truck rolled over me, very tired and disturbed.

June 22, 1979

Work is tough and less meaningful. Am thinking seriously of quitting and doing the writing trip. Where? Taos? Mexico? Red's cabin? Alaska?

June 23, 1979

I flew alone out to the practice area. It was fun, but scary. The airplane sounded different. When I came back George had gone to lunch. Just cut me loose. In the midst of the emotional turmoil, I

June 29, 1979

flew anyway.

At the laundromat last night, I sat next to a very intellectual looking type who was drinking a Pearl beer and reading a hardback book with big words. The giant egg salad submarine sandwich I was eating kept falling all over the Dell horoscope magazine I was reading. I watched him watch me and thought how looks deceive. Maybe he wasn't an intellectual any more than I was only a horoscope reader.

June 27, 1979

On the walk back from the stadium this morning, there was a blue bird perched in some violet tree flowers. For an instant, the colors and life-ness of it soared my flagging spirits. Walking reminded me of Nepal.

There are no rescuers. One major male/female difference is that men seem to approach life concerned with how they will take care of themselves and the people (wives, children, parents) they will ultimately be responsible for. Women, on the other hand, assume they'll be taken care of and hence become bewildered when, like me, they look around at thirty-one years and spot no one but themselves.

June 30, 1979

Finished *Coming into the Country.* Do some people look upon writing a book the way Cathy does raising children? Where and how do each of us leave a mark for better on this world? And how does one decide? I'm thirty and a half and have produced nothing of lasting value and am not on any apparent path to do so. What does that mean?

I've become a loner. My sister's kids were fun and enjoyable. But I'm too selfish to be a good mother. When I told Mother that, she said kids teach you to be less selfish. Somehow I think men don't think about all this in the same way. Even if we career women take only minimal time off from work, we still view parenting as a different experience. Biology may be more determinative than many of us care to admit.

July 3, 1979

An important tie was cut tonight. Sheila and I have cut loose, although I'm not sure she understands it. She is in the "in-love" have-fun stage with Clay. That's neat. But she doesn't want to hear "pissing and moaning." Although I generally agree, this is a time when I need her as a friend to talk with, but she is too busy.

July 4, 1979

Fourth of July again. This diary writing on the fourth is getting ritualistic. I'm happy today. How nice to write those words. Ran with Luke an easy two miles at the lake. Flying is getting exciting again. I go cross country with George Saturday. Am looking forward to it; makes me smile to think of it.

These anxiety downs are cyclical; I need to learn that and get on an even keel. But also for me they are beneficial. I work something out, just not quite sure what.

July 6, 1979

Could I really make it on my own in a cabin near Albuquerque? Give up the ego investment in lawyering, and just write?

Things to take on a mountain sojourn: books to read; Spanish grammar; typewriter; pens and paper; scissors; camera and film; *How Things Work* book; Instrument Ground School books; stamps; guitar.

July 7, 1979

Just went on my first cross country with George. Tiring but fun. It rained on us twice, so now I won't be afraid of a few raindrops. George never had children: "Considering the state of the world, I don't regret that decision."

July 10, 1979

Ran with Sheila. Her long slender legs made me envious.

Journal II

🌿 *Bob*

🌿 *Bob*

January 3, 1981

It's starting up again, the games between men and women, the attraction that distracts. He said he'd had a hard day. I wanted to be with him, find out what had happened, comfort(?) him. But when he asked me to join him, I said no. He tugs at me. A familiar feeling.

January 10, 1981

When I ran into Bob Armstrong with his children, I winced, glad to see him, but with the full recognition of problems of married men even though he's been separated from his wife for several months. Bob says he and his wife have definitely decided to get divorced, but that he is moving slowly. He has moved out, but wants the transition to be as gentle as possible for his three children. And given his high profile job, he doesn't want to flaunt his separated status in public. Mixed reaction. How can I even contemplate such a limited relationship after experiencing the pain of Tim?

January 15, 1981

Bob came by; laughing and smiling, we listened to Neil Diamond tapes. Did I detect a growing tenderness in my worldly-wise friend?

January 20, 1981

I'm not sure I want to continue seeing this man. We've been

acquaintances for years. (I vaguely remember sitting by him at a Friar's breakfast at the University.) Why now are we thrown together and something different begins? He wants to meet, talk. But is that all? Of course not. We both know it.

What makes the magic? I don't know Bob well enough to have any full-blown realistic feelings about him as a person. So I really must be falling in love with the feelings of being in love. There has to be a better balance.

Georgetown: We walked the Texas land; it feels right.

January 25, 1981

And what of our semi-secret status? I feel like I'm starting an affair with a married man, even though he's separated, living apart, and getting divorced. It's sort of schizophrenic. Some places we can go together; others are off-limits because of politics. I don't like *it*; but I'm in deep like with him.

February 2, 1981

Saturday and Sunday were fine days. Saturday at Bob's ranch in the rain. Not the slow two inches we need, but wet enough to take our shirts off and naked feel the wind. We laugh a lot. Slowly I'm returning to a "happy" state as normal.

That's a good lesson from Bob. We enjoy each other, do things and although talk of "heavy" matters at times, don't spend overmuch time at it. He jumps topics when we talk. Like me, he gets sidetracked in his own stories. The diversions and details, while interesting, make it difficult to have a conversation (as opposed to a monologue punctuated by appropriate responses). I recognize it because I've done it too. Poor Sheila! The hours you've spent with my meanderings!

February 4, 1981

Bob on the inclusion of the Lower Canyons as wild and scenic rivers: "When population grows, you have to make rules you didn't need before. Some special places need protection."

February 8, 1981

Bob came by, but on a short time schedule. I tried not to clutch at him, but I sensed his backing away, so I did too. I can't afford to be hurt by/with him. He's spending a lot of time with his children, and that's good. I want eventually to be comfortable in that part of his life.

February 9, 1981

Brown and white are his colors. Earth tones—cows, tousled hair against the pillows. We share and grow.

February 11, 1981

I'm learning to make love. Passion controlled with gentleness. Exploring with my mind as well as body. Bob said I was gorgeous for a moment. Being with him makes me smile. "Be comforted that you're loved." The words don't come easy for him either. I don't lose myself in him. Rather I gain new places. Damn, he's good for me! And I face his absence for a week unanxious even knowing he's to see (perchance to sleep) with an old girlfriend. The feeling is less one of non-jealousy, than one of security.

February 12, 1981

On feeling down at Bob's leaving town: What we choose to share and not to share is important. Although I become upset at our lack of time together, I'm focused on the wrong thing. Rather, I want to focus on the present time and if all is not said, *enough* is said. Similar to the Snow Leopard: to know he saw us is enough, even if we didn't see him.

February 20, 1981

Today was a gift. Time un-stolen together in the sun/wind-filled Texas hill country. For the first time in my mind, timelessness almost. Sitting together in the thin winter warmth, I felt no compulsion to use words. Being was enough. Usually with him I feel frustrated by lack of time to say it all. Today, for a moment, the moments said it all. Driving up, following his truck, I realized how much he gives me even without futures. Perhaps that limitation frees us both to give and receive totally within the parameters.

February 25, 1981

Another "awesome" evening at the ranch. Two pictures: Bob wandering among the cows, surrounded, as the bull let him pet his head. Later, worried about the donkey, he stopped the truck, walked toward the white animal in the open sunset field and reached his hand to touch her flank. Even from my vantage point in the truck, I saw a faint quiver, then *saw* the calm flow from his hands through him to her. Gently he stroked her, examining. In a rush, I felt those hands caressing my body, too.

Although I would have enjoyed going to sleep with him at my side, I felt no sense of loss at his leaving tonight. Bob and I meet in a transfer time. We'll spread out and apart sometime, but that will be okay too. Writing that, I feel no sadness, for I see two whole people going their separate paths, their own ways. Ah, but what wonders while we're one!

Bob walking to the truck, kisses me. "I kissed you on the mouth out of loving, not out of pity, or out of compassion." The man with whom I've marveled at martins!

March 1, 1981

Bob told me, "I love you." He also told me he had slept with someone else while I was gone. I love him, but am afraid to be caught again in romanticism. Lying in his arms, curled, we drank deep of each other, and I, wounded, could not cry for feeling close anyway. It's strange to be so "in love" in a non-crazy way. My wits are still very much about me.

1:00 a.m.: I haven't been able to get to sleep lately. And I feel (am!) fat again. Damn.

Tonight I resent men. I'm hurt by Bob. And I don't want to be close enough to be crying again. But here I am, in the middle of the night with tears, alone. When will I learn to be with someone who feels more like I do on that issue and stop making myself miserable? I'm not sure what upsets me so much. It's not really the sex. Some of it is jealousy, but at least as much jealousy for men being able to let go and screw with impunity while I cling to strange rules I've imposed upon myself. And he told me she was coming and said he wouldn't make love with her. That hurts. Even when he said it to me the other night, I felt something not ringing true. Don't make promises you can't keep.

On the other hand, I'm glad that I can sleep with people I want to. It's just that right now I don't want to, or if I do on occasion, I figure it's just not worth it.

I was trying to hide from the reality of this situation. He's not moving quickly to get divorced. He claims it's his concern for the children, that he wants them to have time to digest the separation. I don't understand; not having children, I can only guess at his feelings, and tentatively try to trust him.

I need to pull back and see and involve myself with other men. Otherwise I'm going to be *really* hurt. I feel so sad. After all the hysteria and resentment and anger and hurt and tears, I think what this may really be all about is that Bob has the power to hurt me, power I willingly give him. I just didn't realize how much. So it's my responsibility to slow down and if possible, take some of the power back. Maybe we can do it together, I don't know. How much can I explain to him? How much do I really understand?

March 2, 1981

Bob, unable also to sleep, appeared at my door at 5:00 a.m. We talked. It worked. We slept. I had said, "If you change your mind about Sherry, that's okay." If I didn't mean it, I shouldn't have said it. I wanted to mean it. In the morning shower I thought it was good I was leaving for the weekend. We are so intense, each moment is full and ripe and we both need space. He is an equal, and meets me at every turn.

March 4, 1981

I'm falling in love. The crazy way. I want to be with him. Trying to be realistic, to temper my feelings, I think of things I don't like:

(1) he's always late, (2) sometimes he rambles away from his points. If that's all, then that's not much. Thinking of him, I smile. It's difficult when you reach the stage where you don't care. There is a funny buoyancy and lilt to my life. But this time being-in-love has not made me lose myself as much. I'm actually sitting in my office chuckling and grinning!

Yesterday on the phone we couldn't talk.

March 6, 1981

I went to see Paul again. For therapy or acceptance?

On BA: "Denise and I drove by a field, 'We ought to buy some land.' Then I thought 'Why do I have to acquire things I like?'"

Later BA speaking: "Sometimes you have them without acquiring."

This morning he looked at me and with his voice matching his body, said, "I love you." The words floated right into the mantra "I love you" that my eyes had been repeating. Never has it been so beautiful. I fear words which are so inadequate. I'm in so deep, I worry about either going deeper or falling *out* of love. Too much analysis. If I do, I do.

March 7, 1981

A note left on my car bearing a single inscription "Yes" just happened to be torn from the corner of Bob's calendar notebook. Unplanned by him, it was my birthday date. Two Scorpios.

March 9, 1981

Ranch day—unexpected time: In the truck I sweated as we joined a neighbor and chased a horse. The first time I'd driven the truck: I ran it over a fencepost. Embarrassed, *I gutted it out*. Ever so afraid to fail, awkward in his world, but I stuck it out!

The sun set as we watched. I'd never seen it go so quickly. Stunned, I tore my eyes for a moment from the now empty sky to his smile. Tipsy, we talked long and deep. B: "If my divorce were final today, I'm not sure I'd want to run off and marry you now." I forgot to ask why not. Guess I didn't want to know.

March 10, 1981

Barely knowing what pliers are, I helped with the mesh fence. In contrast, he heaved the metal sections and salt blocks with the easy knowledge of a body used to such moves. His working hands twisted the fence wire with hardened grace and elegance of movement.

Perched on the front of the truck I sat lost in my own thoughts, but totally aware of his presence in the cattle pen behind me. Separate, but partners. (As he left for the weekend, he whispered all three words in my ear. Yes.)

March 12, 1981

He said "no twinges." And so, instead of twinges, a smile lurks beneath my consciousness. Wherever you are, right now, at 10:38 p.m. I'm sending a quiet loving feeling to you.

March 15, 1981

Last night we talked. From the heart and soul and intellect.
BA: "I am beginning to realize how deeply you feel about me, and I will be even more open." I sense us both so vulnerable, yet just beginning to reach a new depth. Exploring him, his *person*, is extraordinary.

March 18, 1981 (El Paso)

Morning awakenings were a ballet of soft limbs, moves of deliberate spontaneity. He found my lost earring! Mountains and moon were one. Why Paris? We almost drove off a precipice. Magic—deep. His thoughts turn to moderation also. Once again, at every turn we meet. If everything contains its opposite, do we meet and part simultaneously? But my feeling is one of beginning, not ending, except an ending each day of that moment as we move on to the next.

March 19, 1981 (On the plane El Paso-Albuquerque; then in Albuquerque's bus station)

Through the circular waiting room from my seat on this airplane, I see the tail of his plane. We've now broken every rule; New Mexico *is* the Land of Enchantment. There may be no twinges, but my God, what a giant wrench of my heart. I miss him in the pit of my stomach. It hurts. I'm trying hard in this bus station to be rational, to figure out what I really want, but what I want right now is him, here.

Having made the decision to go home earlier, I can calmly look forward to tomorrow at Taos. The attack of ultimate loneliness has fled. Oh, but I'm in deep.

March 23, 1981 (Austin)

L: (in an attack of raw honesty) "I'm not sure I'm more afraid that you'll get divorced soon or that you won't."

B: "I feel that way too, and that's why other factors enter into the equation, like kids."

March 24, 1981

Bob had Houston meetings. He looked exhausted at 10:30 p.m. when he stopped by. The miles and battle scars showed on his face. A tired set to his shoulders spoke of long hours negotiating reasonably. I wanted to let him know how much I respected him for the job he does; how totally separate from my personal feelings. As a citizen I'm glad and grateful he's the Land Commissioner. At these times I glimpse the dignity of public service. But as he talked of politics, I was scared again. Left over Tim feelings perhaps. A confusing jumble of thoughts. I wouldn't like him if he weren't happy with himself and his public contribution, yet the politics will keep us apart eventually—maybe.

It's okay to feel sad and lonely and missing Bob sometimes. To deny the hard parts isn't any more realistic and honest than to deny the ecstasy. B: "The only way you can keep from being torn up when a calf dies is not to ever have calves." That's true, but this is a different kind of vulnerable.

March 26, 1981

Last night I gave Bob a bottle of sherry:

L: "This is not because I love you, but because I respect you." (after Houston negotiations for two solid days.)

B: "I love you."

Later, B: "Do you always feel 'up' when you're with me? Because if you don't, or it isn't easy, that's okay."

Thinking about it, I want to be the best person I can when I'm with him, although not consciously strain every minute to do so. Usually I'm just glad to be there. On occasion I hold back the down/hassled feelings, but less because I don't want to dump on him than that I've learned they'll go away or get me under control and I don't want to waste time or emotional energy with him. Also, it's critically important that I handle my life alone on one level. I'm not, or haven't been in the past, essentially self-contained and emotionally self-reliant. It's taken so long to begin to stand firmly planted in myself, that I'm protective. And, of course, I fear that if I show Bob some of the clutchy, non-up moments, he'll think less of me or leave. Both of which probably aren't true. I hope.

I don't know how to directly and openly ask for help and comfort from any man ever in my love-relationship life. Why? With friends, male or female, I can ask; but I'm so afraid of being rejected or becoming even more vulnerable in love relationships. A not entirely unfounded fear, given past history. Somehow I'm not sure this is like the calf-dying analogy.

Bob said he aches too sometimes. Eventually he will confront why his marriage failed, really. I hope he doesn't perceive it as the glass slipper breaking. I have no vision of what he'll do, not do, etc. But although I sense some big rocks, I think we'll both be okay. Thought: I'm not ready to be married anymore than he's ready to be divorced! But at least they're separated.

March 30, 1981

On missing each other: B: "If you hadn't had all the wonderful times, there wouldn't be anything to miss. So think of them instead."

Planned Parenthood lunch. Luke was there. Two young attractive doctors gave short presentations. I felt tugged. No desire to meet them more fully, but wishing Bob and I would plan futures, sort of. We talked some this weekend. It's good to say those words to each other, but oh, so difficult for me. This relationship is the most self-contained I've ever experienced. We talk to each other, not third parties.

Saturday, we flew to Matagorda Island. In his plane, I marveled that we both were pilots. And I actually flew between clouds. Later when he flew, the plane became an extension of him. At 1,000 feet above the beach, he dipped and turned and played with the plane like a lover. It's the hands again. He's beautiful to watch flying. Like touching the donkey.

The new horse ate out of my hand! At the island we ran for thirty minutes along the beach. But we floated effortlessly. And knew enough to stop to pick up a seashell "baton." I used to be afraid to live so long at this level. For fear that it had to end and then I'd crash. But why not gulp? In the midst of the incredible pace and magic, I don't feel cramped or hurried. He's taught me about calm in the middle of oneself being sufficient to let you totally enjoy the outside world and gulp life. Two gulping Scorpios.

Enchiladas and vegetables. And port. And flying again. And a sand-dug message on the beach. And fireworks when we drove into Houston to begin again.

April 2, 1981

Paul session: Am I prepared for the pain and ending? L: "Why does there have to be an ending?" P: "At the least, one of you will die first." We were not communicating very well.

B called me three times from different airports. We're on such different levels. Wherever you are, "You are my morning."

April 3, 1981

A glance outside to brilliant blue, white clouds, sunshine, in a plane high above. I think of an afternoon trip to Matagorda, smile, and peacefully, joyfully, quietly am with him.

Later, legs crossed, I glimpsed a mole in the center of my bare heel. Instantly I saw him looking down at me sitting in the living room chair in a green nightgown. He touched my dangling foot and said, "I love your feet." Oh, the utter sweetness of instant feel/memories!

April 4, 1981 (Colorado)

We've learned to be apart, grow, enjoy and come together— later. Amazingly, although I miss in the sense of wishing I could share, I don't hurt. Maybe it really is possible to love unpainfully. It is good to be apart. It forces me to get perspective and to stand alone. Reminiscent of the El Paso weekend.

April 5, 1981

Bob called me in Colorado. His voice spoke with the same longing as mine from Albuquerque. It was good for me to hear that he feels that too at times. Although I don't want him to feel pain, I was forced to see that yes, I am affecting him similarly. Somehow I never can believe that he feels like I do. On the other hand, I was relatively fine away from him this trip. Loving, caring, can be *not* painful! I missed him to share with, but not the incapacitating missing of New Mexico. Part of it is a sense of real security of the relationship. At least for now, he won't intentionally hurt me. There is a curious freedom also. It's like being married. At the seminar there were interesting men, several of whom I'm sure I could have slept with had I wanted. But freed from the desire to sleep with new people, I was able to just enjoy myself and them.

April 6, 1981

It's time to begin integrating my life. At first I hesitated letting anyone else know of Bob. But eventually the need to share outweighs the positive side of secrecy. Kathie's hug and "I love you" meant a lot to me.

Part of what's happened is, I think, that we've entered a new stage in the relationship, but haven't had the time to explore it yet. So separately and apart we try to live it and get a handle on it, but relationships take two and time.

My friends said I'll be hurt. Eventually I'll want more than I can have. That's probably true. But he'll be so too. So as the changes happen, we'll just have to figure it out and help each other through. (The only problem with that theory is that sometimes helping means not seeing someone and I can't face his absence.) When I write like this, of endings perhaps, my stomach gets cramped and I'm so scared.

April 7, 1981

Picture: Bob like a kid with a new toy stands in the kitchen with new size thirty-four bluejeans on. We've evened off to a steady incline in feelings, while we're broadening the root structure and becoming richer ("fuller"-his word). This morning, I almost slept cradled on his shoulder. That's never before been a comfortable position for me. Am I less afraid to appear vulnerable? Later, I looked long into his face, memorizing him. Why? He left and I went down, sat at the kitchen table and stared at the fact that yes he was still married and no he wasn't going to divorce soon and even if he did, it wouldn't or couldn't be *for* me or *to* me, and I wasn't ready for that responsibility anyway. One of my patterns with men is not believing what they say. That's what I've been engaged in with Bob. Secretly, I've thought he would want to marry me. There, it's on paper. I must listen to him and believe the words, or else it will be like Tim and Luke. I must also find some paths that leave us friends. As long as I feel no great need to live with someone, to plan futures, we're fine from my side. But I sense this is temporary. Even as I write that, however, I recall the wonderful feeling of going to sleep alone in my own bed last night; it was delicious. Just as now, in the silence of the home I've created, I'm at peace. This is essentially a selfish existence—no husband, no children whose needs conflict with mine. I'll luxuriate while I can. It's a good medium for growth.

In New Mexico, Bob found a toy white horse on the cabin floor and gave it to me. Weeks later, miles away in Nevada, he called me from a pay phone. In the dirt outside the booth was a small white horse chess piece. Oh, the magic.

April 8, 1981

Bob and I were madly in love in a shopping center in El Paso. He put his arm around me. (Ordinarily he stays physically apart from me when we *do* things, e.g., ranch. He uses looks, not hands, to communicate.) I looked up and asked if he would teach me how to catch him if he were catchable. He replied that he wasn't catchable, but that if he became so, sure, he'd teach me.

Eating two pizzas we talked heavy, but today, strangely, I can't recall what about. Somewhere in there about Washington. It became all garbled in my mind with leaving him. I remember; I said I thought next January was the end. Why? The real answer I suppose, is that I don't want to live like this much longer. Today I'm so tired, hungover. My life moves too quickly, and I've begun to fight unnecessary battles within myself. There are enough crisis decision points without creating them. Sometimes I sense my feelings about Bob are in that category. It's as if I want to force him into a choice just to see what he'll do, and yet I know already his answer. That's masochism. And if I ever were to really live with him, I'm not sure I could take the pace. It would be difficult to live *my* life. His life seems more important and more fun. Of course, that's not really true. I'm having a relapse into the being-second syndrome. But when he talks of going to the political events, I'm upset/jealous/hurt that I can't be there publicly as his friend. Examine that. Why do I want that? To bask in his glory? Not good enough. Why can't I sit back and smile to myself and be happy he's happy? I should learn from Wanda's children that each of us has a place, unique in this world. Writing this calms me down.

All of these thoughts come together at the question of value. Did I say something last night to Bob about the certainties? (This is almost scary not to be able to recall precisely what we said.) In this small room/office—drab, with empty steel boxes and regulation desk—I'm on my path again, centering, beginning to regroup and trust my own judgment. The question I must answer is whether there are, underlying the daily tasks of work, a value and a certainty. Slowly, I'm trying to create my life to be rich with those. And figure

162   *A Woman's Odyssey: Journals, 1976—1992*

out what they are and how to live them in the daily ordinariness of
life. Presentness. I used to approach it non-directly and try to identify
what wasn't important in the hope of isolating the important. Now
I want to gulp the important—fully.

One day we flew both airplanes to check them out. Beneath us
was the Georgetown ranch. What does he feel *flying* over a piece of
land, Texas, that's his?

April 9, 1981

Things are not right between Bob and me. I'm not sure if it's
work pressures, time pressures, his family, etc. Or in part that it hit
me that I really do want more on a public, regular basis. He looks at
the good side and I feel small and petty for concentrating on the
negatives at times. But I'm not always up! I don't want to fall into
the pattern of endings again. But I feel as if I'm fighting to keep my
head above water, going upstream. I've put expectations on the relationship; expectations that it is by nature not equipped to handle.
I look to Bob to satisfy too many needs; I become dependent, then
fight with myself to stay apart and alone. Then become resentful
that he isn't all the time here.

April 10, 1981

Finally I came back up again. I ran yesterday morning alone
and things just came back into perspective. Austin is my home and
I don't want to leave. Thinking and imagining D. C. threw me into
a tizzy. Also was becoming obsessed with Bob—marriage-relation-
ship, etc. That's just part of my life, albeit an extremely important
part, and often of late the most rewarding. I keep losing sight of the
fact that I must live with myself all the time, so need to make decisions and actions that fit my value system and not worry about
others' reactions. Perhaps that's why I'm so troubled about Bob these
days. The secrecy element has begun to cause basic conflicts for me.
He's too important a piece of my life to keep it hidden from friends
and the world. He's been sick and looks tired. P: "You're falling
more in love with him aren't you?" L: (Pause) "No, I've been more
'in love' with him at other times, but I'm loving him, deeply now,

and that scares me." P: "Are you content to be Lara? That means you must always have an apartment to run away to." L: "No." (Later, rethinking, that's probably a correct answer, but I really don't know what kind of a relationship situation I want. Not traditional marriage, I don't think, but more than living together. I can design my own institution with someone else! It never occurred to me that I could choose whatever way to institutionalize a relationship. That's what Bob and I are doing now. Only we just (or maybe I just) didn't consciously know it.

P: "Some people decide not to date 'unavailable' men, not because of moral judgments, but because it takes a lot out of you and it's a strain."

L: "But until now, it's been worth it. And I want to figure out how to continue it that way. But yes, it's a strain. Sometimes I want to tell him to stop seeing me for a while, concentrate on his divorce and get that resolved. God knows I've been where he is and I'm worried for him."

As I was leaving therapy, Paul said, "You're a nice person." That meant a lot.

Later: Bob and I talked finally of my scared feelings. I look at his careworn face, hear him say he wouldn't get divorced for me and wonder if he knows that I've weighed that into the equation. Which is part of the reason I can't promise any more than he can. He doesn't want to spend all our time talking of endings. Neither do I. Funny, that's the first time he's ever outwardly been upset with me. Under control, but seemed irritated. I think we could maybe have terrific fights. That thought would once have frightened me. Tonight, it seems only logical that eventually we'll fight with the same passion with which we love. And like slowly finding that passion, we slowly become secure enough in each other to risk differences should they arise. Even though limited, a *growing* relationship is wonderful.

After reading the diary, he said he didn't realize things had been so rough. His comment surprised me and I felt awkward. It's been a long time since anyone has known those things and felt something—sorry?—for me. I'm sure he's had some similar times.

April 11, 1981

Morning run: three miles with Bob. He talked of his children, and the love and affection came through. He glows when he talks of the girls. Landis remains a mystery. It must be fun to have him for a father, doing things with you, running, working the cows, playing guitar. I really have no sense of family at the age his kids are. From seventh grade on, I was a parent. That's why when I meet people that age, I generally treat them as adults rather than children.

Sheila thinks I should be open to a non-married man. Start seeing other men, etc. She says we deserve someone who's one hundred percent committed. Although I basically agree, I think it's more complex. As much as I want someone full-time, I can't imagine a "good relationship" like that, with kids, etc. P might be right that when Tim ran off that night, I didn't just lose Tim, but a dream.

April 12, 1981

Tonight at the Georgetown Candle Factory in the truck:
L: (so very afraid but needing to know) "When do you think you'll get divorced?"
B: "But I'm not sure what I will do when I get divorced." (Saying the word is difficult for us both. It sort of chokes on the tongue. Funny, at one point "I love you" was the same way.)
L: "It's a hard question to ask, but I need to know."
B: "You should act as if the answer is 'I don't know!'"
My body doesn't sit by the telephone, but my heart does.

April 13, 1981

He says he's not as fragile as I think. I'm not sure what he means, but rather than mull it about, I'll just ask. Does he really want me to say, "Hey, I can't. I've got a date?" But I must listen to what he says and not only hear what I want to hear. So he really must want that.

April 14, 1981

Four miles: 36:52!
UP! UP! SMILE! SUNRISE! CHOOSE TO LIVE EACH

MOMENT! TOGETHER AND APART! YES! I'M CREATING MY OWN DREAM!

April 15, 1981

As we lay draped (words can't capture the exquisite touch of his body next to mine, all along one side, shoulder/head to feet and toes, each exactly where it should be at that instant in time) in the "jungle" weather, wet, rainy, but cool enough for bodies to feel good against each other, I realized that the reason I've been hesitant as of late is that I'm plowing very new ground. Although I've let other people "in" before, it's never been on the levels Bob and I inhabit. I'm almost trusting him in a significantly different way. Other times I've been carried away by being "in love" or infatuated and given totally of myself, but maybe because I didn't know the other pieces to share, I didn't give them. With Bob I'm choosing to let us explore (if he continues to choose the same path with me) whole new places. I have moments of tremendous misgivings about doing this because it gets me in even deeper to a situation where extrication will be painful at best. It is important in a whole different way than I initially understood, that we each respect the other's personhood, respect our relationship, and act accordingly.

I like him. He is one of the *nicest* people I've ever known. And although I know he is perfectly capable of "playing hardball," I'm becoming convinced he won't play it on me. Guess I'll find out.

We flew back from Dallas. Flying is special. Wish I could remember everything each time. He told me later that that trip was the first time he'd felt totally at home and nonapprehensive at all in the plane. He ran his hands across the controls and said he knew he knew all that he could about that plane. He's in his "passage" time also.

April 16, 1981 (Pasted into diary from a scrap of paper written on in a phone booth on Highway 29)

Two cows missing. He's in a white dress shirt. Brown and thin wrists poke out the rolled up sleeves. His fingers dial phone numbers with assurance. At Georgetown, light rain.

He's taught me of living life fully. Today he's flown through a storm on instruments, met with oil company people concerning royalty issues, drawn wonderful funny pictures, looked at the cows, lost two—and its only 7:09 p.m. His confidence and competence in dealing with his world are awesome.

In people, like cattle brands, you need to leave room for blood to circulate so they can grow.

April 17, 1981

Everything is moving too fast.

P: "I wonder why you're still coming, too. With Bob, you've found you can view a man as a person. When you leave therapy, you can always come back later if you need to/want to. And I'll remember you." (I hugged him.)

Bob was hit by a cow last night and thrown to the ground. Important time. Immediately I became sober, and concerned for him. His face was white as he continued to fix the fence. He raised the barbed wire and tacked it into a nearby tree. I held the wire up, watched his face and hands intent on his work, and realized his separateness and importance apart from me and our relationship. His kids came to my vision, flashing faces—and I knew how connected he was to them. Work, cows, airplanes all rushed past, then back to just Bob, hammering. He washed his hands in the pond. The sun was setting, his shirt was stark white against the green and brown of mud and grass. He stooped to reach the water and I ached inside, loving him. Because you can't keep cows from knocking down those you love, unless you keep all cows away.

April 18, 1981

Bob says he never forgets work information. (He'd forgotten I'd told him of Liz's second pregnancy.) I react the same way. But it points out priorities. You remember what you think is important to remember. Like choosing how you spend your time. Suddenly I lost sympathy for men who forget wedding anniversaries. And women who forget that the major hearing is next Monday. I have not always been a good listener. But I'm working on it.

On passionate lovemaking:

B: "Why is it so?"

L: "I think really good sex is like fidelity. The underlying essence is that it's freely given."

He spoke of Landis when I asked. But I still have no sense of him like I do the girls. The question, "Tell me about Landis," was answered mostly in terms of sports and then Bob wandered off to another topic. Does a son make different demands on a father than daughters do?

April 19, 1981

There's another level lurking around in all this. Of course, not every moment will we be in love, or thinking solely of the other. But just because the feeling comes and goes doesn't mean we've "ended." The old tales were that once this feeling began to ebb, one settled down to a "loving, comfortable" relationship, "grew into mature love," which somehow translated, for any of us gutsy enough to say it, into taking each other for granted with more or less consideration for the other, depending on the relationship. That's not good enough. And I don't think life/relationships have to be that way. But I sure could use a role model! Was it not so long ago I wrote "create your own dreams"? Well, kid, here goes!

Bob thinks I'm laughing and singing more these last two weeks. It must be my internal well-being, since events have certainly been chaotic. He grinned that funny little side grin across the truck when he told me. He looked strong and fragile all at once. He's getting thin. Those green eyes look so incredible sometimes, with the eyelashes on his left eye curling ever so slightly, just enough to be seen when he looks straight.

April 20, 1981 (A grey day)

In Durham Park, after following B on the tractor, we met the man who was picking it up. His woman was in their truck to follow him to Georgetown. I looked at her, silently. We women drive the trucks and watch and listen to our men transact business. Not in the mainstream of life, but providing the strength and stability underlying it all.

April 21, 1981

We're breaking out of old molds. Not just our own personal ones, but world views. Choosing one's existence in this world is a terribly creative and awesome task, but so fine, fanciful and fun. Ordinary relationships "should" cool down and eventually wrench. Ordinarily sex levels off. A man and woman explore the surface of each other, drink the first cream and settle. There are other ways. When I finally recognized Bob as a complete and separate person, then I could begin to learn non-possessiveness and understand the process of structuring a relationship for good.

Picture from yesterday transferring the blue tractor: Bob in blue shirt, wind-blown hair from the open tractor, sleeves rolled back, both arms outreached in a giant V, with two-fingered equal signs. From my vantage place in the truck behind him, his back and the set of his body radiated freedom and looseness and joy.

This journal has become a love/story/song. Hmm. It's hard not to write for him. Once again I'm understanding that it's okay, normal and probably even positive, to have soul pieces kept totally within and unshared. Not out of fear or hoarding, but because the human condition really is one of aloneness. We can touch bodies, minds, and (rarely) souls. But perhaps never as closely as we touch the wind on Enchanted Rock. Stripped of the complexities that make us human, the molecules of animate and inanimate objects combine for the void. I don't know what it all means.

Bob and I have that whole world left to explore about/with each other. The feeling/thought walking along the dike at Luther College still catches at my insides. Do I want to chase the parameters of that sense of truth with my life's time? Or be in the world? Lately I sense that although I could learn to be so much more competent and involved in the community and lawyering, some of the ledges left to reach may not be worth the climbing time. Were I the head of a large company or agency, I doubt I'd have any greater satisfaction or heartaches than I have now as a lowly bureaucrat with our staff of fifteen. So choosing one's challenges is important. If I'm lucky enough to control so much that is external to me.

Bob is more serious now about the complications. And so am I.

April 22, 1981

Bob's first five-mile run with me: 48:20. He gave Landis a hunting jacket with lots of pockets. I smiled when he told me.

Bob cried with me tonight. I cried at the stereo. Why? Neither of us fully understood. We talked of dreams and last sessions with P and walked through Profit's house and ate pizza and he said he wasn't ready to be divorced and I wrenched and the sunset was beautiful along back Texas roads with not enough rain yet to make the creek run. And Butch considered selling/leasing his oil land and Bob advised him.

Bob said the difference between me and Jean (his first love) was his appreciation for my professional side and for my women's lib feelings. I wonder if he'd love me if I weren't a lawyer or took time off to have child. So complex, so rich; may I have the wisdom for the moment to live and love and learn and handle it! Please God, I'll give back later if I can have an extra dose of strength for today!

April 23, 1981

Bob is not placing rules or demands on me, but the restraints are there anyway, self-imposed. The conflict situation, I guess, is obvious. If he were free and available, I'd never pursue other relationships. As it is, I feel vaguely as if I "ought" to do so and stop being so emotionally dependent on Bob for all that part of my life. And I never want to look back and feel resentful that I didn't seek a long-term person, anymore than I want Bob to wish I hadn't interfered in his marriage. Oh, it's complex. I'm awfully ready to see him. . . .

April 24, 1981

Last night we both lied to other people in front of each other. He, on the phone; I, in person. The hard part was having the other hear it. I was really uncomfortable. When I'm better within myself, the lie alone will cause discomfort.

April 25, 1981

In a moment of lighthearted liberated madness, Bob fell to his knees and clutched my leg. His comment to my similar move yesterday and my remark that my liberated women friends would think I'd sold out.

The rain on the plane window makes my insides wrench. His plane may not be able to fly to meet me. A little bit of non-Bob goes a long way!

April 26, 1981 (Sitting alone on the hill overlooking the valley at Liberty Hill)

The last time I watched a sinking sunset was in a car (truck?) looking at Bob silhouetted against it. Tonight, he unloads feed while I touch base with Texas earth and am quiet for a moment. Pink and perfect roundness was the sun. Lightly pink sunset cloud tendrils streak across the pale blue sky. This rock is white and solid and stark background for purple wildflowers and "dove weed." Listening, I hear cows and night sounds and the faint roar of a far off engine. And I know that in any of our life's trails, I'll be neither closer nor farther from him than I am at this moment.

The first star appears a tiny speck among the smokey blue evening clouds. And I, in my attempted wisdom wish not for Bob's happiness, nor my own, but for both of us, calm acceptance of each other, love and life. Will I someday laugh kindly and fully and wholly at youthful seriousness and attempts to understand life's richness and mystery?

A green and black striped caterpillar picks his way over the small rocks near my feet. Feeling his way. Gnats love my forearms. Harmless reminders that "perfection" includes reality and its bumps. Suddenly, I long to see the green eyes. There will be oh, so many times when feeling that, I won't be able to walk up a hill into his arms. Here I go!

I found him on the porch, hot and nicely tired, watching the same remnants of sunset sky as I only moments before had done. Quietly, I sat beside him and in silence we listened to the coming night sounds. Together.

In silence, he took my hand and showed me the "Equalamente" constellation. Forever for me to be known by that name rather than Pegasus. Equal signs. In silence he built a small fire, and I watched the shadows spread light and dark across his face and hands as he worked. The log caught and yellow flames and red coals became blueness. We sat in silence for more than an hour. At times I wondered what he thought, but always I was more at peace and as comfortable than ever in my life. We were as together, as close, as two adult people who understand separateness can be. Time telescoped and I glanced at our entwined fingers and saw old hands. Suddenly, I knew that I was feeling "ten-year-ness"; that if I were with him ten years hence, it would feel like the present moment; therefore, I didn't *have* to have the ten years if they didn't come, because all time, past, present and future, was totally contained within that moment. This quiet man beside me I'd waited over thirty years to love.

In silence, I thought of ten years, then twenty years hence. Of his dying (probably) before me. And calmly, without fear, I realized I'd learn to live and deal with that. That any time together would make me so rich and full I'd have more than enough strength to create a different richness later should I need to. And I wondered if he could understand how even loving him with every give-away-able piece of my heart and soul, I could contemplate these things. Hold in my mind at the same moments the beginning and the end, the total presence and the total absence, each opposite containing the seed of the other.

May 1, 1981

This morning Dear Abby had a column on younger women having affairs, claiming that the man hardly ever leaves, and if he does, what makes the second woman think it wouldn't happen with her too? It jolted me. Although we have mountains and ledges I never knew existed, we are on another level engaged in one of mankind's oldest games. Both of us come to this relationship with checkered pasts. But do these pasts predict our futures? Echoes of the Leonard Cohen song: "I know that we are not new, in cities and in forests they've loved like me and you." All of which is merely to put this in some small way in perspective.

Bob is the best man I know about women.

May 2, 1981

Bob had a good day. I was glad for him. But I wanted to be serious. I asked him if there were any skeletons in his professional closet.

B: "The worst thing I did in public life was fly over my ranch coming back from West Texas to look at the cows. And once I took a roll of TP from the office because we were out at home." Does he have any idea how *rare* he is, what an incredible public servant? I'm proud to know him.

May 3, 1981

Sometimes I'm jealous of the loves in Bob's life, of the women stories, canoe trips, etc. And I think that if I wouldn't come with him to the ranch, he'd find someone else for company. And I can't always come with him and won't when I don't want to. What does it all mean? (Written while watching his face through the windshield as he cleans the glass. Ah, my love!)

May 4, 1981

You can promise behavior, but not emotions. That must be why marriage vows are geared toward actions.

May 5, 1981

At Enchanted Rock, I shared my wind/place with Bob. We ate bakery goods and laughed and sang and drove through hill country and talked and ran out of things to say and both later admitted to the other (s)he was aware of the running out. We talked of leaving each other with dignity—my thought on a rock as he pulled the soft heads of the Indian grass.

May 6, 1981

Bob is going to battle with the special interest groups. I reminded him of Jefferson's saying that he had to be a warrior so his son could be a farmer, so his grandson could be a merchant so that his great grandson could be a poet.

From *Gulag Archipelago*: "Gradually it was revealed to me that the line separating good and evil passes not between states, not between classes, and not between parties; it passes through each human heart, and through all human hearts. This line shifts."

May 7, 1981

Last night we went to his office. I read an old memo he had written to McGovern and glimpsed the warrior, the writer in him. Gazing at the lit Capitol from the high window after grazing through the pictures and books of his public life was awesome. I realized I was just beginning to understand how important—in a public sense—he is. It scared me. Ambition and success confuse me after being around Tim and Luke and Susan. Ambivalent feelings toward wanting it personally and trying to break out of the pattern of living it vicariously. I'm woman in transition; for my daughters it will be easier.

The Raw Deal Bar. My first time. It was a struggle to overcome panic feelings of not wanting to face a crowd of people as Bob's "girlfriend." Thinking upon it later, I suspect I was just uncomfortable at not being able to be exactly who and what I am out front and openly. But it was fun to drink a beer in public.

Afterward, we walked to Hemphill park. Man-made beauty of lights twinkling on sewer water. We talked.

B: "Will you just accept that I love you?" (He held out his hand, palm open, and put mine in it. In a wink of an eye . . .)

Listening to Roberta Flack sing "Jesse," I remember that Nancy spoke of lack of history being one of the major problems in the age difference. Perhaps that's one reason I'm writing all this down. An attempt to create my own history; our own history. Tonight, a moment of sadness for Rod and me. So long ago, so far away across town, now unbridgeable distances. The songs on this record make me sad. Memories from days when I believed the key was one person who, if present, answered most questions and, if absent, was the root of all aches. It's better to be oneself, and lean less, love more.

It's good to be alone, to hold on to that piece no one touches; how can I love if I don't retain and nourish the strength of aloneness?

Breakout thought: Bob has shown me a way of loving that is essential. Joyful, not sad.

When Diane spoke of her friend "a femme sole," I tried that appellation on for size. It's okay; beats spinster. Sometimes I feel as if a vibrancy permeates my life such that I can't explain to others who live differently.

May 8, 1981

When he walked by me tonight my heart jumped. Some people choose not to have affairs because of the strain; it has nothing to do with morality.

Part of the disorientation is the sudden sense of his public side coming just when I'm feeling insecure about my work; do I want to be a lawyer, etc. I'm awfully confused and feel alone. Not that I can't handle it, but. . . . Tonight life overwhelms me.

Later: Long talk with Sheila concerning men, Bob, her sense of my losing my identity:
1. She should give me more credit.
2. She's partly right.
3. I have to trust my own judgment here. I can't go to her or Bob (and actually don't want to) for approval of the other.
4. Why can't she accept me as I do her?
5. All of this wears me out.

May 9, 1981

I watched the vet check the bulls' fertility. Interesting.

May 10, 1981

Yesterday I went crazy and invented non-crises. But an important time. Dinner with Lee S. brought home to me that I didn't want other men. Before, I've sort of held a piece out so that I could leave and find someone if necessary. Last night I knew that was no longer true. Bob had come to my office earlier in the day. In business clothes he looks older, and I saw that there really was an age factor. But that it was okay. When Lee came into Pecan Street to meet me, he looked all Lee-ish and three piece young Dallas lawyer and I liked him.

The other men in my life are interesting, etc., but nothing compared with Bob. At dinner, I finally understood what a different level we're on. And I quit kidding myself about involvement with other people. Although sometimes I'd like to "show off" and have an ego trip in bed with some of them, I'm not going to. Because it would affect Bob and me in ways I don't want to deal with right now. And secondly, the people who are worth going to bed with deserve more explanation of where I'm coming from. It would be wrong to sleep with someone else when I'm in love with Bob, without everyone understanding.

So I came home and sat on my steps, waiting.

Someday when I read this, I'll probably think I spent too much time and emotional energy on the relationship and not enough on work, etc. Hey, future self, don't be judgmental! You weren't here to run in the early sunrise bright pink/orange light with a full moon across the field and see a too large *Texas Observer* magazine T-shirt stretched across the curve of his ass.

What Sheila doesn't understand is how alike Bob and I are. He's the first person I've found who is just as romantic and open as I, and just as quietly, internally his own person who could walk away. Hey, writing that, I understand that is the uncatchable part of both of us, and why we may last, albeit tumultuously!

May 11, 1981 (At Georgetown, arranging with the neighbor to pump water to the new tank)

Watching a man retrieve his garbage on the Georgetown lawn

as kids run up and down the street, I'm struck by the different stages one can choose to play on. Southwestern U. is too small now for me. Yet the truth is in "Our Town" where the ordinary births, loves, deaths of living are what it's all about.

Cool breezes blow my hair in the afternoon sunlight and cause shadows to shift across the jeans. Yesterday the light at eventide struck his navel and, laughing, we took his picture.

When I look in the new right hand mirror and see a tired, worn looking face with crinkles around the eyes and a little mascara faded and drooping, I don't understand how he loves me. White crinkly hair among the blond portends a new look for my old age, and the wrinkles already prominent on my forehead are harbingers of years hence. I'm not pretty and in growing old must rely on character, or a twinkle! Vision: I'll be alone then.

May 12, 1981

Driving on errands today, I listened to music and sang. I haven't lost identity any more than he has. There is no *precedent* for this.

May 15, 1981

I just read *The Little Prince* again and cried quiet tears. Last night I met Bob at Georgetown after both of us had long work days. We laughed (so close to tears sometimes, our laughter) through a heavy conversation:

B: "There is a fifty-fifty chance it won't work out."

L: (silence)

B: "I don't mean to be obscure."

Bob told me: He and other politicians were all on a helicopter. Bob had brought *Zen and the Art of Motorcycle Maintenance* and *The Little Prince* to read. The others merely glanced at the pages in amazement.

I love him so. And he can't be captured. By that I don't mean married, etc., but that his spirit is free and can only be willingly shared at moments. That's where possessiveness really matters. It's not of consequence to be possessive of each other's bodies, but neither can we possess the freely given soul part of the other; it's non-possessory. And as soon as either thinks it's possessed, it's gone.

Yesterday after running, Bob talked of beautiful women. I said I wouldn't mind having to "overcome" beauty. Wes talked also of Karen's beauty. He never envisioned himself marrying a beauty. B: "You're not 'beautiful,' but you have a beauty that comes out from inside." (Or something like that. It's hard for me to listen well when he talks like that. I'm embarrassed equally by my non-beauty and by the compliments.)

We ran errands and looked at camping gear:

L: "Well, you may as well enjoy this now, while we're still in that place where it's fun to run errands together and before it goes away."

B: (Pause. Long.) "Now *that's* a bunch of shit!"

May 16, 1981

Damn, he's just like me! Comforting thought in some ways, unsettling in others. All the insecurities, scaredness, etc., and all the confusions. But also all the toughness, the ability to back off to get perspective, and the lure toward other lovers. I can only hope he'll feel as bad as I did after kissing Jim last night, when he does the same thing. A sense of betrayal to the relationship and an inflicting of unnecessary pain or even just unnecessary worry. Thinking back, I understand more what happened to him over Sherry. Perhaps he found out in one big lump what I've been finding out more slowly, that I really don't want to do anything to give him pain or cause this relationship to rock. Maybe it's taken me longer because it is easier on a superficial level for me; I don't respond to particularly handsome men the way he does to pretty women, so generally life doesn't present me with as many temptations.

Lunch with Mary Beth. Just as I get too involved in his world and not my own, something happens like formally setting up lunch for women in politics.

May 18, 1981

Today I understood how important it is to have "work of one's own." Bored with my work and ready to leave, for the last few weeks I've been more involved with Bob's office than mine in terms of after-hours discussion. That is fine for periods of time, but eventually the "housewife syndrome" sets in and I become less interesting to myself and to him. Also, real involvement in the world or one's work is necessary for stimulus. We've almost seen too much of each other. Not that we run out of things to say or do, but each of us can't be all things to the other. Bob's work has been hectic and active enough so that I doubt he feels it as much as I do. Maybe he does. Hard to talk about because it brings out front the public problem.

A first today! We went to lunch at El Rancho, then to Georgetown where he checked the very rain gauge I'd taken a picture of him putting up. I was all dressed up (B: "You look twelve in that dress") and stood on the ridge overlooking the dried up tank, wind blowing my dress into my legs and the space between them, a light drizzle falling, and watched him throw "wild celery" to the fish/snake. And ached with loving him.

DEAD SOLID PERFECT!

May 19, 1981

Coastal Community Hall, waiting for Bob. In the dark, so hard to write. Women wait. I have learned to sit silently, alone and just be. No particularly deep thoughts, just accept the night, its sounds, shadows, and not fight the evening's flow. Not to hurry by worrying or wondering how long until Bob comes out. He'll be "up" and I must switch gears to meet him.

We've come to another evening off place. Why do I assume my thoughts will bore him? It's a thin line between comfortableness and taking someone for granted. He fears the kids will hate him. They won't; or maybe they will for a while, but not forever.

While wave-watching at the Flagship: many ocean waves have I watched. With Rod in Greece, Tim in Mexico, and each time I felt the ocean and was both a part and separate. For an instant as he opened the patio door to the soft waves directly below us, I leaned against the railing and flashed to Mexico. There I had cried and was, after comforting, still alone. Now I am calm, and feel fine, maybe—loved?

Jackie, when I said Bob was delightful and I was lucky, said, "You are delightful, and he is lucky." I needed that.

May 21, 1981

Flash: Buying new running shoes, he acted as if he were skiing down a mountain, knees bent to one side, the cute ass swinging in tune with the twinkle in his eye as he faded away from Rooster Andrews Sporting Goods Store and into some ski run. I laughed out loud with delight.

Sheila is acting differently. More tolerant of Bob and me. I warily tested the waters and told her light stories. Today I understood her permanence in my life. She will be there as will I for her, even when months go by and a man becomes more important in both our lives. We make minimal time for each other even in the midst of our mad passions. The problem with male friends is that unless they are co-workers, your lives rarely allow such continuity (through late night phone calls, etc.). For example, it never ceases to amaze me that men once so incredibly central to my existence live in Austin and we rarely see each other, even though I'm sure all would consider us "friends." Have to hand it to Luke that he does keep up the relationship with lunch or dinner every two weeks or so.

After a long talk of finances, etc.:

L: "I don't have much to offer."

B: (Sounding incredulous) "Yourself. What more could you offer than you have already?"

I'm ready to emerge again as me. Tonight I don't want to be married to *anyone*. Wherever I go lately, to the ranches, the Sea Rim, the Big Thicket, I glimpse an understanding that each place is just as important as the Himalayas. That the moment watching the sunset alone at Liberty Hill was truth: no more, nor less in tune with the world. That although each act matters, nothing matters. What is, is.

May 22, 1981

Bob showed me the old Department of Interior Book. He was

afraid I'd love him because of all that. In truth, I suspect it's about the same as his loving me because I'm a Friar lawyer—a piece, but only a piece. Wow, interesting thought: if he were happy doing it, I think I'd be perfectly happy for him to be a rancher with no public life at all (or lawyer or whatever). It's the bundle of complex characteristics, warmth and wit and intelligence and depth that I love. Where he applies his energies isn't critical to me. One, because I trust his values enough to know he'd use them for good, and two, because I trust his judgment.

May 23, 1981

Each day is so full. Another Houston experience. Flying down yesterday was exciting. He looked so concentrated in the heavy Hobby Airport traffic. Dinner at Skippy's (a gambler?) and my first martini! Our dancing left something to be desired, but I love dancing with him. I'm still too aware of him to be completely relaxed. I step on his feet.

May 24, 1981

Flying back from Dallas with Bob, we talked about VOR stations emitting radio signals to help pilots navigate. They're hard to spot from the air, but what once were merely small round white buildings on the ground assumed significance when I knew what to look for. That's true of most everything in life. Daily events become humorous, trees have seven shades of green—when one knows what to look for!

Even as I write this, Bob is inside the airport checking on weather. He said he had a clutch as he saw all his children seated in one plane.

May 25, 1981

A difficult day. Liz is in town, I had work problems concerning automobile ads, hard conversation with Tim about jobs, helped host the women in politics luncheon. At lunch I was confused, the old lack of confidence came again. It's as if I'm very small and not as accomplished as everyone else. Ridiculous, but felt it nonetheless.

Trying to figure out the feeling, I discovered one root is lack of integration. It's schizophrenic keeping such an important part of my life so separate. Yet when I think that, I wonder if he feels even more split than I. The old feelings of deriving self-worth from others, rather than inner self-sense, washed over, almost drowning me. I want to explain this to B, but am fearful. Although we've had time together lately, we haven't had "talk-time." I feel driven to the mountains, to some time alone, away. To be challenged and make it on my own. I don't know who to believe. Trust my own judgment? If I believe "life doesn't have to be painful," we're half way home.

He's so thoughtful. He called immediately upon leaving Liz to let me know I need not be jealous or worried. I wasn't. Her comment: "Total honesty can be a game too." Bob was surprised, but I understood what she meant.

May 26, 1981

Bob made the difference yesterday when we headed for the country. I've begun to face better that Bob may not get divorced in a time frame I can live with. Hard. And I need to live my own life, not his. Even as I write this, part of me would like to marry him and have a baby. Would that be running away?

May 27, 1981

Wet rainy night; lovely; good for the oats. Bob and I followed the waterfall creek on a silent late spring walk. Nature specializes in displays of virtuosity for us! As I followed him, I remembered so many trails behind men or alone. I "saw" all the Mo-Ranch nature trails I'd walked with an ache in my heart for love. It would be nice to have that place in my life filled permanently and peacefully.

Finally, I went alone to gaze at the waterfall. Beauty and peace. Rocking back on my heels, I sought the balance point where pressure from my knees against the jeans counterbalanced the backward thrust of my body. Water trickled down, a butterfly lit on a lush green droplet-heavy branch, and for a space in time—timeless—I was in perfect equilibrium and harmony with the world. Gate, gate, paragate, meshed into the Lord's Prayer and into a soul song of

joyful thanks for knees and eyes and health and balance—and Bob.
He had taken his chamois shirt off from May heat and the sweat
from his back made the little curls in the small curved place dark.
Cows were brown and rich in late afternoon colors. He walked into
the scene and, shirtless, he was brown and rich and cow-like, part
of the perfect oneness.

June 1, 1981

I told Bob I would marry him. Not even sure how I arrived at
the statement, certainly not through calm and rational analysis. Bob,
however, had not asked me to. He's changed. He still is very careful
with future words. When I came home tonight, he gave me letters
he'd written but not sent to me over the last month. The first one
said he'd begun to think thoughts of a life relationship. I was so
tired and shocked that his words didn't really come through until
we drove to Fredericksburg and I reread his letters alone in a hotel
room. We talked hard talk driving back to Austin, and still I
remained calm. He feared I'd issue ultimatums on a short time
schedule; I feared he'd take years to finalize his divorce.

The next day he went to Dallas; I talked long with Kathie and
out loud voiced my thoughts and hopes and fears. Good time. Things
began taking shape as I tried to articulate feelings.
1. I'll make it as a person, a human being, regardless of Bob's timing.
2. It really is his decision now. That makes me unbelievably vulnerable, but I have to trust that he won't hurt me unnecessarily. And I
must let him know that his decision can't be based on being fearful
of my vulnerability. I'll survive.
3. I'm afraid for him. There is so much he must deal with.
4. It won't be easy, but I'm willing to try. Each of us is a neat interesting person, but together we're magic. Probably our best attribute
is that we bring out the best in each other.
5. We each have the other totally defenseless. I suspect I could manipulate him and try to force a quick divorce. Prey on the love. Ugh!
But I never would; what good would that do? There will be plenty
of times of legitimate resentment he may feel toward me. If he wants

me, I'm here. But I don't really want him unless he comes to me willingly. That's been the basis of our relationship so far. And it's worked. On his side, he could easily manipulate me so I'd stay in this situation with him for years. He could use my love to keep me tied. But I don't think he will. For the same reasons I won't.

Hard thought: Life won't suddenly become all one hundred percent wonderful even if Bob and I make it. The Himalayas made me understand that there is more to life than just loving one person, although for me, it's essential to the *richness* of everything else, to love and cherish that one.

June 2, 1981

Quick note: In the long run, Bob and I must be comfortable doing politics together. It bothers me that we each go separately and do our political functions. I'm beginning to feel a little like I used to when Rod wouldn't take me to parties. At first I hurt and went alone, then as I became more independent, actually enjoyed going alone more than together. With politics, I have to go alone. He goes alone, and I'm beginning to view the political functions as time for him to be apart from me, and me to have alone time and other people time. If we ever live together, that's bad precedent.

June 3, 1981

We ran in the full moonlight. Both in the same direction having wondered if dealing with the real world and hard thoughts will wear down/destroy the magic.

Someday both our diaries will concern less of each other and love relationship thoughts and concentrate more on objective world thoughts—politics, law, leadership, etc. It takes an underlying commitment and security to free each of us to spend mental time apart. We'll get there. I hope I'll remember (and he too) that it won't mean there's no magic or that we're taking each other for granted; rather, loving has freed us.

He thinks a few months is too soon because of the work and politics. I think several months is too long because we'll know before that. I won't buy the work argument. The problem with politicians is that as a group they never seem to realize that there is always another session or a campaign or a coastal zone management crisis or a steel case trial. Besides, Bob and I know all we really need to know or can know about each other without really living together. It's a matter of deciding.

Will our feelings about each other change if the chase and go-away fears are removed? I wonder if Bob will want me nearly as much when he can have me. I suppose "tactically" it's not wise for me to promise fidelity and commitment in this strange between-time. But I want Bob to make decisions with as much calm as possible. Me too. The more time I spend with him, the more I'm generally convinced it's good and I want him.

June 4, 1981

Wild day together. First I had breakfast with Mark and Diane—fun. Then off to the ranch to move cows. I drove the truck while he worked on cow books. Picture: an intent look, brown cowboy hat, blue plaid shirt, gold glasses glinting in the Texas sun. I drove and was quiet so he could work, and have never loved him so totally, even though he was separate from me.

The truck broke down at a service station and Butch came out with his truck and the three of us finished hauling cows. I drank a lot of beer, my tongue got loose and I talked to them about Nepal. Bob and I sat in the cab of the truck and touched knees and hands surreptitiously. When we came home we drove around town to his different houses. The one he grew up in is so big! Some lights were on and I wondered about his mother whom he's always called "Honey." She seems formidable. The first house looked loving. In the Mt. Bonnell house he decided to run for Land Commissioner. And told his wife at the same time he told their neighbors. Wow. Not a way to tell your family.

June 5, 1981

At dinner I told Katie about Bob. She had guessed and said we were well suited. I'm in like! With Bob, my life, myself—except for overeating! Ugh.

I read in *Milagro* of lives intertwined, of the ordinariness which is the richness of living. And I realize how rich is life with Bob. Out the plane window, lightning makes the dark night sky burst pink momentarily. Somehow my longings turn to the ranch. I want to see the land, smell the rain there, even go alone without Bob if necessary.

June 7, 1981

A difference between us: I feel better after voicing aloud the hard thoughts. He feels better if we don't talk about them.

I don't want to be like April, but I feel somewhat scattered about work. When I made the list for *Seven Stories*, none were about lawyering. Significant.

June 8, 1981 (Midnight)

L: "I'm all yours."

B: "I'm all yours. Think about that."

Usually he says, "You have as much of me as there is available to give."

June 9, 1981 (Early morning)

Lying on the floor, I asked him about how it felt to own the ranch and then why he did politics. His answers rang truer on the subject of the ranch.

June 10, 1981—at Rod's house

Linda Ronstadt's "White Rhythm and Blues" filled the room in his East Austin shabby rent house. The music blared from a thousand dollar sound system and drifted across the bare linoleum living room floor. I smiled to myself at his decorating scheme (if the word scheme could be used—that implied a plan and this looked much more haphazard); didn't even qualify as early orange crate!

R: "Do you want to dance?"

L: "Old music, old love."

I slid into my ex-husband's arms. Falteringly at first, then with remembered moves, we danced round the floor. We were comfortable. Except that I wanted to lead, to see what it was like. Was that a sign of the independence I'd gained after almost seven years of living alone, or merely a resurgence of the lawyer-bitchy side? Even as the thought came and went, I laughed at the introspection. Leave it alone. When you wash your hands, wash your hands. When you go dancing, dance.

It felt good to be together. Solid. We both cared. And for the first time I felt no tinge of sadness underscoring the moments. No one could ever take his place in my life, yet I know I do not want to be married to him. Not in some never-never land story where we met again after ten years, not tomorrow. He's a remarkable man but we brought each other down. Old habits even today reassert themselves.

R: "You'll like Fleetwood Mac. They are like ABBA but much better."

L: (I'd been taping some ABBA songs.) "I do like Fleetwood. I just didn't recognize the songs as ones I'd liked on the radio."

R: "They're better musically than ABBA."

Frustrated, trying to not let the exchange slip into an old pattern, I looked up from my position on the floor by the tape deck, "I know *you* think they are better. That's one reason we aren't married."

It wasn't always like that. Only yesterday he had stopped by my small house on the other side of town. Over morning coffee we visited. He was animated and the happiest I'd seen him in a long time as he told me of his ski trip. The kitchen was warm and smelled of cinnamon rolls in the oven. A friend stopped by and the three of us scrunched into my small kitchen and added background conversation to the warmth surrounding the morning. Politics, law, local gossip—our worlds drifted in and out of the words, connected by circumstances (you can't practice law in the same town and not run into each other) and by caring. Alone again after company left, we poured the last cup of coffee. Vaguely I missed smoking and absentmindedly fiddled with the coffee spoon. A habit that used to drive him crazy.

R: "Well, how's it going?"

L: "I'm happy. This time it's serious. I told him I'd marry him.

Do you remember how it was when we were first in love? That little time ten years ago when aches and smiles mingled daily? Exponentially, that's how I feel. It's deeper than magic."

He looked long at me, "I felt that way for years."

A puzzled look from me.

"About you."

June 11, 1981 (4:00 a.m.)

We went out to dinner at La Tapatia. I got totally drunk. Can't remember all of what I said; a lot of it about kids. He said I should let him pursue me. I don't know how to do that. I'm worried I'll blow it by not understanding well enough the male-female pursuit game.

Our timing may be off. I'm ready to commit, but sense I may not feel like this forever. It's like being one half of a snap and you just hang out there waiting for the other half. If it doesn't come, eventually you just droop down and find a resting place or another snap. Ultimately, Bob will want me. But probably only when he can't have me.

Public things get to me. All this hurts my feelings even though I try not to let it. Should I try not to fight it? I told Diane that she should figure out how to make her lifestyle work, not change Mark now. Same is true here. I need to stop fighting every day the fact that Bob's still not divorced. I can't control that circumstance, but I can control my response and I'm making myself miserable and unhappy over it. In that sense it's my problem, not his. So I have to figure it out myself. On the other hand, it seems pretty normal to me to be a little hurt, jealous etc., when I'm tucked away in motel rooms.

Somehow I think he must view my feelings about the public stuff the way I view his fears of other men. Maybe I'm not ready to stop living alone anyway.

B: "I want to write a poem that says I can't love you always, but for now."

He played on all-ways, always/loving, I was afraid to ask if he meant really he'd love me always.

June 12, 1981

Last night with Sheila I was for the first time really angry at Bob, instead of hurt. Need to leave before my angry feelings drown out the good ones. He came by and we went to the office. I was so tired. Stared at the walls covered with old campaign literature and pictures. Everywhere reminders of his public life I can't share and his private life he can't leave. Thought about telling him how I felt, but decided there wasn't any point; I've said it before. And all repetition does is make *him* feel bad and *me* angry.

Important lesson: My attitude has been—"I feel bad, you have the power to fix it." It should be that *I* control how I feel.

June 13, 1981

Tonight I went through all the feelings again. Yes, I'm as sure as a person can be that I want him. And suddenly I felt sure that I was good for him. Even weighing in the children, Honey, and politics, I'm good for him and can make him happier, so he can make his own life happier. Tonight it seemed I should fight for him. Because we're right.

We really are special. With us, life will always be mysterious, growing. Should I learn to be more impatient? And he's good for me. I don't want to fight for him just to get him because my pride's hurt, or to prove something to myself or him. But maybe it's not good enough to just say "here I am" and offer myself. Maybe life demands more commitment, plunging in all the way, risking more hurt, but gaining more depth and glorious times. When he doubts or is so uncertain of direction, it makes me doubt. But right now I'm strong enough for us both.

June 14, 1981

It's good my job is so demanding these days, because Bob is strong too and part of me just wants to melt into his arms, his life. Truth: I'm beginning to feel that this really will never happen again. It's so special, so real.

During a discussion of honesty: We decided we really couldn't lie to each other. B: "The other day when you said you couldn't remember who told you you were svelte, I felt you knew it was David but hesitated to tell me." L: "Yes, I know you are a little jealous." Wow! We each *know* the other and if we're listening, can detect truth-levels.

June 15, 1981

McNeely and Bob looked at the cows last night.

M: (to B) "You are still one of my two heroes, Mo Udall and you. I still love you."

Two tough men who have the guts and understanding to recognize what's important and say "I love you."

June 16, 1981 (On plane: El Paso-Austin)

I'm angry, hurt. Never again will I ask the Question. Lay it out for hurt. On the plane I ache so much, it's the olden days, and I thought I'd grown since sixteen. After Bob dropped me at the airport, I walked into the ladies room. Took a long look. Fat thighs, tired face, sad, slightly drunk eyes. Realistically, what did I think anyway? I should give up the dream and learn a new one? Work hard. I shouldn't drink; it makes me feel sorry for myself. Yet even as I resolved to try not to hurt anymore, I watched every person board the plane longing for a glimpse of him. I don't think Bob understands this part of me at all.

June 17, 1981

Where are we? At Ruidoso, hard talk.

What kind of situation have I gotten into? More and more I can't imagine life without him, yet he keeps telling me he doesn't know what he'll do. It wears me out again.

Watching GWTW, we're even more than that.

Oh B, let's just love and live together. Tonight I miss you so much I can't stand it. Totally sober. Realistic. Oh, please come home to me.

June 18, 1981

Bob talked to the Governor. I wanted to know how the meeting went. A moment of anger: "You can come over here and have a drink with Bebe and me, or I'll meet you at home." L: "I'll come by." B: "Well . . . you can't if Sarah is still here." L: "I'll go home." B: "Good, that's better."

I was angry because I couldn't share an important moment. Felt stuffed back into the corner. Shabby.

June 19, 1981

Just finished *The Magic Journey* and although I know I should sleep, it seems important to write.

I missed Bob with an intenseness that's frightening when I put the book down. Wandered into the bathroom, gazed at the softly gleaming wooden bedroom floors. The orderliness of the little house calms me. But winds blew and strange noises rattled my calmness. Here at this turning point in my life, I own nothing of great value. But tonight I understand that nothing of real value is own-able. I'm sparse, finally. Without realizing it, leanness has crept up and almost found me. I'm not like Virgil and April; my work, though meaningful to me, does not infuse my existence with meaning. When I search for what does, questioning my activities for value, the closer I come to the answer that the *meaning* is in the *living*. Just and only that. But it's a terrible and awesome joy to live it alone. That's where love fits in. If meaning is in the living, then living is altered, rounded out, made compassionate by loving. Our relationship is the humanizing element, the centering to make life, in its awesome richness, palatable.

What's important to me? We are. I want the connection with him, I want to share and care and lean on and support and love. To know that despite the ultimate aloneness, he'll go through it with me. I not only want it, I need it. And after Nepal, I understand that need enough to leave Bob if I have to in order to find it. Because all the insights into life's mysteries, all the lawsuits won or lost, yes, even the sunsets, pale in the face of one glance, eye to eye connecting us, or one hand, touching mine.

I don't know if *he* understands this. It doesn't matter if he does or doesn't. What matters is that I do, and have learned to cherish.

Tonight, in bed amidst my non-acquisitions, I feel compelled to take stock. In thirty-two years I've nothing particular to show for them. At least outwardly. My wits are more finely tuned, my sense of compassion more discriminating, my living skills much better. I leave no tangible markings on this earth, no great pictures, no novel, no children. In one sense, it doesn't matter. We're all part of the whole and each contributes and is the beneficiary of all others' endeavors. On a less cosmic level, is it important for me to leave something tangible? I sense a "yes" answer, but—not sure yet.

Flowers arch in a long curve, away from the brown bottle that serves as their vase. The curve evokes mind pictures of Bob first sitting, then lying in the New Mexico dusk, trying to capture a fiery soon-becoming-pink sunset. His body was a series of curves: camera to hand, to elbow, to hip, to thigh, to feet. So lovely in his momentary perfection that I ached. And in a drunken state, tried to sketch the curves on the back of a bank statement I'd hurriedly thrust into my purse.

Tonight we lay quietly in a love letter together. He said he'd had a heavy moment driving the twisted road to the lake thinking about our twisted path.

June 20, 1981

Went to Bob's office tonight where he made phone calls and I threw an emotional tantrum. Then as the distance between us was getting big, I reached over and buried my face in his chest. (A neat trick with glasses!) He touched my head and said, "One reason is because we're both tired." And then, words out, (I told him I was angry, upset about the secrecy), I was okay.

There is some dynamic going on. I think I'm testing him to see if he'll still love me through those tantrums. And he meets me at every turn. So maybe now I don't need to have them?

At El Rancho, we talked. About each ripping the other. He was gorgeous tonight. Hair flopping on his face, white shirt, clear eyes, young looking. He said he's afraid I'll rip him and not know it. I don't think so. He held me and said, "There'll never be another you."

Let me write for a moment of the passion. We have found in our bodies, the other half of our minds and souls. Unlocked pieces of personhood before untapped. In the quest and sweetness of touch and taste and smell, there's a reality beyond the words.

June 23, 1981

Hectic work week, but Bob's wonderful.

B: "Knoxie (his Labrador) won't stay in that perfectly beautiful back yard I have. She jumped the fence and now that she knows what's outside, she won't remain inside. (Long pause.) Sort of like life before you."

Last night we bought rubber boots at Academy Surplus, then fed the stock at Georgetown. He put together the Red chain saw while I got high on Dry Sack and read Nemerov and *Labyrinth of Solitude* aloud. We clowned around for a moment. Then he sat down, looked at me and said, "Do you have any idea how much I love you? You women are all alike. You think you're the only ones who know how to love. You're so caught up in loving me that you don't realize how much I love you."

June 26, 1981

At the political reception, I freaked out. Once again I was all alone, facing a crowd of people I didn't know and having to pretend. Couldn't do it. I can't handle planned direct public contacts. Then saw Bob with McNeely and someone else so I couldn't even explain to him why I was leaving. The situation just devastated me.

I drove home trying to hold back the tears and hurt and anger. The place in my chest started to ache fiercely and I began the old "men-always-rip-you" litany. I heard all of my friends and family reproaching me, "You'll get hurt," and felt foolish I'd not heeded anyone's advice. And thought that I never wanted to open up again like this. The risk is too great. I swore I'd get out if this started happening. The pent-up sobs and tears racked my chest. Couldn't go to Sheila; she'd just told me she didn't want to see me go through this. Went to Bebe and stood leaning against the railing to the upstairs and cried, hard.

July 1, 1981 (8:30 a.m., *beautiful*, sunny morning)

We're going to make it. I'm going to make it. The sun is here.

Yesterday we worked cows, sold ten, delivered nine to a buyer. Now the Liberty Hill set of cows is really fine. I've learned to wander in and among them relatively fearlessly.

B: "I'm just as trapped by my situation as you are." That's true, but a major difference is that he *controls* it and can decide otherwise if that's what he wants. B (in front of the fireplace logs we'd finished stacking): "These logs soaked up sun in New Mexico so they could throw it off later in light and warmth here." (And he doesn't think he's a poet!)

It's important to try to lose weight and stay small. Psychologically, right now, that's important because I can handle most things if I don't feel fat.

In the truck I thought, "Why are you so trusting? He'll probably be like all men and you'll be left with a giant hole in your soul." I wanted to talk with him about it, but was afraid to. Need to learn to talk of those things in the sunshine, sober, not at the end of a long cow day when he's just sold $8,000 worth of cows and watched his herd program finally work after so many years. Need to keep joyful times pure. But I also set myself up for hurt. I desperately wanted him to ask how I was, then when he did, I wouldn't tell him out of fear of sounding morose/down/pushy. I can't have it both ways. If I want him to notice and be aware of moods and ask, then I need to be open enough to tell him.

Anyway, as I fumbled in my mind about our life, etc., worried about what I'd do, what had happened to me, I realized that I really don't have a major single endeavor outside of work like Bob has the ranch. And I've never really considered having one other than writing. But that is exactly what happened to Nancy and Diane. Women often don't think past work and babies. Then we don't really explore life's fullest long-range possibilities. I want to think about all that.

When the storm hit last night, we were filling the truck with gas. We heard it coming in the wind. Then rain whipped around us. We had fed the cows in the lightning by flashlight. An incred-

ible sight: flash of lightning to see Bob stark against the lighted nighttime background, kneeling at a bale of hay and surrounded by cows
(good looking ones!). Number 19's calf let me pet him. A bunch. I
want to be *right here.*

July 2, 1981

Can't believe I'm beginning to be totally honest with Bob about
sex. I always sort of hoped my therapist would ask and let me work
through it, but he never probed and apparently I must be as well
adjusted as most, or appear to be. Running, I told Bob I'd always
thought of sex as something that was done to me, not with me, or
for me. A telling statement. That really forms the basis of the separateness. I wonder if I'm alone in those feelings. Do women in
general feel them? Do men?

July 3, 1981

Driving back from breakfast with Mark and Diane, I perceived
that I need resolution soon.

Tonight I ached. We react differently. He plays the guitar; I watch
the white of his teeth gleam as he plays. And watch his naked wedding ring finger dance across the strings. I wonder if loving is worth
the pain. Maybe to be most fully him and most fully me, we need to
be apart, live our separate lives. But then I don't ever want men
again. As I look at this boyish, bluejeaned, bespectacled man, I realize how much is riding on this relationship. I'm ready to close up if
we don't work. Maybe a child really is the only person who can
love you and be loved honestly and without fear, at least in the
beginning. Love and learn. Let go? Or hold back? Sometimes when
he pops in and out like tonight, he's like a shadow. There's not
enough time to catch hold. Maybe that's what was so hard on his
wife. Never actually connecting for a long time.

Sometimes I want to say, "Take your children and your mother
and go home and let my heart heal."

July 6, 1981

On the business trip I realized that just having Bob wasn't

enough to make life meaningful, that my work and other relation-ships were also important. But I don't know how to do it all right now.

July 10, 1981

When I'm out in public and recognized as a person, myself, I feel like a newborn puppy or calf, sort of shaking off the birth, wet and new and glad to look around. It's as if a weight has lifted and I can laugh and joke around and be *me*. Being a shadow to Bob—at the Texas Hatters, when we travel—has been harder on me than I realized.

July 12, 1981

All the pursued/pursuer stuff—that's just words. We're beyond that. We just don't quite know how to express in words where we are. What prompted my remark was his willingness to let me go, and "help you go if that's what you want." Somehow I always thought he'd at least ask me to *consider* staying.

July 14, 1981

When I write like this I suddenly discover I don't know a lot about what Bob thinks or feels. We spend talk-time and emotional time on the wrong issues. He worries I'll run off, and I tell him things or do things to just barely trigger that fear. So that he'll think about how he wouldn't like that. He, on the other hand, concen-trates on the fact of my possible leaving, rather than *why* I might leave. Reminds me of concentrating on being fat rather than being healthy!

Looking at the up side:

B: "Do you think we're going to quit?"

L: "I don't know. It's like being afraid to hope you made an A; if you admit to thinking you did okay, you won't. Do *you* think we're going to quit?"

B: (Pause) "I don't think so."

Of course, I wondered what he meant since he'd just said he wasn't getting divorced soon. Does he mean he thinks we'll just go along like this?

I don't understand why he won't just file. He's clear and says his wife is too, that the marriage is over; that's why he moved out. If children complicate things that seem so simple, do I really want some of my own someday? He says it's love for them that makes him go slowly, with caution.

July 15, 1981

Hysteria day. Absolutely fell to pieces, weeping and wailing all day. Couldn't keep the tears from falling. Talked with Bebe, Sheila, considered seriously quitting with Bob. But know that if I walk away, I have to mean it. Catch 22: For me to leave, I have to decide I won't run back if he whistles. But he probably won't move unless I leave.

Sometimes I think those of us who live alone have gone a little crazy. Thinking all the time. People who live with people don't have that luxury.

I stuck my stomach out; I'm fat these days and it looked pregnant. That's all I'd need. When he called, just as I was feeling like I could go on, he made the ache start up all over again. That's the pain that will wrench us apart.

The problem with books like *Final Payments* is that they don't mention those of us who live forever-suspended in the hurt stage, who subject ourselves over and over again to the same tears.

An old man was hit by a car in front of the Kash Karry. It looked serious. Life's fragility frightens.

July 16, 1981

This morning his face looked old and almost tired when I told him I was thinking of quitting. He said my name. And I knew I could never really leave him on my own. He told me an old story of his entering Landis' classroom saying, "Landis, I'm sorry I drove off with your math books," thereby relieving Landis of any embarrassment. Oh, he's so fine.

July 18, 1981

Thoughts from the women's evening: I like all those women

individually, but as a group, they're too many women without men. KW and P were the only men present and I felt funny. Wondered how Bob would fit in. They talked about him briefly.

July 20, 1981

Bob doesn't tell me how he feels. "Why cut down the most beautiful Christmas tree just because you can't have the star?" L: "Because someday I want a star."

July 22, 1981

Saw Paul yesterday. He thinks that although I've set myself too fast a timetable, my wanting to change jobs, buy a house, and have Bob make a decision, clearly indicate I'm ready for a change. True.

Looked at cows with Mike Levi. Beautiful fire-hot sunset. "Jillions" of cows, calves cavorting.

July 23, 1981

The oneness/consciousness feeling came again two nights ago. Bob and I watched a storm and lightning show at the ranch. Liberty Hill was glorious, lit up by flashes that outlined her hills and valleys. The martin house was stark against the sky.

Bob tossed blown-down tree limbs across the wire fence. Each of his movements was deliberate, calm, effective. Tree limbs soared over the top wire and then as he let go, they appeared to fly into the lightning/night on their own for a moment, before the trajectory dipped back earthbound. Over and over I watched him toss limbs effortlessly. (I tried a small one; it's harder than it looks.)

Bob understands "how things work." For example, arms lifting at just such an angle lifts trees the best. This attitude must infuse his life. He controls his existence through an instinctive gut-control over his environment.

July 24, 1981

After our run, he sat at the typewriter and rewrote a paragraph I'd left in it a few days ago. He wrote at the end that I was a part of his existence, like breathing. Oh, Bob. It's growing.

Yesterday, I asked for the lessons on how to catch him. Never asked before, although the offer's been out since I soaped his calves in El Paso passion. B: "The first postulate is that I have to decide whether *I* want to catch you."

August 1, 1981

Bob looks different. Older in a "wiser" sense. In his eyes, I see some new things. He seems more serious. We were as in love last night at the Sonic burger, as we were in the beginning. Probably more.

August 6, 1981

I sobbed so hard my throat hurts. Alone. Desperately needing Bob. He's unreachable. At a political party, I want to throw bottles at the wall and break them. Scream out loud. Something to make the hurt go away and the tears stop. What's happened to me? I swore I'd never cry like this over someone again. So here I am, hardly able to write as I sit crouched on my bed. The week was too hard, with no time for ordinary fun with Bob. I really needed him and he's not been there. Just making my own life more active and involved isn't the answer. I want some stability and peace and normalcy. This time the tears were sparked by dinner with Luke. He told me of a party last night. And it was so lonely sitting at the dinner table. Couldn't find Sheila or Rod, the only two people I can really go to. Sat at my desk and just couldn't do anymore. So left and barely made it home as the racking sobs came. I can't let others see me like this, because all I get are "I told you so's."

Tonight, I wanted him to know that I resented all the social events lately. I'm as important as they are. It is like Tim all over. He claims he'd rather be with me, then chooses not to. Lately, I feel like a quick stop to be scheduled in. I can't live like this much longer. I'm numb now.

What's the matter with me? I spent all week scrambling for a few hours when I wouldn't have to do chores or work, and now they're here, I fall apart.

"Success is survival." Read *Time*, pondered oil companies, rising prices, inflation. At least I'm calm and tired. And made it through by myself. Need to be in a calm mood to talk with Bob about us.

August 8, 1981

Driving to the ranch, we spoke of the children:

B: "Shannon still talks to me. Martha Louise is going away. Part of it is a boyfriend."

L: "But she'll come back an adult you can talk to differently."

B: "That makes me want to cry."

Someday, ML, if you ever read all this about your father, know that he almost cried thinking of your growing up. As I write that, I can see Bob's face all aglow when he told me about holding ML, "She was just a handful."

I don't think I could live without Bob in my life. He sent me two pink roses, gorgeous, with the card reading, "A rare pair."

August 11, 1981

Bob isn't well. The chest tightness is there; his exposed tooth is giving him problems; sore throat. I wanted to take care of him and put him to bed last night. Sometimes when I think of all the early mornings he comes over here, I'm amazed. He really does love me and shows it. We went to the office together last night, and both worked. I looked over at his worn face in his chair and loved him Beyond.

Oh the exquisite magic of the everyday. Thought about how if we had a child, we'd lose much freedom. I want some years with Bob first.

The Dink calf has lost his black nose.

August 12, 1981

Yesterday at twilight we took a perfect walk to look at Number 8, Mr. Barton's bull. An LCRA gate perched on a rock to relieve the strain, blocked the car from going into the field. Bob carefully put his tan pants leg over the side fence and jumped over. I followed.

We walked through a flint field and looked for arrowheads.

Our inability to do ordinary things together makes me appreciate them more. Do others gain so much pleasure in keeping house, or eating a meal together, as I do with Bob?

At breakfast, Rod and I spoke of the age difference. Rod thinks I may become a "permanent mistress" and attaches no value significance one way or the other to that appellation. I don't think people generally know what I'm talking about when I speak of Bob. And so I've become more private.

At the stoplight, I paused and a chill passed over as I wondered how truly rare it was to love and accept another. In years past ("in my youth" sounds so pretentious), I set out with optimistic abandon and assumed life would be filled with loves and emotions and good people. Now I look about me and see that yes, for me, that has been true. Not so for everyone. K, K, B, S, the women alone who are not content to be that way, pile up in my consciousness. I've been lucky.

August 13, 1981
   Assorted thoughts:
1. On selfishness and work ethic: Lately, I've worked so hard and been so pressured I don't feel particularly selfish. Yet I question whether Bob and I are "moral" in our quest for personal satisfaction in life. The self-centered quest (best represented by these journals?) that is purported to be the bane of American character these days. I thought about this in the context of having children. I'm told children automatically make one less selfish. But it seems silly to have kids to improve one's moral standing.
2. Drinking wine with Bob, I wondered how drastically Bob's and my relationship would change if we had a baby. Bob loves my independence and "lawyerness." Would I be as interesting and acceptable as a mother?
3. Lefty wants Bob to run for Lieutenant Governor. The politics aspect gives me a glitch. First, I worry for Bob. A major statewide campaign is tough stuff. Then I worry because he'd stay married and not risk political consequences of divorce. And if he did get

divorced, it would be some pretty dramatic changes rather quickly to divorce and then run without any recuperating intervening time.

August 14, 1981

I'm discontent these days. Too much pressure at work, although it's getting better. And not enough normal time with Bob. We're constantly doing errands and chores. They're fun, but I never feel as if there is time to just "be" and discuss where we are.

August 16, 1981

Bob cried this afternoon when I told him how much I hurt and how I thought I maybe should leave. Only the second time I have ever seen him do that. After he left, I lay on the bed utterly spent and then panicked at the thought that I might have run him away and might never see him again.

Bob said he doesn't ache. Only glitches when we can't do something. We're very different that way. Part of me was glad he cried today. I wasn't sure if he felt all this. Momentarily, I felt guilty feeling that, but it's not wrong. There's value to touching feelings; not that life has to be painful, but that sometimes pain is a part.

The other side died a little when the tears came from him. I was overwhelmed and wanted him to never feel pain or cry because of me or anything I'd caused. I wanted to hold him and let the sobs come all out and be there and love him and have him know that.

Once on a test, Shannon answered, "My father makes me feel loved." Telling me, Bob's mouth curved gently up and I was proud of him. She also answered that she wished her father would be home more and would not be gone so much. Part of today's hard thoughts for me were based on Bob's telling me that. He hurt or seemed to feel guilty and I thought how is he ever going to be divorced and feel okay?

August 18, 1981

Only because I am assured I will see him in the morning can I sleep tonight.

August 19, 1981

Sometimes I feel as if Bob does to me the same things I assume he did to his wife in not bringing things up or in avoiding hard conversations, but unlike her, I won't live in that pattern. I want more from a partner. Someone who wants to share his hopes and dreams and who wants to know mine.

Earlier, I went to the intramural field and gazed out at the expanse of green we'd covered so often together. The morning was quiet and still. I couldn't make that run alone today.

August 20, 1981

Tonight Bob looked at me clear-eyed as he lay on the bed. I felt assessed. The ultimate question is whether I'm worth it to him. And only he can make that choice. I'm scared.

Considered going back to Paul. But there's not much he could do or say. Career stuff will have to bow out for some personal time. We need tomorrow.

August 21, 1981

As time goes on, I am more and more private about my feelings for Bob. They're between us. He told me he'd like to really live with me sometime. I love him.

August 22, 1981

Ran a slow three this morning. On returning to the house, I slumped over the car's steering wheel and cried again. I no longer believe Bob the way I used to. He's choosing his life and not choosing me.

I'm no longer willing to stand aside and say fine, I love you, do what you need to do. I've said, if you want me you have me—heart, soul, body, commitment. And he's consistently said, I'd like to, but I can't and I'm not sure I want to do what it would take to have you.

Once again, I've not listened carefully to men's words or heeded their actions. It's just like Tim. Not enough time—work, politics, children—whatever the reason. Bob is doing to me now what I suspect he did to his wife for years. With good reasons, shoved each of us back to "have fun" at whatever the current endeavor is. I'm not sure if he knows what commitment means between two adults. I know he's committed to the kids and to the ranch, but beyond that, I don't know. He complains of the pace. But he's the only one who controls it.

August 24, 1981

Strange events. Stared at Mike Whoever's hairy ass through his swimsuit yesterday afternoon at the kiddy pool with Diane. Later, Bob looked tired and gorgeous, decked out in faded blue jeans, blue shirt and white tennies. He's scrunched and pressured and probably needs me not to be. When we got to the office he began reading, and suddenly I couldn't stand it anymore. I got up and, crying, said I was going home, that I wasn't going to come to the office to watch him open mail. We leaned against the side wall in the dark room lit only by the Capitol's nighttime glow and tried to connect. He said he doesn't think of me as his mistress. L: "But I feel like one." B: "I know."

We're both changing so much. Can we keep growing together? In the midst of all the crises occurring, I feel we haven't taken time to take stock of us, of where our relationship is going.

I'm thinking of quitting to write in the middle of all this. Am I crazy? The mother-road-to-Agra story is bubbling up.

September 1, 1981

Finally, yes, there will be a divorce petition filed this fall, but the actual divorce will take some time, he says. This is hard, sad, wrenching for Bob. He's putting a name on the reality of his life. I think worry about the children causes most of his pain. He never speaks ill of his wife, so all I know is the witty, fun side, the great mother, etc. Surely there is a dark piece, but I suspect I'll never know it. All I understand after being divorced from Rod is that no one outside a marriage has a clue to what's really happening.

The day Rod and I got divorced, we went to court, then ate dinner together. We'd been separated a year and were no longer angry, or even hurt as much as we were so deeply sad. The next day I stayed home from work, played old records and cried. Not wanting to still be married, but remembering the early times.

What does Bob think or feel?

September 15, 1981

Heavy work schedule. Heavy politics. Too tired to write.

October 12, 1981

Bob is running for Governor. Of Texas. The second largest state in the union. With some luck, lots of work and commitment, he's got a good chance to win. (In writing, I'm cautious. All along I've felt it to be inevitable that he'll win. My internal questions reach beyond that moment, to ask, what then?)

Important things:

1. The kids are behind him.
2. He's clearly the best man/person for the job.
3. We can walk away intact if he loses because we'll run the best we can and give our all.

Hard thing: Dinner for Manatt in San Antonio—these people didn't care what the prospective gubernatorial candidate stood for—only that they could "own" a governor.

October 26, 1981

Events:

I ran ten miles yesterday—1:41—last two-and-one-half alone.

The night before Bob was to announce, after he had been in McAllen, El Paso and Austin flying through rough weather, the money people came in at 5:00 p.m. and told him there wasn't any money for the Governor's race. And that there was for Lieutenant Governor. Bob listened, then decided to go ahead and run for Governor. Later, the speech wouldn't jell, so we stopped by Sara's for a beer. We were greeted instead by a barrage of facts—on how badly organized the campaign was and how people were upset terribly by me, my existence, etc. It was pretty rough and tough stuff. I wanted to cry, but didn't. Certainly not in front of Sara—and later, more importantly, not in front of Bob when he was committed still to rising at 6:00 a.m. to work on an announcement speech.

Neither of us could sleep. But I *thought* he was sleeping (snoring indicated it falsely he later claimed) and went downstairs to brood. Recalling Paul's advice, I tried to work rather than think, and wrote an outline of a speech. Then, as I thought, it became clear to me that we shouldn't make this race. If it were true that we had no money and no organization, it would be too tough.

But I was afraid to wake Bob and tell him. I called Jackie. She listened without comment. I lay awake until 4:00, trying to decide if my judgment were too clouded with the personal. At 6:00, he awoke; in the shower I mumbled my misgivings. He, too, had been awake. He called Lefty, et al. And he called off the announcement.

That was last Wednesday night and Thursday. Tonight is Monday. The day before my thirty-third birthday. A long year, a tough year, a good (?) year.

Goals for next year!

1. Aim for serenity of soul—seek a quiet place within to give me strength so I can give strength back.
2. Maintain diet/food/alcohol control.
3. Try not to take things too personally.
4. Strive to be less petty in my jealousies.
5. Run one-half marathon.
6. Control my work life more productively.
7. Try to be less insecure about Bob—maybe the losing is reciprocal.
8. *Stop* feeling sorry for myself in down times. *Act*, not mull.
9. Pray each day.

October 30, 1981

Bob gave me a *gorgeous* garnet and diamond ring for my birthday! To replace the stolen one of yesteryear. In the midst of redistricting, he found time to shop and buy it. I'd been in Houston taking Senator Ogg's deposition v. Joe Jamail. We went to Jeffrey's at the supper break. Though tired I was so pleased we could have a real b-day time. Although we've changed in our everydayness, I'm as much in love as ever.

November 8, 1981

1. Gave Bob a Celestron telescope for his birthday. I told him if he intended to reach for the stars, he ought to be able to see them! I managed to organize a surprise b-day lunch at the Raw Deal. He was astounded. He walked in to a table of his oldest and dearest friends—from Butch of the ranch to Reavley, to McNeely, to Mike Levi, Cactus, Lefty, et al.

2. BYO-Bedroll campout with Lena G., Debbie W. and Barbara. The politics is heavy. I'm torn between wanting to express anticipation and concern over the possibility of a race where I'd be a potential First Lady, and fear that anything I say will be misinterpreted because of the impending divorce.

December 10, 1981

Bob announced for Governor December 7. Press response is excellent; money is difficult. Hard day today. Attorney General Mark White is to announce he'll run, too. That means I must quit my job as Chief of the Antitrust Division. I can't work for him while he runs against Bob. Mixed feelings. Good to leave—bad financially. Upset because I can't go through a campaign as the mistress. But as usual, after talking to Bob, things are better. He called back from Longview and said, "I love you." It really mattered.

Risk-taking is a large part of my life.

Christmas 1981

We're together! At the moment, Bob is at Honey's with the kids for Christmas dinner. I went home yesterday—a joyous Christmas with Daddy sober. Mother and I closed the door to my old bedroom and drank the bottle of airline wine she'd saved from Nepal. We reminisced on our trip times together—Guatemala, Nepal, climbing to Lake William, skiing. She said she had learned from me that fun things took effort and determination in a good sense. The rest of the family banged on the door. We laughed and told them we were wrapping presents!

Another highlight was shooting the BB gun with Daddy. Fun! And I sent Nana a little Polaroid camera. For the first time in ninety-four years, she will take a picture! When I spoke with her in California she was planning her first two pictures and promised to send me one.

Bob gave me *cowboy boots*! Hooray! Mother gave us lots of cute cups—labeled "The Gov.," "A+," etc.

Would prefer not to write of it now, but best get it recorded. I resigned my job at the AG's office effective February 1, 1982. There were serious indications that if I didn't, some office politicos would find a "reason" to fire me at a time most damaging to Bob's campaign. I cried. But it's time to leave there anyway.

New Year's Eve 1981

I hurt. No divorce. Ups and downs emotionally have worn me out. Today told J. C. I wouldn't be handling his case since I was resigning. Then at the campaign headquarters it was tense and awkward as they discussed Bob's going to Houston for the mayoral inauguration. Implicit was that I was not to go, as he was going to be in a VIP section. My pain is composed of feeling bad, then feeling guilty for those feelings. Bob couldn't like this any more than I do, but it is difficult not to turn on him in my mind. Being the gubernatorial candidate's mistress is extremely painful. I am beginning to loathe politics and am fearful of telling Bob. What's the matter with me? I'm right back where I used to be before Paul. This sounds too awfully maudlin and melodramatic—but so is my life at the moment.

January 4, 1982

The New Year turned out much better than expected. Bob and I opened a bottle of champagne and sat, cross-legged, on the floor and toasted each other and ate crusty French bread and cheese. Later we took little Shannon to Larimore's for New Year's Eve and then to the ranch. Vaccinated and moved the bulls to Georgetown. Up and down my moods swing. It's better when I don't concentrate on the hard parts. Lefty said I can't go to Fort Worth for Farmer's Union. But Bob did mention getting married!

January 6, 1982

Car stereos robbed, but mental attitude better.

January 7, 1982

An up day! Cold but fire going. Walked into the office after a dental appointment and found the folks all seated at the conference table obviously plotting something nice for the party. Made me feel good.

January 19, 1982

Campaign going on. Tired.

January 26, 1982—4:00 a.m.

I want to quit the race. The lack of money and our living together is killing the campaign and us. Each day I struggle to get through to the next one. Even Bob has become affected. He's been down, worried about ultimate finances. Decided to send Landis to board at St. Stephen's. I know that decision bothered Bob, since it makes it more difficult for him to see Landis for spur of the moment activities.

I am utterly helpless and frustrated at the moment. My existence is causing so many people pain, and ruining the campaign. I told Bob I'd move out to Dallas, or go to Mexico, and more and more that course of action seems warranted. I'm so embarrassed by my life now. Perhaps Bob is right and God is punishing us for the sin of living together unmarried.

The federal Department of Justice ruled that Texas' redistricting was not legal. Ugh.

February 2, 1982

Peyton McKnight, who had announced his candidacy for Governor earlier, withdrew today; Buddy Temple filed to run for Governor against Bob and Mark. Ann Richards filed to run for Treasurer. Actually, she did so after we called her at 6:00 a.m. upon seeing the headlines screaming that the current Treasurer was going to be indicted. I woke Bob and said we needed a woman on the ticket. So he called Ann. She will do well. I hope.

My going away party was fantastic. Picture: mother at sixty-three dancing at the Broken Spoke.

Campaign back-room lines: (1) "Having "Joe Smith" on your side is like having a rabid seeing-eye dog"; (2) "Our prior Governor's appointees had room temperature IQ's."

February 4, 1982

I hate this. I just want to be alone. And decompress. The newest political rumor is that Mark White's political minions are telling women's groups: "He tried to keep good women lawyers—except Bob Armstrong's live-in, Linda Aaker, quit. He was sorry she left; she's a good lawyer."

Lena and Bragg both told me that at the headquarters. My feelings were terribly hurt, but I tried not to show it. I need to figure out what I can do and do it. Today I took some things to headquarters for my desk/workplace, and I was shuffled everywhere. Drifting in the campaign.

February 5, 1982

Up and down days. Discord on whether to do the Buddy Temple resignation press release. Lefty really wants him to do it. Clentine, George Christian advise not to. Lefty intimated he'd quit. My stomach hurt.

Tonight I had a case of the lonesomes for Bob. First time this week. I hope when this is over, we have a life *together*. Slowly I have come to realize I don't have the gut-strength for this political business. It's too hard. Also, I don't want to be Governor and haven't a clue whether I want to be First Lady.

February 12, 1982

The Austin fundraiser was an incredible success. Landis came from school and Mrs. Armstrong came. They looked cute standing next to Bob. This was the first time I've had a glimmer of the "up" side to politics. It must really be a power trip to have all those folks for you!

February 23, 1982

The divorce was granted February 18. Bob seemed more drained than he was willing to let on. Each child seemed relatively okay when he called to relay the news. I'll never feel okay about all of this.

Today, running, I thought Bob might really be Governor. Strange thought.

Lunch with Meg. Intellectual. Should be running herself soon. But tremendous sense of good judgment about her.

Tonight I had dinner with Kay, Kathie and Katie. Fun, calming to see old friends.

Lefty called to say Bob had done dynamite in Big Spring. Daralyn Davis: "Why didn't you tell us in Galveston you could do this?" Also told me he and Bob were going to borrow the $179,000 necessary for media. I felt lonely. These are long nights without Bob. Wonder what he's thinking walking the empty stretches of Texas around Big Spring tonight.

Today I was yelled at by a Legend—Barbara Jordan. I called to ask if she would do an endorsement piece for Bob, along with Sarah Weddington, Martha Smiley, Liz Carpenter and others. She yelled like God. She may be God. But she said, "Of course." And it was okay.

February 28, 1982

Willie Nelson said he'd give a concert for Bob. We drove out to Willie's place at Pedernales Falls and Bob joined Willie and his friends for a poker game. We were really short on cash, and I told Bob he only had $20 to waste. Later, he told me he played terrific poker to stay in a long time on that $20! Willie's new album, *Always on my Mind*, had just come back from the record company. We looked at the proposed cover and talked of the fundraiser:

B: "What money do you need up front?"

W: "Nothing—we'll give you the profits after expenses."

B: "But what can we do to help?"

W: "Why—just show up! And maybe your people can help sell tickets!"

WOW! He has nice brown eyes and a firm handshake. Bob was up. $1,000 from Levi.

March 10, 1982—The Jupiter Effect Day!

Willie said he'd rather give a check. That's okay. It would be $25,000.

Bob is tired. So are we all. The campaign goes well considering how incredibly on a shoestring we are. Bob doesn't ever want to run again. His balance and good humor are amazing.

April 13, 1982

Worried about posture of things. Fear I'm becoming typical candidate wife-type. Ugh. At ranch during filming campaign commercial, decided I didn't want to live this way. Tough.

April 18, 1982

Endorsed today by *Dallas Times Herald* and *Austin American Statesman!* Also last week by *El Paso Herald Post* and *Marble Falls Highlander!* It looks like he'll be endorsed by all but two papers. (Wish people would read them.)

May 13, 1982

Bob lost the primary election. Maybe won in life. Guess I'll go back to work at the Antitrust Division. But not as Chief. There is a price for playing politics.

May 30, 1982—2:00 a.m.

Can't sleep because I'm worried about Landis. Bob talked a long time tonight with some relatives who say the kids paint a story of never having time with their dad—without me being along. They're probably right. But I get pissed at Bob. He talks of missing Landis, but he won't go on a schedule or force the issue and take responsibility for the decisions. He lets someone else decide, and then convinces himself that it's the best way.

And where do I fit in? Tonight I went to a party that made me feel good about myself for the first time in a long while—but instead of having that moment, I'm up at 2:00 a.m. worrying about Bob's kids. And feeling guilty, which I *don't* like. If Bob wants to change things, he should do it. But he was great to help me through the last few days. It must be tough on him.

June 25, 1982

Bob has a beard. I'm heavy, but becoming happier. Ordinariness feels fine, for a moment.

June 29, 1982

Bob sings, I ponder.

July 5, 1982

Have definitely decided I want a baby. Tried to tell Bob. Not sure if he really understands.

The moon is white-faced, full, round tonight with white clouds racing across the inky sky. Chance to see the eclipse.

Gave my mother an electric typewriter for her sixtieth birthday. She was dumbfounded!

September 17, 1982

Wonderful dancing time at Senator Bentsen fundraiser! Didn't want to go, then met Michael Murphy and danced—it was great to let go and just have fun! Bob seemed nervous about it, although I tried to reassure him. Besides, I told Murphy I was safe to dance with because I was "madly in love with Bob."

September 20, 1982

I feel I'm slipping into a depression and can't get help. At least I no longer blame Bob for my feelings. I need to take control of my life—workwise. The success syndrome has caught up with me, and I feel lacking. Haven't made it in the "real" world. Surely I'm not alone in this?

September 23, 1982

Exciting and special dinner with John Henry Faulk and D. Bragg and Bob. J. H. spoke of justice and history and law—and how much having a son at age fifty-six meant to him.

For years I thought my goal was to be the power/person/woman behind the scenes or a man. But I was quiet in my aspiration. Now perhaps I've achieved this and am without a new challenge. Or rather, am scared to take on a new one—or to define it.

October 15, 1982

Strange unsettling times. Work goes progressively better, although I think it is mostly because I have too much to do and can't think about it.

Pat D, Diane, Deb and I had dinner and watched "My Brilliant Career" on TV. We had a WONDERFUL time. Women together are unique when in tune. We laughed till our sides hurt.

I'm bothered still by not being married and being childless. Bob shows no signs of changing that. My feelings are hurt. We're no longer in "magic love." When will men ever learn that the romantic words mean so much and add to the physical intensity of lovemaking?

This is sort of silly. I'm actually fairly happy. Am running well—three miles in 23:14! (under eight's) Permanent done, and am wearing my contacts again!

November 3, 1982—Day After Election

Mark White won overwhelmingly. Bob is ecstatic for the party. I was grudging about it last night; today am tired and resigned. It feels strange to think that I'll be out of politics, or at least that Bob will be now. Somewhere inside I had harbored thoughts that MW would lose and Democrats would rally around Bob. On the other hand, it will be nice to be private.

Very mixed tired feelings right now. Am proud of Bob for the person he is.

November 9, 1982

Gave Bob a diamond stickpin for his birthday. Also a Walkman and flowers. He's feeling old, I fear. After the Y meeting, I was so *angry* at women for not participating more in civic activities to control their environment.

November 12, 1982

Bob asked me to marry him last night at the Chili Parlor. On November 11, a lucky day. I didn't believe him at first. But he meant it—and I said yes. WOW! I'm HAPPY!

November 15, 1982

Everyone is happy about the wedding plans. January 8 is the big day. It is nice to feel calm about it.

December 21, 1982

Thoughts of marriage mingle with thoughts of work-related problems. Bob is wonderful; my family becoming more close and important to me.

December 29, 1982

Much happened in eight days. On the 22nd both Bob and his mother went into the hospital; she with a heart attack, he with ventricular tachycardia experienced while on a treadmill stress test. They did an angiogram that revealed the heart of a seventeen-year-old. But the doctor told me the tachycardia was life-threatening, put him in ICU. Then told me some of the prescribed drugs could have a side effect of impotence. A lot to take in twenty-four hours. That night between 3:30 a.m. and 6:00, I cried alone at our condo. The wild tears of aloneness at 34th St. And I couldn't stop. Knowing there were many friends I could call didn't help. Something in me grew older. The thought of Bob's dying was so deeply painful that nothing and no one could ease it.

December 30, 1982

Last night was the General Land Office goodbye party. Bob's heart hurt; he took two nitroglycerin and scared me. The doctor said don't go to the hospital.

January 13, 1983

We're married! The night before the wedding Bob gave me a gorgeous diamond engagement ring! I was totally surprised. He cut a hole in my cowboy hat and stuck it through, like my giving him a diamond hat pin for his birthday.

The wedding itself was solemn and joyous at the same time. We knelt before the fireplace at the ranch with only the children, Mother and Daddy and Butch and Marie. Bob wore jeans and a guayabera; I, a blue Mexican dress. Dr. Farwell came from Iowa, and Reverend Summers. Each spoke at length during the ceremony. A perfect event.

🌱

Journal III

🕯 *Enter, Will*

❧ Enter, Will

March 29, 1983

Together we went to see Dr. Lancaster and had my IUD taken out. We spoke to him of having a child, age, etc. Bob is wonderful. I was scared. The awesomeness of deciding to *create* life overcame me. Even if we don't get pregnant, I'll be always grateful for those moments today of feeling totally connected to all women, everywhere, everytime, who contemplated birth. The basicness of life is serious joy.

April 11, 1983

I'm happy. Bob is well. He ran three 9's last night! Yes!

April 19, 1983

Against all odds, I may be pg.

May 9, 1983

Things I'd like to do with Bob before children:
1. Visit Missouri—fishing.
2. Go East during fall to visit kids.
3. Isla Mujeres trip.
4. Have each of nieces and David for a visit.
5. Ruidoso for a horse race.
6. Trip through the West.

I guess the Nepal revisit must wait. That's okay.

Mixed feelings about work, jobs, etc. Bob is very sick with flu. I try not to worry, but it's hard.

May 11, 1983 (At St. David's Hospital)

Bob is in the hospital with a 104 degree fever that the doctors can't break. They think it may be Rocky Mountain Spotted Fever from a tick, but can't be sure. I've tried to come by several times a day to check on him, and spend the nights in a chair in his room. It is serious. Bob has gotten delirious. I found him one afternoon sitting up in bed calling people all over Texas. It was weird. Then he lay back exhausted. Last night the doctors wrapped his whole body in ice. He hated it. I'm scared.

May 14, 1983 (At hospital)

Finally the fever broke. The good news is that the doctors decided his heart must be incredibly strong to take nine days of 104-degree fever. They've taken him off any heart medication and say the Christmas event must have been an aberration in rhythm he's always had. Exhausted, I stopped by the chapel to mumble a prayer of gratitude.

May 31, 1983

The end of the legislative session. It has been tense, difficult. Attorney General Mattox supported amending Texas's antitrust laws—the first changes since they were originally enacted in 1889. Steve Baron wrote the bill (modeled on federal law) and we acted as "legislative liaison" to try to pass it. Every business interest group in Texas jumped on us. Carol Barger from Consumers' Union took me aside and patiently explained the basics. Hardly any women lobby on business issues. She and I stood for hours on the hard marble floors outside the House chambers (Rule One—wear flats, preferably with rubber soles!) We talked to every legislator, one by one. And counted votes. Representative Woolens ran the floor fight and was great. In the Senate, I testified before the State Affairs Committee and was grilled for hours by Senator McFarland. But afterward we met and he went over the seventy-six-page bill line by line to make changes and corrections. He may be one of the few members who really understood it. I got to know our bill sponsors—Senator Doggett and Representative Messer—fairly well, but also felt the great gap between us and these men who met behind closed doors. An uneasy alliance. When the bill passed, I *loved* winning. And I wondered, how much do I like what I accomplished for the State, for antitrust policy, and how much did I just relish playing the game—and winning? It's unsettling, not pure.

June 9, 1983

Work is settling down a bit. A new guy has come to help on the Carmichael case as a trial lawyer. It's pleasant to feel as if I'll have help and not be totally responsible.

Bob played at the Kerrville Folk Festival with the Dallas County Jug Band. What fun! It rained hard—lots of lightning. Peter Yarrow and daughter singing old songs gave my soul a much needed trip to the mountains. Bob continues to be my joy. Tomorrow we leave for Mexico (Manzanillo for the weekend). It will be nice to get away. Wonder if I really am pregnant . . . .

June 14, 1983

Manzanillo was beautiful—white Moorish buildings, blue seas. Bob and I had a love-letter weekend. He was so kind and considerate. I was for once in my life sort of the glamorous one. Strange role, but fun.

June 16, 1983

Not pregnant. Good, supportive friends. Bob is sleeping so gently, sweetly beside me. Big love.

July 6, 1983

The sperm test came back with bad results. Low count, low motility, low number of normal sperm. I went away and cried before calling Bob. Perhaps there is a fatal symmetry to life. It is not even reasonably fair and no one gets everything she/he wants.

July 13, 1983

Having a baby is becoming more important to me the harder it is for us to have one. I cry a lot. Bob is terrific about the whole thing.

July 15, 1983

Events:

1. MW wants to put off appointing Bob to Parks & Wildlife. Ostensibly because of Padre Island suit. Hunter people don't want him since he is a "park" rather than "hunter" type person. Interesting statistics: Texas has about a million hunters and twenty million visitors to parks in a year.

2. Baby thoughts are harder and harder to deal with.

3. Ultimately, I'm worried about Bob's health. This is too much stress.

Did my first Nautilus! Arms ache!

August 17, 1983

Salmon River trip was excellent. The best day was the long hike to an alpine lake above Alturas. The rhythm of the hike soothed my mind and ached my body. Bob did fine.

The psychic, Dora, foretold yesterday: three marriages; I was lazy, but worked hard at administration; I was extremely creative and could be famous in the arts should I channel my energies there. Bad situation at work but I wouldn't work here too much longer. Bob would get a change in position and we'd travel extensively, probably overseas. Money would be forthcoming and fine. We'd build a house. No children, but it was not impossible for me to have them. Two major events to happen before October 1. First, between 8/22 and 8/28, an extraordinary fight with Bob. Terrible pain, crying, etc. She warned me to not pick a fight and if engaged in one, to plead "a toothache" and discontinue. Second, there is an accident happening to me sometime soon. Stay away from electricity, falls, etc. But even if I have the accident and the fight, I'll survive fine. She said Bob would have a recurrence of a chronic disease but it would not be serious. He would need my support to help him choose the new position. Someone would die that would affect his job position. When I asked about babies, she replied no chance until after next August. About my work—I wouldn't be working after a few months because we would be redecorating a house and traveling. And she said I was psychic.

At the end, I felt awkwardly ungrateful. The fortune was a glorious one of happiness and affluence, travel, meeting interesting people, but I could not comprehend a life without babies *or* a job. So what or who am I then? Too tied to relationship and work to obtain an identity? But what else but those two compose life? Is there a fundamental existence of each human being that lives beyond or independent of relationships and work? I think not—yet when wind whistles past an ear or brushes lightly over my arm on a run, I glimpse a moment of that reality.

August 23, 1983

We made love to have a baby last night. Perhaps will work, perhaps not. Bob is loving in his attitude. He seems to detect the longing in my eyes when I gaze at children.

In Dallas we said goodbye to Nana, who at ninety-six recognized us and was wonderfully surprised we came up "just for her." After dinner at Janet's, the Norwegian Lee women stood laughing and dancing in the kitchen. The legacy of mother-daughter relationships was passed down to my niece Courtney.

David is maturing majestically. I think he has the potential to be a great person in our society.

John Tower won't run for Senate!

A terrific interview with Bickerstaff, Heath & Smiley; an offer to be considered for Chief of the Insurance, Banking and Securities Division of the office, and a long shot to be named public counsel for the Public Utility Commission!

August 29, 1983

In this middle of life, life seems more a river, wide and broad and deep, than a swift moving trout steam as before. Nothing seems as monumental; everything pours into a whole more readily, easily. The significance of one person (me!) is diminished—but so also is responsibility.

September 1, 1983

Office politics: The First Assistant wants me to consider:

1. Possible conflicts being married to Bob.
2. My loyalty to Attorney General Mattox.

I felt sick. He wants "can-do" people on his team. Ugh.

Later, Steve Baron took me to lunch. He is the smartest male lawyer I ever hired. Emotion-filled, he cried because I was going to leave to go into private practice. I gave him a baton engraved from me to him and said to pass it on when it was time. He said, "You've taught me by example and by interaction that one can be happy in this world."

October 11, 1983 (At a waterfall in Colorado)

Two pyramid-shaped mountains thrust themselves, snowcapped, into the view, framed by yellow shimmering aspen leaves and blue sky. Water trickles loudly from the sixty-foot falls and makes diamond bubbles on the autumn leaves that, being in water's way, got splashed. Yellows, whites (aspen bark), golden fall tans color the scene. Huge cliffs tower above. Clean lined, they are comforting, not menacing. Life is good! This hike is exactly what I needed. My private alone time outdoors. Constants in life are so few; this type of renewal is one constant that works for me.

My new job with Bickerstaff, Heath & Smiley is interesting. A relief to be out of the public sector and read Mattox news from a distance. The people are excellent—helpful, laughing and good lawyers. Already the intellectual stimulation is showing on my mind. Once again, I'm intrigued by the mental functions and writing.

I'm passing into midlife just fine. Hooray! Who would have thought things would feel so good! I'm ready to work hard and accomplish professionally. With Bob I have met my lifemate and the love continues to grow. Reading *The Dancing Wu Li Masters*, I realize that is an apt description of him. Wu Li masters do everything as if for the first time; Bob awakes in the morning to suggest we have "fried eggs with *butter*!"

The sun on my face is the sun of Muktinath, Nepal. Minds empty and patterns of sound, sun, droplets grow exponentially in importance. Me, relationships, work. Meeting up with my old fat cells! A joyous reunion!

October 15, 1983

Appropriate color. A RED letter day! The oil well is doing ok; 175 million in the sperm count.

Mid-life means reaching an accommodation with one's body. I no longer hate it if I'm five pounds overweight. A marvelous feeling.

October 26, 1983—age thirty-four!

I *love* my job. The subject matter is not intrinsically interesting, but doing a good job to solve a problem *is*. My only fear is that Bob and I might drift apart since I am so involved in work. Must not let that happen.

October 27, 1983—Birthday

1. I woke up at 3:00 a.m. and said "Rabbit, Rabbit, Rabbit." Bob responded, "Conejo, Conejo, Conejo."
2. At lunch I ran three miles and watched a duck dive beneath the murky water of Town Lake. Remarkable that I'd never before noticed how the duck totally disappears from view—as if poof! Vanished.

A glorious time to be alive.

November 3, 1983

Waiting for 4:00 p.m. so I can call Dr. Lancaster about results of pregnancy test. Trying to remain calm is difficult. If I can't have a baby, at least I'll have a permanent tomorrow.

All last night I awoke every hour on the hour, thinking about a baby. The adult's version of Xmas Eve anticipation. Asleep at my side, Bob was so peaceful. Love for him overcame me as I gazed at his starlit face. His new beard tickles and made me smile. Finally at 6:30 a.m. I suggested we get up and breakfast at Trudy's. On the theory that it might be our last truly "alone" time if indeed we were pregnant. We did.

The day has gone so slowly. Bob went to the lab with me. The older woman there smiled at him since once again we were back. I joked, "With this crew, it's from one extreme to another!" Our last trips were for sperm tests. She laughed, Bob blushed. I try to be calm.

November 8, 1983 (at office)

No baby. I cried, then had a massage and felt better. Bob has been terrific. I'm really missing him now that he has rehearsals every night for the Gridiron. He becomes each day more precious to me.

I love my job. The new desk came and I like being here.

"I didn't take Bob's name, but I did take his brand." (On my desk, fashioned from ranch barn boards.)

November 14, 1983

Late yesterday afternoon we sat in a treehouse deer blind and watched a golden fall afternoon become dusky evening. Four dirty white tennis shoes bearing sand grain traces from Idaho's Salmon River swung aimlessly from our perch. Suddenly the quiet was broken by the thunderous cries of hundreds of birds descending from the skies through the trees, including our tree, toward some common destination a few hundred yards away. For a magical (mystical?) moment, I *became* the tree.

Before, I'd always considered trees from their vantage point of looking down from heights, never had I considered that they, like we humans, could also look upwards.

It was the relationship of tree to bird that showed me this. Somewhere in relationship lie more keys to life's mysteries. I pray to be open enough to see them.

November 21, 1983

Ranch moment. At sunset we knelt beside a live oak and peered with binoculars around a cedar bush to the deer feeder. Ever so softly, four does approached and cautiously nibbled the strewn corn. Not seeing a buck, we arose stiffly and hiked along the fence line.

Dusk became dark and the red sunset began to glow on the horizon. Suddenly across the open field, on a high ridge, we saw deer silhouetted against the red. Delicate ears perked up momentarily, but we were too far away and positioned correctly windwise for them to do more than merely sense our presence. We watched a long time. Then turning to leave, we gazed to our right and were met with a gigantic fall full moon rising through the trees. Huge, it bestowed a night light that created fanciful moon shadows. The moon was so close and large that with our naked eyes the outline of its craters against the night sky was jagged, not smooth.

November 29, 1983

Friday after Thanksgiving, Butch, Bob and I loaded cows to take to the Georgetown Commission Company for slaughter. Everything about the cowboying worked. They caught fairly easily, we separated them smoothly and finally Bob backed the trailer to the chute. He kept the radio going in the truck cab. Strains of "You're the Reason God Made Oklahoma" floated over the sun-sparkling, crisp pasture. Turning to Butch, I held open my arms and asked him to show me how to dance.

His whole being changed. He crumpled up his knees, sort of in a crouch, clicked his boot to the earth and began. Right there, in the pasture, we danced in the wind. Laughing and in wonderment my eyes met Bob's and we smiled down to our Texas toes.

December 10, 1983

Mike, the beer lobbyist, told Bob that when I came in to lobby the AT&T bill, I was a "hurricane of fresh air!"

January 18, 1984

(Bob's writing): We are going to have a baby!

Can you really imagine this? Yes. Old life, new life. Really a time for celebration. L. is *ready* for this. I'm glad. But filtered with all the real world apprehensions. But it will be *just fine*. Whom to tell? Kids *first*! Then we'll see. I feel calm.

January 19, 1984

This is a strange and wonderful time! I want the baby to know what an absolutely marvelous father he/she has. Will the baby have his crinkly eyes?

Told Katie at lunch. She whooped! Really loud!

February 13, 1984—My nephew David's fourteenth birthday

The baby is beginning to seem real to me. He (she) just finished seven weeks and is now possessed of all the basics—brain, hands and feet, etc. In the morning, I listen to classical music on the way to the office, hoping the lyricism, grandeur and beauty will be transmitted to our child.

Bob is terrific. I've not felt too well—a little nauseous and *very tired*. He's cooked and comforted and consoled. One night he took me in his arms and said, "I'm really glad we're having this baby. At first I was glad for you. But now I'm glad for us, and for me. And I'll help." It was the *absolute best* thing he could say.

At work, I'm heading into the last of the first stretch. When I started work here, I decided to work extremely hard for six months and to put work as the priority. This weekend, Martha and I finished a complicated tax question, and I realized I had accomplished my task. There is a piece of me that is very determined once I set a goal. I'm proud of myself.

Other news: Bob was persuaded to run for chair of Travis County Democrats. A thankless job, but one that needs doing. And besides, part of him thrives on the politics. I loved it that he told everyone that our baby came first, however, and he'd have to be here for its birth.

February 16, 1984

The Outer Continental Shelf decision was announced today at a press conference. Texas got almost $400 million. Mark White was wonderfully complimentary to Bob—said the decision would not have occurred but for Bob's aggressive leasing policies.

Afterward we all went to lunch. Bob told the assembled group

(White, Fainter, Kever, Hubert Oxford and me) all about *pre-natal learning*. I really love this man!

February 20, 1984

Thoughts for the little one:

1. Your dad sent you a separate single rose on Valentine's Day. He gave me flowers and then shyly handed me a beautiful orange/pink rose for "whoever is in there."

2. Your first mail arrived from Martha Louise—addressed to "the 2-1/2 Armstrongs"... (actually 1-1/4 Armstrong and 1-1/4 Aaker) at 6627 Valleyside.

3. Today you are eight weeks old. The pictures are fantastic. Every Monday your dad and I read the baby book at breakfast to check your progress.

Names: Christopher, Colt, Anthony, Matthew, Hunter, Elizabeth, Sky, Lacy.

February 22, 1984

Yesterday, we heard your heart beat! An extraordinary experience. Bob came in and you hid. Dr. Lancaster finally found you again.

I've decided to consciously think each day about the pleasant and wonderful moments of bearing life. This time goes so quickly. When the baby leaves my body will I feel empty and less complete? Only now am I getting a little used to the idea that we share this human vessel together.

My personality is evening out. I am consciously putting harsh thoughts aside so that I waste little time on extraneous matters. Besides, I'm not interested in being in a swivet.

March 12, 1984

Martha came in to tell me how much she appreciated my being with the law firm. She said my comments at the Women's Advocacy speech made her feel how lucky the firm was to have me. She said she almost called me over the weekend to tell me. I awkwardly said thank you. When she walked out, tears filled my eyes. *I'm* the lucky one.

March 28, 1984

Went to the doctor. The baby is doing perfect—we heard the heartbeat. We arrived late (as usual) so Bob dropped me off and parked. When he came into the waiting room, I'd already gone into the examining room. He was, of course, the only man in the waiting room. The receptionist said "Are you waiting for someone?" Bob replied, "Yes, but they're not due 'till September." I heard peals of laughter all the way down the hall!

April 3, 1984

I'm nervous about the amniocentesis.

April 19, 1984

I just re-read Bob's article on mountain flying in Idaho. It's good. Reading it made my heart tighten up with love for this incredible man who married me. (Even if he doesn't pick up his socks.)

I wonder why I'm not writing much these days. With the baby growing, I thought I would write well and often. Instead, I practice law (getting better at it, I do believe) and grow larger.

We had amniocentesis in Dallas last week. The sonogram pictures were wonderful. Tiny arms and legs flailing mightily in the air. Reassuring. The results take four weeks. A *long* wait.

I'm making a new friend at work—Carolyn Shellman. Sort of like Katie in a long-drawn out beginning friendship.

May 4, 1984

The baby is fine! Hooray! We celebrated and bought two new chairs!

May 11, 1984

My sister Janet is in the hospital having a hysterectomy. I worry for her—and pray. When I called her this morning before the operation, she sounded flat and scared. My baby sister.

The trial I'm working on is screwing up. Conflicting settings with the two other lawyers threatening to not let it go to trial Monday. Ugh. We'll know at the last minute.

I want Bob to lose weight and get healthy. I worry that the stress of the baby will be too hard on him if he isn't in shape.

Janet is fine.

May 27, 1984 (at Birus Creek in the British Virgin Islands at dusk on our honeymoon)

The waves roll in much like Corpus, only here it swells over coral reefs. Today I went snorkeling for the first time. Looking at the fish swim by us, I felt as if merely by putting on masks and acquiring the ability to breathe with faces submerged, we had become larger versions of their species. Bob says tomorrow will be even better, as the water will be clearer.

We sleep and eat and repeat the cycle. This vacation, unlike others, calls for just such resting. The baby has popped out and goes "glump" and turns with swimmer's kicks in my no-longer-drooping womb. Bob is his usual delightful self. I feel more subdued, quiet. Partly because we started this trip when I was so tired from work, partly because I'm pregnant and have a sort of basic contentment flowing through my system.

June 3, 1984

I want to get my body in really good shape after the baby. But to start maybe I'll have to begin with disciplined walking. Need to think of goals.

June 5, 1984

Child of my love, child of my loins, I think of you with a constancy that surpasses "in love."

July 15, 1984 (in the middle of the night)

I'm so angry with Bob I can't sleep. He joined the Hills of Lakeway today, just to the end of the year—$650. And he did discuss it *generally* with me, but not specifically. I wouldn't care if he would just get the taxes done and let me know how we are doing financially.

July 27, 1984

Of course, we talked and everything was fine. Sigh. My emotions are going crazy.

Today I panicked because the baby hadn't moved in twelve hours. Went to Brackenridge Hospital ER and the nurse listened on the fetal monitor. Baby was fine—120 per minute. It really scared me. All my worries about anesthesia, etc. paled next to the overriding concern about keeping this baby healthy and delivering him *any* way into the world.

Bob's been in Hawaii and I've missed him a lot. He comes home today. Hooray!

August 8, 1984

Yesterday for an hour I contemplated the syntactical difference between "My baby dropped" and "I dropped my baby." Yes, of course, I'm distracted at work!

August 9, 1984

Watching Bob pick up golf balls at Camp Mabry. He's had a hard couple of days and needs me to be supportive. Instead, I wanted him to help at home and not golf. I think life is full of moments of conflicting needs. In being a successful couple though, we both have to give a little. Often I give my share, but am mentally begrudging about it.

September 4, 1984

I feel a little different today. Does it mean anything? Who is the little person inside? Please, God, make this new person safe and healthy.

Played six holes of golf yesterday.

September 19, 1984 (Bob's writing:)

Well, here we go!

5:18 a.m.—L: "I think my water broke." Sure enough, lots of draining. Called Lancaster. He says "Go." One last shower as a twosome. Went in the new car. Dawn is breaking. Moon is last quarter and high. L won't go to emergency in the car. Wants to park and walk. Everyone is ready at St. David's. Pam and Georgeanne are nurses' aides. Wanda is RN, super attitude. Delivery room is 7!!

Linda is giving urine and getting drained. Wanda says get in bed. L.: "I'm dripping a lot." Wanda: "Well, drip on over here and get in bed." Fetal Monitor is right on *140*. Green striped sox are on. We're ready.

7:55—All hooked up. 150 f/m. Not many contractions. Linda looks pretty and relaxed.

8:03-8:05—First contraction, then nothing.

8:10—Lancaster arrives. Petocin for a while to see if contractions will come and cervix will dilate. If six hours of Petocin won't produce, then rest overnight, try again, and if that doesn't work, then C section. This is the program. L says why not try today and then C section? We'll see.

8:45—Contraction (small). Fetal monitor is jumping. L on phone to Carolyn.

9:30—Contractions are every four minutes to three minutes. But do-able by breathing. L is doing o.k.

The machine is helpful. Lots of confidence from hearing the steady heartbeat of the baby. L blood pressure is 116/72. More relaxed than when she came in.

Called the offices and the mothers. This is it. We are going to meet the new person today or tomorrow for sure. ALL RIGHT!

9:30—Three minute intervals.

10:00—Hooked up for two hours. Petocin for 1:20, boy do I love her.

10:15—80 cc Pet.

10:35—Now slower but stronger. Three-and-a-half minutes. Gave some Demerol. Helped some but still HARD WORK. Lots of contractions. L is SUPER TOUGH. We have good help from friends.

12:30—Lancaster comes—going for Epidural.

1:07—Broke the scar tissue. Up to three-four cm now. Three contractions during the epidural. Epidural complete—six cm. No pain from epidural.

1:20—I'M DRESSED! We're going. Heart rate steady.

1:40+—L is at ten cm.

Wonderful to see L relaxed.

1:50—pushing hard, beginning to bulge.

Lo and behold in came Mickey and Minnie Mouse and Pluto and TV cameras. You couldn't believe it. A local station was doing a hospital special.

Linda works real hard. Begin to see some hair. It's really there. Pushing lasts and lasts. Wanda really helps. Katie and Sheila really help. We all help. Finally, Dr. L. comes. This is it!

Glasses and cameras. We're ready. We hold hands rolling into the delivery room. A little extra epidural first. It goes in a tube, no new shot needle. Dr. L. comes in and things begin to happen. The episiotomy is first. Things really happen fast. First a forcep, then another. Then a pull and a head's out. "You better be ready with that camera," said the doctor. I was. Then a shoulder and then a baby. A whole baby right there. "Cry!" said L to the mass on her tummy; and cry he did. HE! It's a boy! A whaaa then another whaaa. He's here and he's fine. All toes and fingers check out. I'm still taking pictures. He gets wiped off cursorily, wrapped up and they hand him to *me* to take to the nursery. Lancaster is all smiles but has a lot of work to do. I leave and *we* (baby and I) head for the hall where Sheila and Katie are waiting with cameras. I still have on my hat and mask although I *did* kiss L through the mask in the delivery room when she announced, "We did it!" We sure did.

Weights and measures in the nursery—seven pounds, thirteen ounces and twenty-and-a-half inches. Lots of things to do. Vitamin shot. Eye salve for VD. Still lots of blood everywhere. Then we go back to recovery, he and I. There he nurses for the first time. He and L are a pair. Back to nursery for a bath. I bathe him. He likes the water running on his head. (Note for future baths.) Scrub head with brush, the rest with wet napkins. Cleans up real nice.

Back to see Linda. Nurse is pushing hard on her belly. *Big* clot jumps out, like a baseball. (Hope that's all.) Really cleaning out. At some point Will seems like a good name. It just happens.

We go to the room, 325, donated in the memory of David Bouldin. Can you believe this? When I was born in 1932, Dave Bouldin came to the hospital with some quail shot out of season because my mother loved quail. It's the only thing I have been told about my birth, besides the date, and here we are checking our son into Dave Bouldin's room.

October 14, 1984

Will is almost a month old! A time of loving, tears, learning about each other. I was unprepared for how much having him would hurt physically (and have had a tough recovery). But I was also totally unprepared for the intensity with which I love him. There is no rationality to the feeling—it is complete—I'd die for him.

Some random moments I don't want to forget:

In the hospital: Bob to Steve Bickerstaff: "It was the best day in fifty years!"

In church (Will was 2-1/2 weeks), Bob carried him to the communion rail. Will had not said a word, then Reverend Powell put a hand on his head for a blessing, and Will went, "Wa, Wa!" On the way back down the aisle, Barbara Miller said to the person next to her in the pew, "That's a baby that love made."

Bob is wonderful. He slept on a cot in the hospital room with me and Will. One night I had fed Will, and Bob had him on the cot next to him, feeding him water. I was exhausted in my hospital bed. A new night nurse came in and did a double-take at the sight of the baby with Bob in his red flannel nightshirt!

Two days after the baby was born, Bob came into the room with some cookies. In the cookies was a small package. A *gorgeous* pear-shaped diamond pendant with a note that read: "To Mommy. Daddy and I love you, Will." I cried, Bob cried. Will just sat there!

In the hospital, Will was a beautiful baby. Everyone expected him to look cone-headed and mangled since I'd had hard labor culminated by two hours of pushing, finally requiring forceps. But there wasn't a mark on him. He was perfect. Brown hair (not much of it, but enough), a perfectly shaped head, large hands and a great mouth.

When he was put on my stomach in the delivery room, I felt relief and thankfulness that he was ok. The fact that he was a boy barely registered. On my breast, he still hadn't cried. I looked at him and said, "Cry!" He responded with two short cries and then just settled in. Bob and I said a prayer of thanks for his safe arrival. The doctor then wrapped him in a blanket (still bloody) and gave him to Bob saying, "Here, take him to the nursery and they'll tell you what to do!" Off went Bob.

While he was on my stomach in the delivery room, I looked at him and thought, "Here's Will." We hadn't picked out a boy's name, and William had barely been mentioned. I didn't say anything to Bob. When he brought Will to recovery, he said, "You know, my uncle's name was Aubrey William. Maybe William is a good name." I was amazed. So we named him Will.

October 17, 1984

I'm breaking the cardinal rule: Go down, i.e., to sleep, when the baby goes down. However, I'm so emotionally down, perhaps that counts. The physical part of having and nursing the baby is wearing me out. My left breast looks like a meat grinder had a go at the tip. Scabs and open cuts. I cry when I nurse Will. Today I just lay on the couch and cried because I think I starved Will the first three weeks until we started giving him supplemental bottles. I don't hate them at all. I'm grateful he'll take them and get something to eat. Even as I write this, I realize some of the tears are due to hormones. But that doesn't make me *feel* better, only *think* better.

As much as I love Will, I need some time away from him and Bob. The only time I've been alone in a month was driving Honey's car home the other night while Bob drove the car with the baby.

On a better note: Will gained eleven-and-a-half ounces last week! Hooray! And he smiled the faintest little smile at Bob this morning. He can now entertain himself for periods of about fifteen minutes. I really love him. Can't face leaving him for work. I'll think of that later.

October 18, 1984

Will seems almost psychic where I'm concerned. Just when I think I can't stand it, he comes through and sleeps a little extra to give me a break. He's so cute!

Children make one grow up. I went to get the minor surgery done on my leg and back all by myself since Bob had a meeting. My stomach was in knots, I was so scared of the pain. But I did fine. Maybe I'll even get to passing dogs without panic.

October 20, 1984

Our maiden trip to the grocery store ended with the checkout clerk offering to write out the check for me as I held a squalling Will! This from the woman lawyer who's handled rooms full of negotiators!

October 21, 1984

Bob was worried before Will came that he wouldn't be able to hear the baby. Since he has taken the 2:00 a.m. feeding though, he wakes up upon Will's small cries before I do. I think it must be conditioning. If you know it is your responsibility to feed the baby, you hear him. On the other hand, in the afternoon when I try to nap with Will, the slightest moan from his room causes the adrenalin to flow immediately and jerk my body almost rigid. I never realized having a baby was such a basic, instinctive experience.

Good news: the left breast is getting better. Mother is here for the weekend. She's great!

October 23, 1984

He smiled at me.

October 26, 1984 (my last day of being thirty-five!)

This is the most contented time I've ever spent in my life. I'm doing exactly what I want to be doing at this moment in time—taking care of my son. Life moves in a rhythmic pattern based on hours between feedings; time and future have a distant dreamlike quality. It feels good.

October 27, 1984

I am thirty-six years old and happy! We took Will to the airport so Cathy could see him, then ate a hamburger at the Sonic, fed Will in the car, and dropped Bob off to do an ad for Russ Tidwell's House race while Will and I went to visit Honey. Then back home Bob watched Will while I took a long two-mile walk and stopped at the bakery for a piece of carrot cake. And it started with a call from Farwells! And a sung Happy B-day from Mother and Daddy. Nice, contented time.

Goals for forty:

1. Become partner at BHS.
2. Build a house.
3. Have China trip under way (at least planned).
4. Try to keep my eye on the big picture—not sweating the details (e.g., no one ever died of dirty dishes!).
5. Become civicly involved again.
6. Have some land purchased (maybe pay off Aaker's acres).

October 29, 1984

Tonight for a few minutes during the movie "Amadeus" I forgot about Will. It was strange. For the first time in weeks, I didn't have him in my thoughts constantly. He's gotten so big. No longer can he fit in my lap from knees to waist without his feet kicking up against my chest. It was sad to think of that—he'd grown without my knowing it. I miss the Will that was, while welcoming the Will that is.

October 30, 1984

I really think I'm ready to wean him. My chest is so sore. After six weeks, I'm tired of always hurting! Will doesn't seem to care whether it's me or the bottle.

November 3, 1984

We had Chris Harte and Kay and Mike Levi and Anita over for champagne and cheese before going out for Chinese food. Will was terrific. We put him in the infant seat on the table and arranged all the food dishes around him. I said, "Will, you're being a good boy." Mike said, "Good! He's being super!" Unsolicited comments like that make a new mom's day!

I knew Bob was really thinking about the baby when last night he told the other diners that he needed to sit at the end of the booth "in case he needed to do the baby," even though I had Will with me at that moment.

November 7, 1984 (Bob's fifty-second B-Day)

Will and I are up now at 4:00 a.m. He's fed, changed and laughing and cooing in his infant seat on the table while I write thank you notes. He is my joy and delight. He "talks" and plays now, kicking off blankets and being fun.

November 28, 1984

What a wonderful day! Sonja Kever and I took Jenna and Will for a walk and laughed and laughed afterwards as we did a few casual exercises. She is a good solid person. I've learned a lot about mothering from her. It's wonderful to have a friend around the corner whose child is *exactly* the same age. Jenna is only a week older than my Will.

Will had his two-months checkup. Twelve pounds twelve ounces. A little chunk! The doctor hurt him at the checkup and I almost fainted. Thank God, Bob was there. They also gave him the tetanus, diphtheria and whooping cough shot. He was screaming and wouldn't calm down till I held him ten minutes. It was *horrible*. The first time I'd seen someone I love intentionally hurt. That night in the middle of the night, Will finally smiled again. I love him so much I cry. My heart was so full of glad that he smiled again. I hugged him close and thought that I don't care if he's brilliant or dumb, president or janitor; I just want him to be happy in his life, and not hurt.

We're starting the slow process of separating a little from each other. Will is already an independent baby. He cuddles, but while in my arms he looks around the room taking it all in. When he wants to be held, he clings tightly to my neck and grabs a handful of my hair.

Today I left him on his blanket crying while I finished carrying groceries in. He cried so hard he wouldn't calm down to nurse. It was awful. I felt like a terrible mother. I don't ever want him to cry like that. Perhaps that's what colic-y babies do. That would be hell to live with.

The law firm will let me go back part-time—Hooray! I'm ready to rejoin the world, but I wouldn't have minded staying home full-time a bit longer. Having Sonja Kever and Jenna around the corner makes being home fun. All alone, I'm not sure I'd like it.

Last night I saw a PBS special on the starvation in Ethiopia. I cried at the children's plight. The last year I've been totally self-centered, trying to work at my new job, be pregnant and be a new mother. My social cause commitment has fallen low and I need to rekindle the flame with some action. There is more to life than conspicuous consumption.

The breast feeding is going great!

December 4, 1984

Will smiles and gurgles. He is so cute I can't stand it sometimes. I love him *totally* beyond reason.

January 1, 1985

Last year was the best year of my life. I predict '85 will be joyful because of Will.

Goals:

1. Weigh 114 (from 120).

2. Exercise regularly—three times a week.

3. Buy a house.

4. Be single-minded at work and stop being insecure. I'm at least as good a lawyer as I am a mother, and I am one hundred percent certain I'm a good mother.

5. *Enjoy* Will—don't sweat the small stuff (I've been running an experiment, and life goes on fine when I play with Will instead of

cleaning house).

6. Write more—somehow I'm too busy living to write.

January 7, 1985

Today I left Will for the first time with Janet (the English nanny) at Honey's. I cried from 7:00 a.m. to 1:00 p.m. It was like leaving a lover. That intense horrible feeling of wrenching separation. He did fine.

January 10, 1985

I totally, absolutely love Will. He's doing very well with Janet. I really like her. She notices things about him. "He moves his legs when he tries to use his hands." Four-month checkup today. He weighed fifteen-four and was twenty-five-and-three-fourths inches. We're supposed to start solids.

Both Bob and I *forgot* our anniversary! Two years. I sent him two red roses in Tahoe where he was on business. He sent me a dozen long stemmed roses with a card, "You are and always will be." I love that man.

It's good to be away from Will part of the time. The key to leaving him is to have good times with him before I drop him off.

January 17, 1985

Bob: "Will, I've changed more of your diapers than all three other kids combined—and you're only four months old!"

At the Shivers funeral, someone said to Bob, "I'm surprised you didn't bring the baby. I've heard you're never separated!"

Going back to work has been great. Will sleeps a lot in the afternoon, so we don't feel so guilty. Also, he's up till 11:30 at night, so we really spend time with him.

January 24, 1985

Bob of Will: "One smile is worth a thousand diapers!"

Will is becoming his own person. I left him for a whole day. When I returned at 6:00 p.m., he would only go to Bob.

February 4, 1985

We saw "The Killing Fields"—a movie of Cambodia. A+ film. Will has deepened my life immeasurably. War takes on an entirely different dimension when I see pictures of lost, wounded children, frightened and dazed. With the advent of heightened loving, he brought also heightened empathy and fears.

I wondered if I should quit work for a few years and do some hands on work for the POWs. Surely I could roll bandages.

We came home and I rushed into his room. He sleeps peacefully. As he sleeps, I miss his smile. That perhaps is his most outstanding characteristic. When he smiles this winsome, engaging smile, all the Armstrong in him leaps out. Folks are glad to have seen him; he leaves them happier, somehow better just because he happened to them for a moment. Bob has that quality. He says his dad did too. I love them both beyond reason.

February 7, 1985

I just spent my first night away from Will. It was surprisingly easy. I enjoyed the opulence of the Four Seasons robes, shoes shined, etc. A long bath while I practiced my speech. The speech was about a B-. Why, oh why do I speak so fast!

Good line from another speech. The cabinet posts are switching so fast that the standard instruction in D. C. is, "If the boss calls, get his name!"

Bob took Will to the Land Office reception last night. Will had his first nametag—attached to his back. Apparently the "guys" did just fine without me.

March 5, 1985

Will was the hit of his first campout. The other night he learned almost overnight how to sit up by himself. When Bob came home later, I proudly put Will in his new position to show Daddy. Bob said he nearly cried because Will, as a little sitting being, was not really a baby anymore.

Will has his first cold. I feel terrible. Ugh.

March 31, 1985

Will can sit by himself, almost crawls by putting his bottom high in the air, and "walks" if you hold both hands. No consonants but lots of babbling. He is an absolute charmer. We've taken him to political rallies and parties. Everywhere, people love him. But not as much as I do! He gives my face large sloppy kisses and recognizes the word "open" for eating. He gums tortillas at breakfast at Trudy's.

When I came home from running today, Bob and Will were in the bathtub and Bob had "parted" Will's hair with the brush to wash his scalp. I couldn't tell who was more pleased with himself.

April 23, 1985

Two mornings ago, Will called to us—from his proud position *standing up* in his crib!

He crawls, is always on the go, pulls up on anything and *loves me* totally now.

April 28, 1985

Sonja, Andy, Martha, Rick, Bob and I went to the University Club for dinner last night. It was absolutely the best evening out for dinner I can remember having. Socially and businesswise, it was wonderful. I'm coming out of being only a mother.

Will has had two *tough* days. Out of sorts, crying, maybe teething? Tonight we went to a wedding shower. He was fretful. For the first time he wasn't the hit baby of the show—usurped by more pleasant mannered babies. I felt a pang—equally for him and for me. There will be so many times in his future when others will outshine him. But it only made me love him more.

May 5, 1985

I was feeding Will rice cereal mixed with apples and pears for breakfast. Bob thought it was corn mush. He brought out his guitar and made up a song about being "corny" and finding out it was rice and apples. Will grinned through toothless gums, I laughed, and Bob sang. We have a wonderful family.

May 10, 1985

I went to the fortuneteller again. Predictions:

1. I'll face a major career choice in the next few months. If I take it, I'll ultimately be rich and famous, but at tremendous cost to my personal life. Bob will be supportive of the advancement initially, so I have to be doubly cautious.

2. Be careful with electricity and machines.

3. Will would be fine—very smart and intellectual. "He makes people obey him."

4. Bob would be depressed about Honey.

5. Our trips would be good.

May 27, 1985

At Martha Louise's graduation from Amherst, I was happy to be exactly who I am!

May 29, 1985

My euphoria was short-lived. The nanny Janet is quitting and going back to England to engage in peace work. I cried for two hours.

August 6, 1985

Will finally got a tooth. Bottom right—about ten months old. He isn't walking yet, but stands without help, if he isn't too interested in scampering off to investigate. I love him beyond my wildest imaginings. So does Bob.

Sheila had a healthy boy. Jeffrey Paul. Pam and Steve Baron had Hannah. Momentarily I wanted another baby, but not now.

Our new house is unbelievable. Twenty-five hundred square feet.

August 12, 1985

Will is taking tentative steps, his face lighting up with accomplishment. Bob is in Alaska for thirteen days. I miss him already (Day 1), but am determined to get thin and try to enjoy this alone time. I could have gone, but was unwilling to leave Will.

August 16, 1985

Daddy has colon cancer. He barked at me on the phone the other night and then later called back to apologize. I'm leaving tomorrow to go to Dallas with Will.

September 11, 1985

A miracle happened. After a gruesome hospital stay, two surgeries and a prognosis of ninety days to one year because the cancer had spread extensively to his liver, Daddy was told the cancer had disappeared. Dr. Harrell, the surgeon, said, "Someone stole your cancer." Not exactly. The colon cancer was removed, but there are cancer cells running around. The new prognosis is three years.

September 12, 1985

I'm healing. All summer I've been sort of depressed, but finally I'm coming back. While driving to Houston for a business meeting (to advise Ft. Bend County on the Fair Labor Standards Act), I negotiated freeways and felt competent. Driving into the country, I saw a white bird soaring against blue sky. It was the first thing I've "seen" in months.

Some of my best times with Will are right before he sleeps. We rock in his room. With the curtains open, I see one star and the tops of trees out his window. His body is sleepy-warm, and occasionally, at rest and not kicking.

September 18, 1985

The night before Will turns one. How do I describe a year of such magnitude, of such splendor in my life? Will came, and nothing remains untouched by his presence. I look back at the intensity of this year, and see our progression toward separation from each other after nine months of utter togetherness. I still love him so *hard*! And I wonder if my mother-love will change over time. As Will grows larger, older, will I love him less intensely? Is this mothering a changing feeling, like loving a lover?

As I write, Will is (hopefully) talking himself to sleep. He doesn't

really talk, he says lots of noises. A squeak toy just made its unmis-
takable sound. He's playing with his cradle gym that I carefully
removed from overhead his crib, and put to one side. Sigh! He'll
never go to sleep!

Will, at one, is defined largely by his active curiosity. He's constantly on the go, trying to see how things work. If he has a whole
yard to explore he heads for the sprinkler outlet, fascinated by the
turning mechanisms. He smiles and laughs a lot and generally is
good natured and funny. He has lots of personality. His smile reminds me of David's. There is an open, vulnerable quality to it. He's
very strong and muscular, but not very aggressive for his strength.
He's perplexed when Jenna hurts him; such behavior is not part of
his general world. He's beginning to be more affectionate, and cries
when I leave. He is always excited when I come home.

New Year's Eve 1985

We celebrated tonight by having Andy, Sonja and Jenna come
over to watch videos of Jenna's christening. Will and Jenna took a
bath together. Things have certainly changed since my single, non-
child days.

Will runs and shrieks with delight as he entices us to chase him.
He is so all-boy. I am not particularly encouraging the male behavior, but he exhibits totally stereotypical patterns. I'm unwilling to
admit genetics is all, but I must confess there appears to be something to those influences. Will says Da-da. He occasionally will stay
Ma-ma, but he makes the same sound for the monster stuffed animal my mom gave him for Christmas.

I worry slightly that he is so terribly active. But he doesn't exhibit obnoxious behavior, just constant exploring. He also is less
affectionate with me lately. It bothers me, but he seems really happy,
just too busy to give as many hugs. It also bothers me that he doesn't
seem to care much if I'm gone, as long as his nanny Carolyn is there.
She's obviously doing a great job, but I wish Will would show *more*
of a preference to me!

New Year's Resolutions:
1. Give up diet drinks for one year.

2. Lose five pounds.
3. Run three times a week.
4. Do sit-ups five times a week.
5. Let the compulsive stuff go (like house cleaning), and play with Will instead.
6. Be more supportive of Bob's activities, less subtly undermining.
7. Work steadily—try to maintain even keel.

January 4, 1986

Finally I finished the Collin County Bail Bond project. It's a good report but scary in its implications. We analyzed the dismissal of several hundred thousand dollars worth of bonds. I enjoy working with Syd Falk. An ex-astro physics professor turned lawyer with one wild eye and a wild mind.

I came home from work late last night and drank champagne with the two Whizettes—Melinda, now in med school, and Meg, now working for Representative Delco. It was fun to be mentor to the two twenty-one-year-olds. Love and commitment (they're scared of both), and wanting more fun from relationships were foremost on their agendas. I'm the only working woman with a baby they know well. They want to see "how I turn out." As we drank, I began to see how very far apart we were in our life stages. It never ceases to catch me up short because women that age *look* like experienced women. But a lot happens to one in fifteen years.

Will and I are having a great weekend. Fed the ducks, took a walk, bought clothes for him. Tonight, for a big Saturday night treat, I moved his high chair to the playroom, ordered pizza and cokes, and we ate while watching *Superman* on TV. Bob called from hunting in South Texas. I think he missed us even though he's having a great time.

We've been taking Will to the ranch a lot lately. He *loves* it. He sits on the tractor and "drives," brings in wood, and practices mooing at the cows. Bob and I took a long New Year's Day walk and went to the south fence, then over to the top hill near the waterfall. It was overcast and misty and eerily beautiful. The perfect way to begin this New Year. I'm feeling better.

January 17, 1986

   The night before Women's Weekend at the Ranch. I'm like a kid before Christmas and have laid out my jeans and shirt and new underclothes to wear tomorrow. Fifteen women will come. I wonder if it will be as fun as I anticipate. The weather looks as if it will be perfect. Bob is great. He cleared out the ranch cubbyholes and filled up the truck. I think he'd like to be there too. But no men or children are allowed. My life is even and well these days. Work goes fine and I enjoy working with Carolyn.

January 20, 1986

   Women's Weekend was glorious. I *love* my women friends, who willingly share their laughter and pain. We're lucky.

February 16, 1986

   Denver Airport. We're on vacation to ski. Last night I cried for half an hour thinking about leaving Will. This morning, I woke him early. He snuggled more deeply into the crib and curled his legs tightly into his red sleeper. My little lump resembled a left-over valentine. At the airport when we left, he cried as I buckled him back into his car seat. I cried to Denver.

   Aspen, Colorado. Will's nanny Carolyn said he cried only until the car started!

   Women like me go through life waiting to have a baby to "complete" themselves, in some vague but persistent feeling that having the baby is somehow necessary to selfhood. But today I realized that it's a paradox. Now that I have Will, without him I feel incomplete, and yet will spend the next twenty years teaching both of us how to get along without the other.

   Before Will, I could glory in aloneness and fly blissfully off to foreign places to seek adventure and read books. Now my steps are tentative down the airport ramp. Every child reminds me of Will-o. I miss him. But I like these few quiet moments without him to record thoughts. I've missed these times too.

   We're meeting interesting people. Scott is our host, a flying ace who lives year-round in Aspen, runs marathons and lunches with famous physicists. Last night his friend Janet joined us for dinner. She was the first and only woman to compete in the Indianapolis 500.

The night before we left for Aspen, Bob and I went to a party at Syd and Julie's (Syd is a lawyer at BHS) and stayed late listening to music and playing with the Lounge Lizards, a guitar group composed of lawyers and law students. We had a great time.

Both experiences served to remind me of how narrow my vision has become since going into private practice and having Will. Everyone I meet lately seems so accomplished at things. I need this time to regroup.

March 23, 1986

I ran the Capitol 10,000 in sixty-seven minutes—much to my surprise, since I trained so little. Intended to run just two miles and then walk, but got caught up in the excitement.

Will and I had a marvelous day together. This morning he woke cheerful and funny as always. But he "talks" so much now. He's so happy—he has a mama and dada and a "bob-ble" and a warm cozy bed (ours!). What more does a person need! He kicks his legs like a little gymnast on a pommel horse. He's been waking at night, I think because of teething, and gets scared. So he cuddles on top of me and I let him fall asleep in bed with us. All the books counsel otherwise, but he's too afraid to send back to his crib.

Bob went to West Texas to view Halley's Comet. I probably could have gone had I hustled a babysitter and worked all day Saturday. But I really didn't want to leave Will. And I am exhausted from racing around. Will fell asleep at 6:00 p.m. and may sleep through the night. I cleaned out my closet, wondering if someday I'd think I was crazy to miss an up-close view of the comet at McDonald's Observatory for the chance to play with an eighteen-month-old baby and clean closets! But I feel great!

Mother, Daddy and Janet went to Santa Fe to get the old brown station wagon. They're having a ball. Mother said, "I wish I could put you in my pocket and take you along."

March 25, 1986

Bob called. West Texas was my kind of trip. They climbed Mt. Livermore. I was envious, and not as nice on the phone as I could have been. But I *did* make the right decision, and should let this one go and move on.

April 6, 1986

Will's vocabulary: Mama, Dada, more, slide, outside, row row your boat, moon, balloon, app-um, fish, peez, ga-ga (thank you), gate.

At the ranch Bob leaned his weight (two hundred pounds) against the old wooden martin birdhouse to see if he could affect the lean. After he walked off, we glanced back to see Will leaning all thirty pounds of himself mightily at the post.

When he smiles, I can deny him nothing. Such joy he radiates!

I don't want to go to work tomorrow. I want to play with my Will-o!

April 28, 1986

Will sat on Bob's stomach and rubbed shaving cream over Bob's belly button. With the studied intensity of a great artist at work, he splayed his fingers across Dada's body and observed the growing white design. Bob, all the while on the telephone, fought to keep laughter from dissolving the stomach/easel into a quivering, giggling mass. Oh, my two guys—how I adore them both!

Carolyn and I tried the first of our developer cases (sewer and water CCN applications) and did a *great* job. Our client even wrote us a neat note about it.

Everything is going well in my life right now. All I need is time to exercise and to lose five pounds.

We went to the San Jacinto monument to celebrate Texas's 150th birthday. My folks and little Shannon went with us to the events sponsored by Parks and Wildlife. It was interesting—a bit too social, but we saw the *Elissa*, a three-mast sailing ship, and had cocktails on board.

Bob helped write Barbara Jordan's speech. I flew back to Austin with her in Lt. Governor Hobby's plane. When they tried to put her in the small Cessna 410, she got stuck halfway in the doorway and a long painful struggle ensued. Her clothes were disheveled, her dignity challenged, her sense of humor unscathed! It was painful, embarrassing to watch as I sat helpless in the plane. She is a truly great lady.

May 19, 1986

My life overwhelms me. Will has been up two nights. So I go to work on four hours' sleep and try to handle major cases. Plus arrange child care, groceries, pay household bills, check out schools for Will, take primary care of Will's clothes, dinners, bath, etc. No exercise. I'm exhausted and feeling sorry for myself tonight.

June 18, 1986

I found this diary! Hooray! I thought I'd lost it!

June 21, 1986

We cut Will's curls. He looks nice, but older. I wanted to do it, but feel a little sad. Bob marked the sun on our porch for the longest day.

August 24, 1986

At the ranch, I stripped and walked in kneesocks and tennis shoes to the waterfall. The wind on my bare body replenished outer and inner cells. It rained. As Bob, Will and I ran for cover under trees in the four-wheeler, Will joyously yelled, "Umbrella!" He talks in complete sentences. *All the time.*

September 2, 1986—Will's First Day of School

He went off to Athena Montessori School this morning in a red shirt, blue jean shorts, and sneakers, carrying a red backpack containing his extra diapers. At the door I feared a scene as he left me. His teacher Mary Ann came to the school door, behind which was a long corridor leading to his room. She opened the door, and my little guy ran into the school with nary a backward glance. Bob and I looked at one another, both almost in tears. "I feel like we're giving him up to the world," said his daddy.

Bob went by to talk to his teacher after school was over. "Perfect" was the report. He hadn't cried at all. Tonight, at bedtime, he's crying piteously, "Mommy, rock." He's still little. I hope tomorrow goes as well.

I'm losing weight and my good humor is returning. One hundred fifteen and one-half pounds.

October 8, 1986—on plane to Denton to negotiate sale of hospital

At the firm retreat last Saturday, Steve Bickerstaff announced the partners were asking me to become a partner in January. I called Bob. At the firm dinner that night, Bob made a wonderful toast about how I wasn't at all blase about it. (Of course, when I came home from the meeting earlier that afternoon, I was greeted by a note from Bob saying he and Will were flying to Giddings for a P&W function. When they arrived in Giddings, he hitchhiked from the airport to town, and at the party was the only person accompanied by a two-year-old and with a diaper stuffed in his back pocket!)

Work thoughts: I enjoyed getting to work with Jane Hickie and Martha on Capital Metro projects. We managed to stave off until January an attack on CM's one-cent sales tax. But it wasn't easy!

Today I met with Dr. Shirley Chater, Texas Woman's University's new president, a bright, savvy woman I liked immediately. I think we'll have a good project.

I've been on a roll at work. It's going well and I'm doing interesting things.

Will is splendid. He talks like a real person now. School has gone well for him; so far I think he really likes going. Today, however, he didn't want to go, but rather wanted to stay home and "play." He's funny. He lures me out of the shower with, "Mommy, go potty," then jumps in and wants to keep the whole shower to himself, laughing uproariously. At the ranch, he "drives" the bulldozer, examines bugs, moos at the cows, and generally has a ball.

He has a good life. I've been traveling more, so Bob has had him a lot. I miss Will, but I think the time they spend together is good for both of them.

Bob and I have both gotten thinner. He's lost twenty-two pounds (now one hundred eighty-eight) and I'm down to one hundred thirteen. We're both sexier.

Bob had been taking Will to school for two weeks straight since I'd had early morning meetings. When one morning I finally got Will dressed and breakfasted, Bob looked at us preparing to leave and said, "I thought all those mornings that it was kind of onerous to take Will to school. And now I miss having him to take."

Scene: Will opening the door to the heater and examining the pilot light with great seriousness and a steady stream of conversation.

October 26, 1986

Will woke us up yelling, "I'm finished night-night!" We had a *wonderful* weekend at the ranch with the bow hunters.

My life is lovely now. Will is great, Bob and I had an enchanting four-day float trip in Big Bend, and I have made partner.

I thought we could go one more year without Trick or Treating. Nope. Tonight he told me he wanted to "get dressed up" in a "costume" and be a "cwom" (clown) and "go Halloween." At church today, we snuck back into the sanctuary between services and watched the choir practice. Will directed from the pews!

December 7, 1986

At the airport we honked in vain for the electric gate to open. Finally it did. A little voice from the car seat said, "Tank-you, gate."

About a broken toy: "Mama, it's falling apart."

When asked by Santa what he wanted for Xmas, he replied, "A lollipop." At the mall, we *had* to go to the video games place. I entered a male domain, and realized this experience was part of the mysterious journey I'm making as Mother-of-a-son. Scene: Bob in Hawaiian undershorts stands on a chair attempting to put a new lighted star on our Xmas tree. Oh, what a glorious season!

December 29, 1986

Will's second Christmas was a success. He enchanted the grocery shoppers by bursting into "Happy Birthday to Jesus" in front of the zucchini. Fall is my time of year. I'm loving Bob a lot lately.

January 5, 1987

Putting Will to bed tonight, he wanted me to "yie (lie) down a yittle (little) bit." So I did, and in the grey darkness he turned and looked long into my eyes. He seemed much older than merely two. And I imagined how someday, some woman would lie there as his lover and see the same depths. The time goes too quickly.

The long time off from work due to the Thursday Xmas and New Year's Day gave me needed perspective. Bob and I went to the ranch and played with Will. We took him to the San Antonio zoo, where the highlight was the porcupine and the playground. He made a joke to Carolyn—told her the elephants were "yittle," then laughed and laughed since elephants were "big!"

February 1, 1987

Me: "Will, do you want to try to wear training pants today?"
Will: "Yes."
He then looked at the pants *very* carefully, inside and out.
Will: "Mommy, where's the train?"

I fell and sprained an ankle. Then got a bad case of sinusitis. My mom responded to my SOS and came for the weekend to help with Will. I'm lucky to have my mom. Hope I'm as good a mother as she has been over the years.

Bob has been terrific—helping through these hard/sick and work times. The legislative session is starting with a bang, too quickly. Cap Metro is *too* hard.

April 13, 1987

Last night we all three awoke to thunder and lightning.
Will: "It's thunder. God makes thunder. Mommy, where is the button?
Me: "What button?

Will: "The rain button God makes thunder and rain with."

Where does he get his ideas?

We won first round of AT&T bill. We settled SWB bill today. Shirley Chater was inaugurated President of Texas Woman's University to great acclaim. I'm lucky to be associated with her. But the personal cost of this session has been too high.

June 3, 1987

Will was playing Animal Lotto and saw a picture of a big brown feathered chicken. "Mama, that's a bar-b-que chicken!" he exclaimed.

After we lost the AT&T bill votes in the House, I invited Claytie and Modesta Williams, Bill Clayton and Carol Barger over for caviar. Exhausted, feeling down, we trooped into my kitchen, only to be greeted by the sound of a vacuum cleaner and wails of Will. He stood sobbing before us, dressed in a once-white shirt, suspenders and shorts and oxfords—covered with ashes and soot from our fireplace. While Bob had showered, Will had climbed into the fireplace, taken the little shovel and proceeded to shovel ashes all over the living room floor. Such is the life of a woman lobbyist.

June 15, 1987

I had a terrific legislative session professionally, but never want to work that hard so long again. The problem is that it's like having a baby—after it's done, you lose sight of the pain in the wonder of the accomplishment.

Going back to work today, I was glad to see people, but missed my sense of autonomy. I think Andy has found that within the firm. Perhaps I shall too. Perhaps I already have.

June 30, 1987

It rained twenty inches this spring. At the ranch, we drove the four-wheeler under some tree branches and were splattered with raindrops. "Mommy, the trees are crying," said Will.

On the stairs from our bedrooms to the living room, Will paused in mid-step to exclaim that the sunset was "beautiful."

August 13, 1987

Will: "At Eastertime, Jesus is napping."

Will: (Upon watching me pee)—"Mommy, where is your penis?"

L: "Mommies and girls don't have penises."

Will: "But Mommy, what *happened* to it? Who took it?"

A classic: Will to Bob: "Your tummy's big. Who lives in there?" We had neglected to explain only women get pregnant!

Bob looks great. He's lost twenty pounds, has moved into offices down the hall from mine. Landis worked as a runner for ten days, so we had the whole family here.

I'm serving on a Bar committee to screen candidates for county court-at-law judges. It's been a fascinating experience, and humbling. The minority candidates are so far some of the best qualified. It has made me realize how far away I am from ever being a judge. Hubris to even consider running. The committee appointment came at an opportune time. I was sort of stale professionally and it has been invigorating to talk about clinical law and procedure and see another side of my chosen profession. As years ago in the Grievance Committee I would return chastised to my caseload and keep better records, etc., I return now to my desk and want to become a better practitioner.

It is time to reconsider goals. What do I want the next few years to bring to my life?

1. Take Bob to Nepal/Tibet/China/New Zealand.
2. See Alaska and Canadian wilderness.
3. Get financial plan for us.
4. Tile the ranch.
5. Begin to look for artwork for home.
6. Enjoy time with Bob and Will.
7. Buy Mom a car.

I have fewer professional goals and that's fine for now. Just see how things roll. So far in life, it's been fine!

Little Shannon goes in for surgery Monday. Hope it's okay.

Daddy is doing better. Out of wheelchair.

August 17, 1987

Will: "Does God have a penis?"

Will, upon handing me a little rectangular piece of plastic to play in his "band": "Mommy, you play the "hor hannika." A new Jewish swear word perhaps.

September 16, 1987

Will, after leaving Matagorda Island and the Gulf: "Mommy, did we remember to turn off the ocean?" Ah, the egocentricity of a three-year-old.

Lately, things are very slow at the office and I am restless to quit this legal world and stay home, out from under unstated pressures.

Read *Children of Alcoholics* and was amazed at the description of myself.

September 28, 1987

Bob and I were in bed at night, reading. Will refused to go to sleep. Suddenly he appeared before us at head level. His ears were stuffed with strips of cotton hanging out and he carried a tray from which he offered us "Chicken fajitas." We both laughed till tears came. What a little hoot!

His birthday was fun—the Tonka bulldozer is the big hit. Someone ran over the back wheel to his tricycle. But Will loves it anyway and rides it up and down the street with the funny bent wheel clanging slightly.

Insight flash: Mom and Dad wanted to have retirement time together, and now they can't. Bob is correct in playing golf and enjoying life *now*. I'm going to try to do the same.

October 15, 1987

It was bow hunting season. Bob dressed in his camouflage, strapped his bow and arrows to the four-wheeler and went to climb a tree in the pasture. Will raced after him, his face in tears, dismayed that he too couldn't be a hunter. So we wiped off the tears, strapped his tiny bow and arrow to my four-wheeler and drove down to the far pasture where a large oak tree had fallen many years ago. Our tree climbing consisted of my boosting Will to his tree seat, weapon and all.

I explained that most of hunting is learning to look and hear. Quiet sitting is not Will's long suit, but he tried his best. Suddenly, to his delight, we heard a muffled rustling. Not a ten-point, but a suitable object to hunt when you're three—a huge armadillo came skittering around the dead tree branches. Will breathlessly took aim, and missed all three times with his little arrows. Armadillo survived the (I'm certain) unprecedented assault. Will and I climbed on the red four-wheeler and drove into our Texas ranch sunset.

Bob didn't even see any deer close enough to have a shot.

October 27, 1987

Thirty-nine years old today! My life goes well. Will and Bob are great. Law practice is slow, somewhat scary considering the October 19 stock market crash/downturn.

November 20, 1987

I bought Mother a car—a 1986 Taurus—thirteen thousand miles—for $10,115. I'm *really* excited. She comes tonight and I'm surprising her with it. The firm is having a tougher time financially, but we'll make it. I'm tired tonight. Women's weekend is this weekend. My anticipation is that it will be calmer than usual.

Irony—Sheila, Ms. Feminist, has married two men with money who've supported her. I, who've never been motivated by money, now make a lot. Also, *Texas Monthly* named me and Bob one of Texas's ten most powerful couples. Bob and I laughed—who would have thought.

Thanksgiving Monday

1. Mother was overwhelmed by the car!
2. On the spur of the moment—literally within an hour—Bob and I decided to take Will to Taos to ski over Thanksgiving. It was a wonderful family time. Will skied in the kinder program. He cried when

we left him, but wouldn't let us teach him. Later he skied "under the rainbow" and was all smiles. A *great* family time.

3. Cana, Will's babysitter, put Will in his Irish fisherman's sweater. Two hours later he told her goodbye, then, "Actually, Cana, when I go fishing I wear a T-shirt."

4. Will wanted some of Bob's coffee.

B: "It's hot, Will."

W: "I'll blow on it." So he did. "It's still hot. I'll blow louder."

December 4, 1987

One night I tried to go to bed early. Bob was going to tell Will a story and put him to bed. Just as sleep beckoned, Bob came to my bed, "What's the ending to Peter Rabbit?"

I went to see a fortune teller. She said Bob and I were soulmates. Accurate.

The Day After Christmas 1987

Will got a holster and toy guns from Santa. He put on his pajamas, then the guns, and asked if he could sleep in them! We explained that the guns were only for the ranch.

I figured out, at almost forty, the secret to the wonderful Christmases at my mother's house: everyone in my family is more excited about *giving* presents than getting them.

January 1, 1988—at the ranch

Will and I just returned from hunting together. He rode in the truck with me to a brushy area beyond the campground—and promptly fell asleep. I sat motionless and listened to the cold winds whip each branch into what appeared to be a fourteen-point buck. At some point in each hunt, when the silence has finally gone beyond sitting still, and entered one's soul—at that moment the trees and brush hum with expectancy. And as the sun fades, each fleeting sun-shadow turns briefly into a magnificent buck. We had that kind of hunt. I've taken a week off from work. Instead of doing something exotic, I've just hung out with Will and Bob and our families at Christmastime, then at our Austin house, and at the ranch.

Friends have joined us at the ranch; David and a friend shot deer here and Will watched them skin and butcher the deer. Sheila and Clay came up and brought some calves. She and I watched the seventeen-year-olds and their hunting talk, and wondered how long the blink of time before Will and Jeffrey replaced them.

On New Year's Eve, I made a terrific dinner for us and we drank a good bottle of champagne and went to bed at 10:30. All three of us.

Tonight, Butch, Marie and the kids came up and we shot fireworks off the back porch and twirled sparklers until the adults were coughing, then roasted marshmallows over an enormous log I found in the pasture and took back to the house. What a marvelous way to celebrate the New Year!

Next year goals:

1. Get in shape—with aerobics and running—maybe get back to one hundred fifteen pounds.
2. Go on some four-day weekends with Bob.
3. Pay off some debts—the cars.
4. Put cream on my hands daily.
5. Stay as calm as possible.
6. Be confident.

I worry about Bob's knee. He was up all night with pain. But he suffers so stoically. Tonight he cleaned up for dinner and was gorgeous. We ate Swedish meatballs and drank wine. No fancy restaurant could be better.

January 4, 1988

Will announced he knew where babies come from—New York! (He has misheard "the stork.")

Going back to work was awkward, yet okay. I feel as if my "real" life is with my family, yet I'd never give up the economic freedom that earning money gives a woman. The workplace does not applaud folks like me, however, who are unwavering in desire to have a normal home life.

Tonight there were two political functions. I didn't want to attend either one because Will went back to school with Carolyn today and I didn't want to have a babysitter. But my male lobby friends would take that as a sign of weakness. I am becoming more aware that I'm not cut out for all of this on some fundamental level, but because I do it very well anyway, I continue.

Will said that when God visits the earth from heaven he comes on a giant ladder with five steps. He's also begun to mimic being an old man and walking bent over. What a character.

March 8, 1988

Will was in the bathtub. I asked, "Did you remember to wash your face?" "No." "Did you wash under your arms?" "Mommy, I guess my name is just 'forgetful.'" Then I took him bundled in a beach towel to Bob on the couch and relayed the exchange. Bob: "You've got to write that down somewhere." A little voice started singing, "Somewhere over the rainbow." We just roared.

At Lena Guerrero's fundraiser, Will was out of control, high on a nutritious dinner of coke and nachos. As we three climbed into the car, Bob tried to get Will buckled up, while Will wanted to hold two glasses of ice and orange juice. Bob, exasperated, said to me, "I don't have any control here." Will promptly reached for the parking control card: "Here's the control card, Daddy."

Since Bob was Governor Babbitt's Texas person, Bob was in demand after Babbitt dropped out of the Presidential primary race. Senator Gore called three times in the evening to our home. I was startled each time I answered the phone to hear, "This is Al Gore. Is Bob in?" What a class act. A politician who makes his own calls.

Tonight after work, Will, Bob and I played with the ball and bat on the sloping green grass hill behind the Four Seasons Hotel. The swans were out, the sunset orange and gold, the air cool. Will threw the bat and rolled the ball down the hill. Bob left for a P & W meeting and Will and I ate at Newport's. He ordered his usual—rainbow trout, and tried my lobster. He didn't like the lobster, but insisted on taking the claws home. At the end of dinner, the waiter told me that the man at the next table wanted to buy me an after dinner drink. I turned to my benefactor and asked, "Do you think I need it?" (The man and his wife were from Kansas—home of Dorothy and Dole!)

March 16, 1988

Will used to drink a water bottle at naps and at bedtime. Since we're working toward no nighttime diaper, I pretended we'd left his bottle at the ranch and he'd have to use his nice Peter Rabbit cup to put water in beside his bed.

In the middle of the night, I heard his squeaky, padded footsteps in my room. He carried his three favorite blankets and his little empty cup. He deposited the blankets on our bed, walked into the bathroom, turned on the light and filled his cup. Then very carefully he came to our bed and placed the little cup on the nightstand beside the bed. Only then did he crawl in for a snuggle. Oh, where is my *baby* boy?

May 9, 1988

Will: (while tree climbing at dusk) "I want to climb this tree so high I could steal the moon!"

Will: (watching a TV show where a man fell from a ship) "I hope he knows how to kick and pull!"

May 10, 1988

Will: "I'm a vegetarian and that means I'm allergic to girls."

May 17, 1988

I put on a new swim suit and put my hair up in clip. Will saw me and said, "You don't look like a Mommy!"

June 1, 1988

We woke up this morning to Will peeking at us in bed. He arrived in his blue-footed pajamas and his Davy Crockett coonskin hat.

July 5, 1988

Will: "I can't eat grilled cheese sandwiches—I need boy cheese sandwiches!"

We went to Rockbridge, Missouri, for three days and had an idyllic vacation. We fished for trout. Will was wonderful! Bob and I laughed—Mom enjoyed us all.

It's been hard to get in the swing of work today.

August 4, 1988

Weight affirmation worked out with Carol Barger: I am a whole and complete person whether I eat this food or not.

Will toasted Honey on her ninetieth birthday: "To the future."

August 28, 1988—in Colorado Springs

A stream of consciousness of goals and dreams—
to have a daughter; have more time with Will; take him to school and pick him up; learn to play good golf; exercise five days a week; run three eight-minute miles; weigh one hundred fourteen; have clear skin; read lots of books; take pictures; fix scrapbooks; learn to make videos; more time with friends; dinner parties once a month; play golf with Bob; work fewer hours; be home when Will comes home from school; pay off debts; own home; enough money to send Mother and David regularly; be more productive at work; be less upset by external work problems, people's perceptions; be less critical of others; travel to China and Nepal with Bob; go to Alaska; camp with Will and Bob; explore spiritual life at church; fix up ranch with new north bedroom; have summer place in mountains; help make law firm more profitable; do more work that I'm good at, less that I don't enjoy; deal with people/clients more; figure out hopes and dreams; learn about Bob's hopes and dreams; laugh a lot.

September 4, 1988—at RHD Memorial Hospital, Dallas, 5:30 a.m.

Reveries of hopes and dreams have been interrupted by present day reality. Daddy may be dying. (Strange way to phrase it, since he's been "dying" for thirty-eight months since the cancer began. Perhaps in that sense we're *all* dying—we just don't know the name of the "what of"—old age, etc.). I came to Dallas expecting it to be the last weekend. After two days at the hospital, I think Daddy is about to pull another miracle out of his seemingly unending bag of medical tricks. He's had two surgeries for a perforated ulcer, he's supposed to be immuno-suppressed from three years of chemo, yet his white blood count jumped from one to six overnight. He's been in lots of almost uncontrollable pain. We children are ready for him to die. Mother is ready for him to be out of pain, but not out of her house—she fears living alone. So would, so do I.

The best thing to happen about this event was meeting and talking with Ed Schulz—the hospital chaplain who knows my dad better than anyone. If God has an emissary to my family, this is he. The same eye contact intensity of Reverend Chuck Myers (the death expert). We talked for a long time. He met Daddy last year when Daddy was so ill with the perforated artery in his groin. He introduced himself as the chaplain and Daddy tried to throw him out. Ed picked Daddy up in bed by the hospital gown and told him he wasn't leaving, and that he was different from other pastors. He made Daddy open up as no one in his life before. Daddy told him of growing up, Luther, the Navy. Those childhood experiences led Daddy to the insanity that became his life until cancer. The drinking, emotional distance with us—all were offshoots of his fundamental lack of self-worth. Ed made him see that someone could know all that about him, and still love him. And, at least from Ed's view, that God could still love him. Over the last year, Daddy began to help other people, cancer patients and families. It helped. He'd never had much to give before, but now he did.

Ed analogized God's grace to a courtroom scene, where the defendant is judged guilty and he is in fact guilty—but God has decided to bear the sentence—if the defendant will let him. Ed told Daddy there would be two great surprises awaiting him: (1) when he opened his eyes and realized he was in heaven and (2) when he realized how much God loved him.

It was so good to talk to Ed because he knew both sides to Daddy—the ugly and bitter and hurtful and the soft inside that had so little time to come out. It was good not to have to be defensive about *either* piece. I believe he must be a phenomenal therapist. Or could it be that God was at work through him. Powerful thought.

In twenty minutes I felt better about myself and Daddy than I had in years.

This was interrupted by Daddy's hallucinating. It took five of us to hold him down—it's now happened three times.

Funny hospital *tale*! Nana fell, cut her head, went to the ER. They x-rayed her bottom. As the doctor tried to get the picture, she exhorted, "Take an extra picture of my ass. I'm sure it's prettier than my face. Make it in color and I'll frame it!" From a one-hundred-and-one-year-old lady!

Bob has been wonderful with Will and my mom. She doesn't want to be alone at home, so he keeps her company. After watching all this go on with Daddy, I'm (a) positive I made the right choice to not be in medicine and (b) not going to do any sustaining life measure on myself. This is no way to exist.

September 10, 1988—at the ranch

Daddy died September 7, 1988. The four of us decided to remove the oxygen, all medication except for pain, and all IV's except for one. We took all the machinery out of his room and pulled a sheet up to his chest. He rested peacefully, and died four hours later. Mother, Cathy, Janet and I were with him. The funeral was two days later. I spoke. Bob sang "Amazing Grace," Ed Schulz preached. At the burial, the funeral director folded up the flag that covered Daddy's casket and presented it to Mom on behalf of the U. S. Government. She got up, walked to where the pallbearers were standing, and gave it to David. He stood tall in his Academy khakis, cropped hair, with tears down his face. Al played taps.

When the service was over in the sanctuary, they opened the casket for the family's last look. Cathy placed a small airplane on the pillow next to Daddy's cheek. The whole experience—hospital and burial—was hard but strengthening for my mom and sisters and me. We talked all night at the hospital about the good things and the bad things. We laughed, we cried. Exhausted, we were glad we had each other.

September 19, 1988—Will's Fourth Birthday

Four years old! Impossible. It underscores my resolve to quit working this hard and spend more time with him.
"Leadership is the ability to empower others."

November 1, 1988

My fortieth birthday was fabulous. Bob gave me a Rolex watch. I couldn't believe it. Carolyn Shellman organized a wonderful work-people party and they played "How well do you know Linda." Jane Rundquist flew in from California for the weekend, and we had a great time.

Our counseling is going well. I'm discovering I can get mad. I'm not sure Bob yet feels that way. We almost fought healthily, last night. I want to take afternoons off from 3:00 on, and spend time on myself and on Will and on Bob. Surely that is accomplishable. Bob said he always thought that being a professional woman was really important to me. It is.

November 6, 1988—Beautiful Sunday Morning

Yesterday at the ranch, I took Will hunting. We loaded the blue four-wheeler with my gun, binoculars, Will's Ghostbuster equipment and took off for the campground. He wore his camouflage clothes and a too-large Parks & Wildlife gimme cap. Cowboy boots completed the outfit.

Crisp, sunny air surrounded us and Will scanned the treeline for deer. At the corner of the open campout field, we parked the vehicle and hid it behind trees. Butch had made a small fort-like enclosure under an oak tree where the two of us climbed in to sit and wait for deer. I propped my rifle on the stacked dead tree branches, to steady it in case the extraordinary occurred and I actually had a shot at the elusive ten-point. Will sat beside me, legs straight out in front of him, body tense and alert for deer. We listened to birds, rustling armadillos and falling leaves. But saw no deer.

Off we went to sit on our armadillo hunting tree. We drove over the bumpy fields and climbed up on our special tree place. Bark was peeling from the fallen trunk, and Will began to tear it off and play a counting game. He spotted two yellow butterflies and tried in vain to follow them through the binoculars. We watched the breeze turn the grass stalks into ocean waves, and Will practiced listening for the leaves rustling. "The leaves are falling; that means it's autumn, Mommy." He was so proud of his announcement. We laughed, listened, smiled and hugged. A *magic day*, an ordinary day with my Will-o.

Later, we went shopping for my dress shoes. Out of the blue, Will asked how old you had to be to go to college. "Eighteen," I replied. "When I go to college, I'll be an astronaut and then on my first spaceship I'll go way up high and get Papa and bring him back. I'll visit heaven to take a look around." My heart ached for love of Will and loss of Daddy.

November 16, 1988

Therapy has stirred up emotions; made me aware of my enabling behavior. I'm trying to be better, but not totally succeeding. (Who ever does?)

The weather finally turned cold and winter's chill seems fresh to me. I'm taking pictures again; still dreaming of writing. I've begun to realize that I take pictures and write out of a need that is apart from public praise, although that is lovely, of course, when it happens.

February 1, 1989—at Angel Fire, New Mexico

Skiing! We drove through a genuine blizzard last night in order to get Mother to and from Taos hospital where a doctor looked at her knee she twisted on the slopes. Torn ligaments, not too serious, but it hurts and, of course, worries her about how to get to work, etc. She's a good sport at sixty-six!

Bob said he couldn't see the snow falling outside the condo through the windows. Will explained, "You have to put your nose against the window to see the snow." The blizzard was scary. Cars were going off the road in droves.

Will also painstakingly wrote a message on his placemat at dinner: "Bob, I love," then asked me how to spell "you very much."

June 29, 1989—on plane to Austin from Fort Worth

The session is complete. All my clients came off okay. I actually enjoyed a lot of the work. Smaller mountains to tackle mean smaller headaches.

I survived a breast biopsy and cancer scare. After a day of being poked and cut the good news was that everything was benign. It made me focus on unfinished business.

Will told Sonja that, "Mommy had surgery. They put a needle in her nipple . . . or her hip . . . ."

July 23, 1989

Will saw a wedding on TV: "Mommy, I'll marry you when I grow up."

Me: "But I'm married to Daddy. You need to marry somebody else not in the family." Will: long pause—"Well, I guess I'll just have to marry Grandma." It was worth a call to Mom in England where she was visiting Cathy!

December 6, 1989

Will: "How do you cry in Spanish?"

His teacher Mary Ann Torrance wrote on his report card, "When Will puts his mind to something, I don't think there is anything he cannot accomplish. I often think of him as the number one student because he tries so hard both at learning and at interacting positively with other children. He is sensitive and proud. I think he internalizes feelings sometimes, but will discuss them when approached in a caring, loving way. Will is an inspiration to me in all ways. He is what being a teacher is all about. We love him."

January 8, 1990—seven-year anniversary

Bob and I each, unbeknownst to the other, sent seven roses to the other. I guess we must be in tune on some level!

Leadership Texas wants an anonymous form returned listing our (1) goals for the coming year; (2) long range plans or goals.

Goals for the Coming Year

1. Go home at 5:00 one day a week.
2. Have more *fun* with Bob.
3. Exercise four times a week.
4. Write six chapters of a book.
5. Plan financial goals.
6. Go to Australia.

Long range

1. Financial security for retirement.
2. Travel more.

February 1, 1990

Nice things are happening to Bob!

1. Elected to the Board of Directors of the Trust for Public Lands.
2. Letter from Ed Wendler saying Bob was the only ex-politician with integrity that everyone wanted to see.
3. Letter from someone in Saudi Arabia commending him for Big Bend purchase.
4. He was listed in *Ultra* magazine as one of fifty people of the 80s who made a difference to Texas.

But I was mad at him for not being home to pick up his clothes before a party for the firm's law clerks.

February 20, 1990

Will threw a penny into a wishing well. Later, making idle conversation, I asked what he wished for. "For God to give the poor people more money." The totally unconscious sincerity of his reply made my eyes sting. He is a remarkable five-year-old.

April 16, 1990

Will at Snowbird on our spring ski vacation, outraged that Bob began to wash his hair in the shower without telling him the shampoo was going onto his head: "You could at least have *informed* me!"

The Easter Bunny came to our hotel room. He left a small stuffed bunny. I asked Will what he was going to name him. "Well, I was going to name him Harold, but that isn't a good name for a bunny, so I'm just going to call him Bunny."

First utterance upon waking this morning: "Mom! I don't think William Hunter Aaker Armstrong is a good name. 'Will' is okay for a kid, but not a grown-up." "What would you like to be called?" "A grown up name like Dad's, you know, like 'Bob.'"

April 30, 1990

Will asked, "Was I damaged?" when I told him he had fallen out of a swing when he was two years old.

We have a new nanny. I asked Will how she was doing. "She's coming along just fine. I directed her to Luby's cafeteria."

I talked to Andy today about going part-time so
1. More time for me.
2. More time for Bob and me.
3. More time for Will.
It felt incredibly freeing to talk about it.

Summer 1990—July (At Akumal, Yucatan, on vacation with Bob and Will)
Ideas for writing:
1. Parenting is like flying—minor corrections, initial years/time spent in flight check—preflight/immunizations, dentists; maintenance is important.
2. Will is defined by his passion for *learning*—anything from number relations, to God-questions; from how does the sprinkler work, to how does the universe work. Bob is defined by his passion for

doing—acting, whether it's sports—golf, skiing—or politics, Parks & Wildlife, Land Office. He experiences the world through his senses.

I'm more defined by my passion for feeling and observation. I experience the world internally. My mind's life is as teeming as my outside existence. Part of what makes Will such an interesting child is the striking combination of the two.

This vacation is rich in visual memories. Tulum ruins were a perfect place for a small boy to experience his first archeological enthusiasm. He ran from stone to stone across the plain. Easy to spot because he had his red bandanna and red baseball hat on his head. Foreign Legion style.

Bob put "LA" on his own back in tape and created a sun-brand. Wow!

We went ocean fishing. No fish. Will fell asleep on my lap. He was covered up against the sun in one of my long-sleeved T-shirts (ironically, from "Legal Writing Seminar") and I held him as we bounced through rough late-afternoon seas. For an hour, I watched the peacock-blue-ink-colored water and the brown back of Will's neck. It reminded me of the hours of nursing him. *Then* I knew every hair on his head—literally—because I stared at it for forty minutes, every four hours, for what seemed years. Now, short, fine blond hairs cover his neck. Several small dark moles have appeared on his back, next to an occasional chicken pox scar, that only a mother would notice. (Or maybe, someday, a first lover.)

The snorkeling is amazing. Schools of multicolored fish everywhere. Feels like you're swimming inside an aquarium.

July 4, 1990

Will in an innertube at Diane and Rowland's pool after a 4th of July BBQ dinner with Kevers: "Life doesn't get any better than this!"

July 30, 1990

I want to write about secondary women. Peggy, Sonja, me. About our trials and tribulations.

August 26, 1990

It's too hard right now. My job is hard. It's not fun. But Will is fun. I love him.

August 27, 1990

At least Bob and I are both getting thinner. Bob's lost sixteen pounds, me five. Today was better. Our lifestyle is too hectic and needs changing. But when things go well, it's an exciting, vibrant world.

Will is in a big growing streak. His speech is remarkable. A local pediatrician couldn't believe how advanced he was. Physically, he's in an absolutely gorgeous stage.

October 10, 1990

Will: "How did you get out of the shower so fast? It must be Mom Magic!"

Being a mother means looking at every person with new eyes— because each of them was some mother's baby. Someone knew each hair, each tiny wrinkle, each fold behind a little ear.

January 1991

For the next several months, I am going to mainly concentrate on writing poetry seriously, and will not write much in this journal.

August 1991

The Democratic Leadership Council (DLC) organized a luncheon at the Headliners for Bill Clinton today. He's been Governor of Arkansas now for what seems like forever. Before, when he's come to Austin, Bob and I have had Mexican food with him, or he's come to the ranch. We've just sort of laid back and laughed a lot. The only really serious time I recall was an airport discussion held standing by the wing of his plane, and Bob and I were giving him our pros and cons of whether he should enter the 1988 presidential race.

Today was different. Bill gave an hour-long speech and Q and A to about thirty people. He was eloquent, thoughtful—and seemed very confident of his positions on various issues. But the confidence was more mature than that of the cocky young Attorney General I'd met fifteen years ago.

After the speech, we talked on the sidewalk in front of the building. He wanted my opinion on whether he should run for President. "No," I told him. Bush is riding high, and the campaign will be brutal for Hillary and Chelsea. I told him if he announced, we'd help, of course. But I really hope he doesn't run.

December 1991

Hi, journal! I'm back, sort of. I did write poetry more regularly, and submitted a couple for publication, but got rejected. Maybe my sixth grade English teacher was right when she gave me a B on my poetry (my first B in English) and wrote, "You would have been more at home, and more able in prose." Yuk!

January 8, 1992 (Our Ninth Anniversary)

I stopped to pray on the way to work. The rains had washed out the stream bed by the park where I usually park my car. I try to quiet my insides so I can talk and listen to God. Today I tried so hard to concentrate on the quieting, that I felt the top of my head in my brain start to open up. It was as if someone was pulling on my brain to pull it out of itself. Then I heard birds sing and I flashed for a moment on whether they were God's messengers to people like me. Maybe listening was at least partly listening to the nature we have been given. Then I tried to open my heart, not just my head. I had another vision/feeling of my heart inside my chest being literally opened up, bleeding, but open to the air, vulnerable, waiting for comfort but with every expectation that it would come. The Holy Spirit? Then I lost my listening concentration and drove to work.

Will's recent sayings:

1. "Do you remember when I went to school at Mary Ann's (his preschool) and there wasn't any early and there wasn't any late?"
2. "I was a very lucky boy yesterday, Mom. I was writing and the pencil just stuck me in the eye, but I was writing so it was the eraser end." (Here is the child of his ever optimistic parents!)

Saturday, July 12, 1992 (New York, New York—for the Democratic National Convention)

An unplanned trip! Governor Richards was asked to be chair of the convention, and she asked Bob if he wanted to go with her so he could see his candidate accept the nomination for President. At the last minute, I decided to come, too, and work as staff for Ann. We arrived in New York at 2:00 p.m., with a staff meeting at 3:00. I was assigned the states of Arkansas, Ohio and Wyoming to monitor. Sort of act as the Governor's representative as chair of the convention to see if they need anything.

We're staying with Martha Louise and her new husband George. They are so young and in love. It's fun to be with the kids as grownups. We took them to see *Man of La Mancha*. The music was as great as I recalled, but the show is old now. Sitting in the theatre balcony, I remembered the first time I saw it. When I graduated from high school, I went to New York for a week with my then boyfriend. (Actually, he was a male friend. I remember negotiating—and getting—separate hotel rooms.) I was in a thin stage, and wore a blue dress, and yes, false eyelashes. What possessed me to wear the eyelashes, I don't know. The performance was masterful. When Don Quixote sang "The Impossible Dream," tears streamed down my face, and inevitably dislodged one of the eyelashes. I looked like one-half of a Maybelline Velvet Eyes commercial. And was mortified.

Tonight, I was not even wistful for the girl-that-was. Sometimes now, I don't even wear mascara.

Sunday, July 13, 1992 (New York)

We overslept, so raced (literally down the streets) to the 9:00 a.m. staff meeting in our sneakers and shorts. Afterwards, we decided to stop by the Intercontinental Hotel and see the Clinton headquarters. We took the elevator to the top floor. It opened. Right in front of us was Bill Clinton. He scooped me into a huge hug and pulled Bob with us into a corner where he proceeded to quiz Bob about his perception of Bill's choice for Vice President, Al Gore. I couldn't believe it. I thought we'd never see Bill and Hillary again.

Bill left and we decided to shop for a pair of comfortable shoes. Cole-Haan had a sale, so we stopped in. While trying on shoes, I heard a familiar Texas voice, "I knew all the best people would be shopping here." It was Ann Richards and her son Dan.

Outside the shoe store, people were lining the sidewalk just to look at our Governor. She's really become a celebrity—bigger than politics. A TV crew was following her around—filming her buying shoes! She invited us to go with her around the block to her taping of the next morning's "Today" show. Inside the studio, while Ann waited for the technical details, a young schoolgirl stood earnestly holding a clipboard, obviously wanting to interview Ann. The Governor walked over to her, grinned and said, "I know the answer, so you have to have the question." Everyone in the room laughed, and the little girl was put immediately at ease. Ann's got it.

Tonight was the Governor's big party at the Supper Club. Jane Hickie assigned me to escort Hillary to the party. What a *great* job! But the party was a major event; everyone wanted to come, and there was limited space due to fire hazard regulations. People were lined up for blocks demanding to come in. When Hillary came, she was swept into the crowd by handlers so fast I barely saw her. She's become a celebrity, too.

Monday, July 14, 1992

Things are moving too fast here. Notes will have to suffice. After a *late* night, we were up and at delegate caucuses at 8:00 a.m. Made a speech at the Ohio caucus. (Arkansas wouldn't let me in!) Went to Emily's List luncheon for the beginning reception. Left a note for Harriett Woods (NWPC). Drew credentials for Monday night. Went to convention. Ann Richards' speech was great. Ran into Rep. Paul Ohgren (Minn.), Sandee's husband who crafted Minnesota's Health Care Reform legislation. Off to a McGovern reunion. Met Frank Mankowitz, Gloria Steinem and Bella Abzug. (Bob to Bella: "Nice to meet my alphabetical friend from the Nixon's Enemies List!") Collected Molly Ivins and went to Texas delegation party—too loud. Home 2:00 a.m.

Tuesday, July 15, 1992

Up at 8:00 for delegate caucus. Lunch at Time Warner with Bernie Sorkin and his wife; Jane Goldman; Joe Lelyveld; and Bob. Molly had to work, so was a disappointing no-show. Pat got us backstage passes to meet President Carter. Waited at security entrance for Margo, "a black woman dressed in black with white tennis shoes." She's head of all convention security, we discover later. When staff asked President Carter if he wanted to see Bob Armstrong, he said, "Absolutely."

Short visit, went on to the convention floor and visited all around. Fun. Stayed with Lena Guerrero backstage in Jesse Jackson's room while she prepared (nervously) for speech. Went to Carter reunion dinner. Fancy. Saw everybody. Frank Moore, Scott Burnett, Hodding Carter, Jody Powell. Loved it when Sam Donaldson left his group hunkered down at a table to see Bob! Met nice couple, I think ordinary. Turns out he's part-owner of Bulls Basketball team in Chicago. Tried to get him with Clinton and Richards. Home 1:30 a.m.

Thursday, July 17, 1992

Slept in. Off to Intercontinental for credentials. Again, ran into Bill Clinton at fourteenth floor. Perot had just announced he was dropping out of the race. BC asked what we thought. Folks worried about timing, wanted Perot in race longer. I told BC, "The operative word is OUT" (of race). Asked Spence to take our picture with Bill. Bob was sort of embarrassed that I'd asked.

Lunch with Carter people at Peninsula Hotel Rooftop. George comes. Rory Benson (NAB) gives him and Martha Louise passes. I buy books for folks who helped us. Bob to AR staff room. Harriett calls to see if we want to go to Kennedy reception at Water Club. Cast of famous folks. Harriett is Senator Metzenbaum's cousin. Lots of senators, etc. Senator Culver's daughter is a Luther College grad married to Scoggins (Olympic diver—living in Austin!). Back to change. Off to convention. Meet ML and George at convention. Sit in hall on steps of convention floor and listen to Bill Clinton, Gore.

At end, I cry. Go to skybox. B. Rapoport tells me how great Bob is. I say, "Yes, we've been married ten years and I wake up each morning delighted to be with him."

To Sheraton for dinner with Entergy. It's 1:00 a.m.! Room unconsciously packed. Dinner—Entergy men and wives, Senator Bumpers, me and Bob, Jane and Deece. Funny scene with someone who just sat down uninvited to the table. Bill waves at us (we're right up at the stage). After speech, we surge up to see/wave at him, Hillary and Gores. BC reaches down to clasp my hand. Secret Service moves him along. He goes a few steps, stops and he, HRC lean way down to us. HRC, "Bobby, can you *believe* we did it!" BC holds both hands with me and gives big grin. Home at 3:00 a.m.

Friday, July 17, 1992

Up to see papers. Hear rumors that Perot may divulge economic plan on Larry King live tonight. A friend in the Perot camp thinks BC should call Perot. Spend morning calling BC folks to try to make that happen. Give them Perot's direct line.

Off to airport for home. We're tired. Too old to do this schedule for more than a week.

August 3, 1992—British Columbia—at our Gold Claim at Squaw Creek

What to say about these vistas near the Yukon, where vast distant mountains look impassively at the torn up creek below and at we mere mortals trying to dig through the land's past for gold for our future? And why gold? Is it merely for money? Each of these men could make more money, or at least steadily more money, in their chosen worlds, than they can here.

Squaw Creek, so named for the Indian women who panned and found gold here years ago, now resembles something out of modern rock video. Desolate vehicles are left among the rocks, to rust or be vandalized. The old machinery leaves a record of the previous tenants. Some left their cast iron troughs with shattered dreams.

Others left too happy, ready to count their catch immediately, and never returned to reclaim the monsters of homemade metal that facilitated the new-found wealth.

Not much has changed, fundamentally, since the days of the Wild West gold rush. After a hard day's work digging a stream channel, welding the sluice-box, fixing three good meals to keep energy and hopes high, talk still turns to honorable and dishonorable men. The men play poker and tell tales of human transportation. The names of the vehicles have merely changed from horses to airplanes. How fast, how far, who to trust, when to hold 'em. The male version of female chitchat rises and falls throughout the long evenings where night never really falls, only softly beckons toward the next twenty hours of daylight.

Shades of purple flowers grace the hillsides—both the natural and those made of cast off stones. They stand proudly, too, on the linoleum table in the cabin—ubiquitous in their splendor.

August 1992

Soon I will join the Clinton/Gore Campaign bus as it travels through Texas. Then later Lucia W. and I will visit secondary newspapers for the campaign. I can't write in this journal and also record the trip for the office. I want my law firm, BHS, to understand what I'm doing (since I'm not billing).

August 29, 1992—Memo to Bickerstaff—Campaigning with the "Clinton Road Warriors" on the Clinton/Gore bus to Corsicana, Texas

I used to just read history; for the past day and a half I've participated in it. Here, on a bus filled with intensely competitive young men and women, American politics is being reshaped.

In Austin a huge crowd covered the LBJ Library fountain area waiting for the man from Hope—to bring hope. It had rained hard all morning; our worries were needless as the Texas sun burned off the cloud cover.

Bob flew in from Colorado and we met up with each other briefly. Will (it had been his first day of third grade) gave his dad a grand "hello" hug. Afterwards, we followed the Clintons and Gores through the LBJ library. Hillary had never seen the letter Jackie Kennedy wrote to LBJ the day after JFK's funeral.

The bus left Austin and headed up I-35. At Georgetown, a non-scheduled crowd of 300 lined up at the WalMart. We stopped. The Clintons and Gores walked the crowd, shaking hands and apparently gathering strength from the outpouring of support. A Baptist minister brought his teenaged daughter on a respirator to see Clinton. They were proud people who sought hope in a worldly sense to match their belief in a spiritually hopeful future.

At Salado at sundown, the light was gentle, the day had cooled and the small grassy field was filled with kindergartners in an old carriage, carrying signs and shouting, "We want Bill." The drill team—pert young Texas girls in red and white—called for Hillary, who has become a minor political cult figure since the Republican convention when they made the mistake of bashing her.

It was a Norman Rockwall painting when the two young men and their blond wives stood tall and in shirt sleeves proclaimed a message for change, for hope. Cynical politicians—Ron Brown, Garry Mauro, Bob Squires—we all felt goosebumps in the gentle magic. Was it nostalgia or a glimpse of our future?

Bill came into our bus and rode eighty miles to Waco. He sat next to me and regaled the eight or ten people on the bus with tales. We talked old times, politics, policy. Each time I see Bill in a setting where we can actually visit, I assume it is the last time I'll ever be able to have a normal conversation with The-Man-Who-Will-Be-President. And each time he remains the same extraordinary—but ordinary—guy I've always known. Passionate in his convictions, hard-hitting in his humor, compassionate towards his friends. He's still real.

Waco. Baptist territory. The crowds lined the river and the bridge. He shook every hand and crossed the quarter-mile bridge in forty-five minutes. On the bus, he told us he wanted to go bowling! We didn't. Instead, eight of us (not Clintons and Gores) went to George's (a restaurant) for chicken fried steak and beer. No taxis run in Waco at 1:00 a.m. on Friday. We stood in a darkened parking lot, with pebbles prickling our shoes. So we hitchhiked with a young man in a jeep back to the hotel.

Today we spent lots of time in Waco at the Texas Utilities plant. We waited while Gore gave seven live interviews by satellite to Detroit. Bill gave a press conference on the lies Bush tells about the Arkansas tax record.

An hour and a half late for Corsicana, we nevertheless stop at two tiny Texas towns, Dawson and Hubbard, where the whole town turned out to see the caravan. How can we not stop for a sign that says, "Give us eight minutes and we'll give you eight years!"

Amid the Clinton signs, there is a group of Bush supporters with signs. But they're stopped in front of a cemetery! In contrast, across the road, an elderly lady had wrapped a sheet around a hula hoop and spray-painted "Welcome Bill and Al."

Way behind schedule, we now just wave to the people who line the road at each small hamlet.

I am stunned. In August, people are standing for hours just to wave at a bus behind whose impenetrable windows sits a Presidential candidate. *We're going to win.*

October 6–7, 1992–Memo to BHS—On the road in Central Texas

Cool. The edge of August's heat has been broken.

Driving north on the interstate in one little car with two other women is a far cry from August's buses loaded with candidates, staff, press. Now is the lonely time. We are retracing some of the bus tour stops to visit local papers and communities to talk about the Democratic Leadership Council (DLC)—the think tank type group out of which grew the moderate Democratic Party movement. Both Clinton and Gore were founding members.

Texans are tough—and not particularly forgiving. At the first gas station convenience store, I test the political waters. "How is Perot playing here?" Haughty sniffs worthy of Buckingham Palace are the reply. No articulation of the reason is given. He quit. (Bill is just the opposite: he's like the Energizer commercial and just keeps on going, no matter what.)

This scene is repeated over and over. Perot is just not a factor. I'm mystified by the polls that show he's getting *any* support. They must be taken in Dallas.

Killeen's last big media event was the Luby's slaying where a madman gunned town the citizenry at dinner last year. We visit a few days before the anniversary of the event, which seems much more compelling than the Presidential race. The editor is pleasant, impressed he actually received some pertinent information from Clinton's Little Rock office on military spending issues. As we turn the conversation to DLC issues, I am hopeful.

Up the road, Temple is doing just fine, thank you. Here at the home of the famous Scott and White Clinic, the economy has not been impacted negatively by Republican politics. I guess people get sick under either party. The status quo reigns here: "The reason business is in business is for profits—not to create jobs." The Deming of America has not reached central Texas.

This is much harder than following the adoring crowds who surrounded Bill and Hillary a month ago.

In Waco, the Democratic headquarters are open year-round. And *organized*. The workers tell us how impressed the Clinton advance folks were with Waco. When the bus tour came through, the advance team finished at 7:30 p.m. the night before the event, and sat around telling campaign stories. Unheard of in advance annals. Mementos of the bus tour—pictures, articles—fill the headquarters. A month later, we are a blip on the political screen, but provide willing listeners to the volunteers' tales.

The next day in Bastrop and La Grange, we are grilled about Bill Clinton and trust. Here in the country, people don't want Bush, but are uneasy with Clinton. It is difficult for us who really know Bill to respond. We have known him. We trust him. But how can three middle-aged women in a rent car filled with press packets and Diet Cokes change minds, or influence this election? Somehow in civics class, they didn't say the democratic process would be like this.

A fun moment. We look up, startled, as we whiz through *Hope*,

Texas. Based on nothing, our spirits soar. The La Grange editor said the Democratic Party beat the Republicans in one critical way—they could weave a vision of a dream better. Part of me feels we're living in a dream.

The Clinton/Gore headquarters in Victoria is manned by a Republican—not a convert, he assures me, but a Clinton supporter for this election. He may be the living proof of Governor Richards' line about some Clinton supporters being Republicans who voted for Reagan and Bush, and who still aren't rich. He can't direct us to the Democratic Party headquarters, but he can point the way to the newspaper's building. There, we are *news*. We meet with the managing editor and two reporters. The staff photographer snaps our picture. Hey, maybe we *are* accomplishing something!

Buoyed by success, we travel swiftly through ever smaller Texas towns, dropping information by the weekly newspapers and chatting with whoever will talk with us. We find the papers the old fashioned way: if the address is Church Street, we look for a church; Water Street is near the river. The theme we hear is universal: "Clinton will win, whether I've decided to vote for him or not, and I probably will."

Tired, talked out, we share a hamburger at the Gonzales drivethru Whataburger. No state dinner could taste better.

Yes, we really may win Texas.

Friday, October 16, 1992—Memo to BHS—San Marcos

We parked our rent car at McDonald's and walked three-quarters of a mile in high heels along the weeds of the frontage road. Bereft of our Clinton memorabilia, buttons, etc., we marched over to hear Barbara Bush address the crowds in McCoy's parking lot. I'm sure some passing cars thought we were nice Republican women taking their lunch hour to hear the First Lady. Actually, we were spies. But polite ones.

The sky was threatening and the Secret Service stopped us before we could get very close to the bus. George Bush, Jr., spoke to the crowd in English and Spanish. Why in the world would the Hispanics in the audience think they would be better off with Bush than Clinton? Barbara Bush took the podium. She stressed the choice between two very different men. So far, so good. I agreed with her. But then she began a harangue about all the defense projects her husband brought to Texas and chastised Bill for his lack of support for the Superconducting Supercollider. Is the latter true? I don't think so. When she described the importance of the Republicans winning their "home state of Texas," I rolled my eyes at Lucia. Home state? A hotel room in Houston?

It began to rain. We loved it. Hurriedly, we grabbed two posters and carried them above our heads to prevent ruin of our Republican-type hairdos.

To reach our car, we took a short cut and walked along a stretch of railroad under the Interstate Highway. In the early romantic novels I'd read, boys merrily walk along railroad ties carrying fishing gear and having deep adolescent talks—usually about sex or baseball. Lucia and I traipsed through the rocky, pebble-filled shoulders of the railroad tracks, high heels scuffed up, Bush signs for umbrellas, and talked politics. Middle-aged adolescents.

Emerging from the underpass, dodging Interstate traffic to return to the car, we share a serious moment. Funny, wet, bedraggled as we are, we still represent a bedrock idea of this country. We are the people the Constitution was written for—ordinary citizens who have the right to speak out, support a candidate, call on newspapers, and yes, even attend the other side's rallies. It is still a *free* country.

October 19 & 20, 1992—Memo to BHS—Forging into Deep East Texas
A new warrior is added to the group. Nan, the government relations person from Motorola, has just returned from a week in Chicago living and breathing the hardnosed business world of corporate America. From meetings with the CEO and Chairman of the Board, she is now with me traveling through Taylor and Thorndale, Texas. When we walked into the Taylor paper, we asked for the editor or the political reporter. The young woman gazed at us somewhat critically and responded, "I am *the* reporter." Actually, our visit went well.

Down the road, to reach the Rockdale newspaper, one has to walk through a printing supplies shop. Past the legal pads and the yellow Post-Its, beyond the pencils and the ink pads, around the corner and into the bowels of the building are the newspaper offices and production plant. The editor explains that his county always goes Democratic, but our message of moderation from the Democratic Leadership Council "sure makes it easier this time."

After Rockdale, we drive to College Station, the home of Texas A & M. I visit briefly with the editor of the *College Station Battalion*, the student newspaper, in the heart of conservative college land. He seems surprisingly interested in the DLC. The Vice Chancellor's wife has offered to host a small gathering of women in her home. We meet while the florist decorates the house for an evening University event and we discuss politics. I am struck by the strength of women. Our hostess is an epidemiologist by training, teaches, produces major dinner parties, and still finds time to meet with women on short notice to see what she can do to help the campaign in College Station. In particular, she, unlike many women, loved Hillary Clinton's remark about cookies. She relates a tale in a similar vein that happened to her as a university administrator's wife. These women come up with a brilliant idea: On October 28th in conjunction with the Women Light the Way for Change event, they will have a candlelighting ceremony in front of the George Bush Memorial Library site. I love it. We visualize CNN covering the event!

As we drive to Crockett to meet up with the other "Road Warrior" car (Lucia and Karol) we try to hear bits and pieces of the Presidential debates on our radio, whose signals crackle because of the pine forest surrounding us. (No one thinks of Texas as being wooded. They are dead wrong.) The other group has had a successful day—speaking with three newspapers and making drops of press packets at two others.

The next morning delights us with a brilliant sunrise as we walk around the parking lot of the Crockett Inn to get some exercise before we head for a day in the car. Nan and I travel to Lufkin, home of Temple Industries, lots of forests, and the editor of the paper (who is further to the left than we are and wants to talk about welfare reform and abortion issues). We are amazed as we discuss the issues with this thoughtful man. Leaving town, I dash into Angelina Junior College for a brief visit with their newspaper editor.

On twenty-four hours' notice, the women in Huntsville have convened at the Steak and Spirits Restaurant for lunch. It's an exciting crew that includes the woman who is their past mayor as well as the university president's wife and various other community activists. These women ask hard, substantive questions. Where is Bill Clinton on the details of how he intends to convert defense jobs to nonmilitary jobs? What kind of federal job training dollars will be available for those efforts? What exactly is the plan to reduce the deficit while increasing investment in America? How will higher education be impacted by Governor Clinton's plan? I answer the questions as best I can with Nan rescuing me on a few.

At all these gatherings of women, I have brought my homemade picture album of snapshots from the Clinton-Gore bus tour. Each time I bring them out I am worried that people will think they are, as my son says, "dorky." But people love them. It makes the Clintons and the Gores real. I explain that my husband has known Bill Clinton for twenty years and I have known him for fifteen, and that he is a brilliant man with the integrity and leadership skills to make a great President. But these women are also hungry for details about Hillary. I tell them about our puddle jumping tour through West Texas last spring where the schedule got all mixed up and Hillary handled it with grace and extreme competence. These women can hardly wait for Hillary to be First Lady. We explain that we need everyone's help to make that happen. The women agree to raise money for a radio ad on women's issues if I can get the campaign here to cut one. I make that promise.

After the women's meeting in Huntsville we catch up with Lucia and Karol. We meet in a restaurant that is beneath the Republican Party headquarters. Giggling, we take pictures outside the restaurant decorated with GOP banners. Inside, the four of us revamp next week's Texas tour and make plans for West Texas and Beaumont trips. This group is covering a lot of territory.

We travel on to the paper at Conroe and stop at Prairie View A & M and then begin the drive back to Austin. The day is getting long. But the campaign is getting shorter. Thank goodness.

October 23, 1992—Memo to BHS—Austin–Dallas–Austin

In this campaign, no one is too good to make the coffee. The last time Bob debated on the University of Texas campus, he debated John Tower in the Reagan/Mondale race. Last night he appeared on behalf of the Clinton campaign before a group of pre-law undergraduates and debated the Bush and Perot representatives. The Bush man's claim to fame was a lost City Council race. When Bob began his opening remarks (after the other two presented canned, earnest appeals) and spoke of leaving his first job in 1960 to help John Kennedy run, I knew we'd won the audience! We couldn't find any Clinton/Gore position papers on such short notice, so Bob studied an hour over the DLC packet the Road Warriors use. Our influence is spreading.

Today, Lucia and I met with the owner of seven suburban Dallas papers. His office was covered with Republican pictures—him with Reagan, Quayle, Clayton Williams, and a handwritten letter from Kemp. Because he had known Lucia as an old Duncanville girl (she lived there almost ten years), he was willing to do a piece on "Local Girl Makes Good as DLC Executive Director" and allow us to meet with reporters to infuse the article with some DLC substance. His credenza contained a panoply of campaign buttons and materials. He voted for Buchanan but playfully attached a Clinton button to his lapel for picture purposes.

Over lunch we discussed Dallas/Texas politics. Like everyone else, he believes Bill will win. But he thinks Bush will carry Texas and Perot will garner a percentage in the high twenties in Dallas, low twenties statewide. That remains to be seen. His brand of Republican honesty assesses the economy as getting better—six quarters of increased growth. According to this publisher, Bill will be a two-term President because he won't mess up what is already beginning to get better.

After three weeks on the road, I'm convinced that while there exist themes and melodies of this strange campaign year, the variations on the themes are as intimate as the people we encounter. What a country!

October 26–27, 1992—Memo to BHS—To West Texas—lots of road for the Road Warriors!

Before we left Austin for our West Texas trip, I went to the doctor to get antibiotics for a raging sinus infection. Do Bill and Hillary ever get sick on these trips? What do they do? We can't just stop. It's like having a child. You fix dinner no matter how you feel, because the baby needs food.

Thus, our leaving was inauspicious. With a roll of toilet paper for kleenex, we loaded up the Clinton-mobile with DLC folders, Ten-More for Clinton-Gore forms and our briefcases full of work for our real-life clients. As Lucia leaned over to pack the car, two black buttons popped off her dress and escaped forever into the black dirt of the flowerbed. We hooked her together with various Clinton-Gore buttons. Onward to Lampasas!

The local paper lay spread on the news counter glaring the front page story that the school children of Lampasas overwhelmingly chose Perot for President. Buried in the story were the national statistics of the school poll. Clinton won by a landslide. The bespectacled editor in a button-downed lightly striped Oxford shirt admitted he was a Republican, but listened to our message. Hard to get a real read on Lampasas.

Goldwaithe, Texas, has a small paper. Lucia chatted a bit and left a press packet while I figured out if we were going to make it to Abilene by dark. In Brownwood, we visited with a large woman who funneled the assignments to reporters, but who wouldn't write anything down herself.

By Abilene, we were ready for a big city paper. The plant was in a high rise building and there was even an editorial staff. But the woman city editor explained that the political reporter had taken these last two weeks off! Excuse me, we said. The two weeks before the Presidential election? Yep. He'd be back for Tuesday night. We wondered if he'd have a job. Guess everyone doesn't take this stuff as seriously as we do!

Although it's late, we decide to drive to San Angelo. A mistake. We look for a motel with only one condition—room service. Lost, we end up at a Whataburger drive-in asking the squawk box for directions to the Holiday Inn. The hamburger folks thought we were joking. We find the inn, which has no room service and only pizza available for delivery. Soggy pizza it is. These are the nights that I will recall when Bruce Babbitt tries to tell me the airplane tarmac tours are tough!

The next morning I awake to a phone call from Bob and Will singing happy birthday. I am now forty-four years old.

Lucia and I throw on jogging clothes for a quick walk to counteract a month of hamburgers and road pizza. Small houses cluster behind the hotel and we are excited about a neighborhood stroll to replace our motel parking lot routine. But two women walk by carrying large sticks. A strange looking man passes us. We jump into a Stop 'n Go for toothpaste and casually inquire about directions. "I wouldn't walk around here. We had one shooting two nights ago and a mugging last week." So much for crime in San Angelo.

This drive is interminable. In far West Texas, when you drive around you *know* you are in West Texas. Here, between Brady and Mason, it feels like no man's land. Out here even our phone won't work. The Cellular One company doesn't even have a contract for a cell. People here are into visual aids. One store had ten-foot renditions of farm and ranch implements painted on the two-story structure. We almost missed the San Angelo paper because it was housed in a low-slung building adorned with a picture of a large orange rooster in an oval plaque with the words "Standard and Times" on either side of the crowing bird. I thought it was a distribution center for fried chicken franchises. In Brady, lest anyone miss the fact we were in God's country, the paper's emblem is in the shape of a cross with the words "Standard and Herald" emblazoned on the sign.

Fredericksburg, two papers in Kerrville, and we head for home. Six more days to go. Surely we will all make it.

November 8, 1992—Memo to BHS—On the plane to Seattle for Leadership America Meeting

Our friend Bill Clinton is President-elect of the United States of America.

On election eve in Little Rock, we went to headquarters where Begala was ecstatic, when for a few hours it looked like Texas would join the electoral landslide. We were with the staff while Koppel interviewed Carville, who wiped tears away. Carville cried and when asked what he had contributed, somewhat surprisingly but accurately said, "I taught this party how to fight."

Wednesday morning, we went back to headquarters, visited briefly and cried tears of joy with Betsey Wright. But it wasn't until we saw President-elect Clinton on a TV monitor in Dallas at the layover that the enormity of this election began to sink in. The President-elect was putting the world community on notice that we as a nation were strong in our resolve and that we had one president at a time. Bush was President until January 20. Any country's first signal of good will to the Clinton Administration would be support for the Bush presidency during the transition.

The speech finished. Two old black men in the airport lobby with us applauded. America had a new President.

It is now five days after the election. We've celebrated during that time: (1) Bill Clinton's election as President; (2) Will's second soccer goal ever; (3) Bob's sixtieth birthday; and (4) reaching Leadership Texas' year's goal of getting two women appointed to corporate boards. Our home is not dull.

The sign on my in-box is correct: "A ship is safe in the harbor, but that's not what ships were built for." The campaign gave me an opportunity to sail, and I took it.

Life *is* the process.

December 8, 1992—On plane from Austin to D. C. to attend DLC Clinton dinner

Lady Bird Johnson held an enormous eightieth Birthday Bash in Austin last weekend. Liz Carpenter orchestrated two days of black tie dinners and tributes from Barbara Jordan, Bill Moyers, Ann Richards and others. Seven hundred and fifty people were invited, Bob and I among them. The event celebrated Lady Bird's extraordinary commitment to beautifying America—and any environment she occupied—by her mere presence and serene calm. It was an impressive, nostalgic time.

Standing in the receiving line while surrounded by practitioners of the Great Society, I felt on the cusp of history. Will Lucia, Karol, Robin, all the Clinton campaign folks, be like these Johnson men and women twenty-five years hence? Would we have as much cause to celebrate? Will we have our Head Start, Civil Rights programs and yes, our Vietnam (Somalia)?

My favorite part of the Lady Bird program occurred when seven women (including the daughters) read aloud excerpts from Mrs. Johnson's diaries. She writes very well, and her observations about her life with Lyndon and power were humorous and insightful. I was struck by how much richer most women's accounts of historical events are, at least to me. She placed anecdotes of the personal alongside the event, and like women's lives, showed how we're always operating on several levels. For example, when LBJ decided to run for the Senate, he tried to call her, but missed as she was alternately carpooling children and constituents around Washington.

Mother was visiting for the weekend, so I took her as my date for the Saturday LBJ seminars. Liz Carpenter regaled the audience when she chaired a panel of aging women reporters who covered Lady Bird. Their lives, too, were interwoven with kids, husbands, job deadlines. Liz once picked up the wrong dog from the vet, and didn't know it until she got home!

In the final tribute, Bill Moyers had us almost in tears. He told of being the young aide sleeping in the hotel bathroom on a cot in the Johnsons' room. He described the vicious incident at Dallas' Adolphus Hotel when a mob of pretty Texas women surged and spit at the Vice President and Lady Bird. When he later asked Lady

Bird about the incident, as the two stood, shaken, looking out the hotel window with curtains slightly pulled to view the still wild mob, she said she would be okay but that, "Nothing will ever be the same." And it wasn't.

December 31, 1992—New Year's Eve 1992, Magnolia Beach, Texas, at Cathy Bonner's and Ken Wendler's coastal hideaway—with Cathy and Ken

The morning rose gloriously today. Clear, gorgeous, hot sun, cool breeze coast day. The water is clear. Perfect for fishing. Will, Bob and Ken left to go across to Keller Bay in a small boat loaded with camouflaged men, Granola bars and a dog. The plan called for fishing, then duck hunting. There wasn't room for me in the small craft, so I'm on the pier, taking a break from rigorous pursuit of the fish.

Before the "men" left, Will and I took a long walk on the beach. I intended to walk briskly in an attempt at exercise, especially since the bathroom mirror here reflects (full-blown on the door) thighs of forty-four years. Will was garbed head to toe in camouflage—a mini-Bob as he picked his way across the shell beach. He dawdled. "Hey, Mom—see this?" A regular oyster shell. "And this one!" A simple stone washed smooth by eons of waves. Taking a deep breath, I realigned my thoughts and plans, cast exercise aside, and entered the wonderment of an eight-year-old's world. We meandered along, found a dead mullet (supremely fascinating to a young boy, especially because one eye had been gruesomely eaten away). He spotted the birds first. Three different kinds of crane-like animals were poised in the sand reef near the backwater ponds. The sun was to one side and silhouetted the delicate necks and slender beaks and legs. For a moment, I felt I was entering a living Japanese parchment painting, notwithstanding the rented pickup trucks with three-day-old-bearded men cruising by.

A woman strolled by with her dog and her casting net to try for some bait. Will watched each cast and encouraged her when the net approached a perfect circle. Eight-year-olds know few strangers.

When the guys left, I took my fishing gear and headed for the pier. Nostalgia hit me. This will always be my Mom and Dad's fishing place in my eyes. Ken and Cathy had them down the summer before he died. Daddy was quite sick, but *loved* the fishing and the camaraderie. He and Mother spent hours on this pier making endless casts.

The pier was locked. I asked a neighbor for a key, and feeling quite competent, let myself in. I walked on the wooden boards dragging my shrimp-filled hook along the bottom and luxuriated in the aloneness. Private alone time is a luxury for working mothers. Probably for *all* mothers.

I've never fished off a pier where you could see the bottom. Each ripple of water revealed new glimpses of the bay's treasures. Was this a rock, or a special fish species unknown to neophyte fisherwomen? But what—a bite! Yes, I caught something, hauled it up, both of us equally startled at the sudden turn of events. The fish looked at me, unblinking, from two eyes on the same side of his head. A flounder? I recalled that when fly fishing, one "bops 'em on the head" for humanitarian reasons. Not having seriously contemplated *catching* a fish, as opposed to *fishing* for fish, I was unprepared. Gingerly, I lifted my prize and made my way to the sink-like-structure that I figured must be used by big fishermen for big fish. I flopped the fish in the sink and hit him with the hose attached to the sink. Not good enough. Worried, I searched through the little bag of lures Bob gave me. Yep. Should have known. There were two pairs of plier-type tools. I bopped him again.

He was caught on a three-pronged hook. Really caught. I considered asking the neighbor for help, but quickly reconsidered in the face of appearing utterly foolish. Surely I can do this, I thought. So I did. Pliers held the hook, while I deftly pulled out the prongs with the second pair. Smugly, I viewed my work, then raced across the open field to the house for an ice chest for my trophy. I felt great!

Now, the day moves on. I eat, lose a hook, put on a new lure, begin to really see some fish, which is like spotting airports when you first learn to fly: Until you figure out what to look for, they're invisible. I see a school of small fish, and of course a great big one that hasn't the faintest interest in my pink plastic lure. Do I detect disdain in the elegant flip of his tail as he swims past my hook?

I'm tired from looking so hard at the water. But I don't like the mindless casting into murky depths which now seems like a silly way to catch a fish. What arrogance leads me to even think a cast into the vastness of the bay will cross by a fish I can't even see? Ridiculous. But I continue to do it.

The wind is cooling off: I've learned to listen to its subtle messages. The waves are picking up. Do all fishermen watch the tiny bubbles, the occasional floating bird feather, a piece of flotsam, and wonder about the mystery of this water? Its comings and goings, its impenetrable depths, its utter disregard for the specks of humans who dally at the merest edge of the organism. A piece of my hair drops into the waves and joins a floating jelly-like bulb. Maybe we really are all part of the One.

❧

❦ Epilogue

In every family there is an anchor. My mother, Pinky Aaker, is ours. She lives her life unconditionally loving, but not unconditionally liking. To her, my two sisters Cathy Swanson and Janet Smith, and my father, I give thanks for putting up with me all these years.

My husband Bob is my soulmate. This book is for him—and for our son Will in whose ways we delight.

My three stepchildren, Martha Louise, Shannon and Landis, have grown in wisdom and grace over the years. I continue to be thankful for each of them.

The people of my law firm, Bickerstaff, Heath & Smiley, have given me room to grow, ideas to argue about and support both personally and professionally—unheard of in legal circles. BHS is a very special place.

Kathie Meredith, my friend and my colleague for twenty years, not only typed the manuscript, she shared the years with me.

My life has been blessed with friends. Some of them are in this book. To all of them, I say thank you for our journey together that inspired these journals.